MASTERS

ANTON SEDER
COLLECTION

A CURATED ARCHIVE OF 100 DOWNLOADABLE MASTERPIECES

SERIES

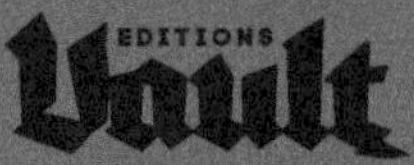

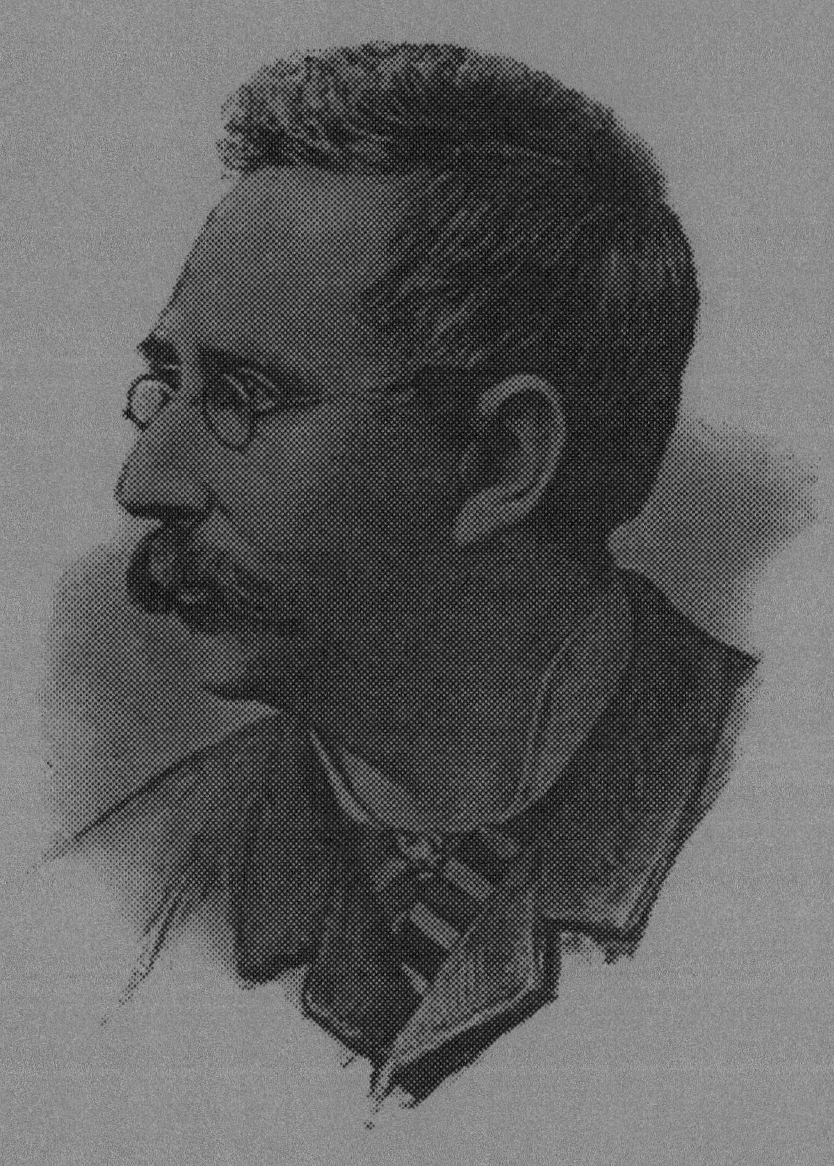

ANTON SEDER

11 JAN 1850 – 01 DEC 1916

ISBN: 978-1-922966-57-5

TABLE OF CONTENTS

Introduction   01
The Animal in Decorative Art   03
(Das Thier in der Decorativen Kunst)
The Plant in Art and Craft   33
(Die Pflanze in Kunst und Gewerbe)
Download Your Files   105

01

INTRODUCTION

"The goal of this work is to provide a vast reservoir of forms for artists to select from, recognising that decorative art is as much about reflecting the diverse expressions of individuality as it is about technical prowess."
-Introduction to *Die Pflanze in Kunst und Gewerbe*

Anton Seder was a renowned German artist and educator known for his contributions to the Art Nouveau movement. He was born in Munich, Germany, on 11th January 1850 and died on 1st December 1916 in Strasbourg, France. Seder was the first director of the École supérieure des arts décoratifs de Strasbourg (now Haute école des arts du Rhin) in 1889, where his leadership shaped decorative arts education and fostered a culture of innovation. Through his commitment to workshop-based training and fresh teaching perspectives, Seder inspired a generation of young artists to embrace creative experimentation, infusing Strasbourg's art scene with energy and vision.

Seder was also an accomplished author, publishing approximately ten works devoted to drawing and painting and co-editing a journal dedicated to the Arts and Crafts movement in Alsace-Lorraine. His most famous works, Das Thier in der Decorativen Kunst and Die Pflanze in Kunst und Gewerbe, are landmark books in the study of decorative art.

The Anton Seder Collection: A Curated Archive of 100 Downloadable Masterpieces captures the spirit of Seder's groundbreaking works Das Thier in der Decorativen Kunst and Die Pflanze in Kunst und Gewerbe, bringing together 100 meticulously restored Art Nouveau images inspired by animals and nature. This collection celebrates Seder's fascination with the natural world and highlights his unique

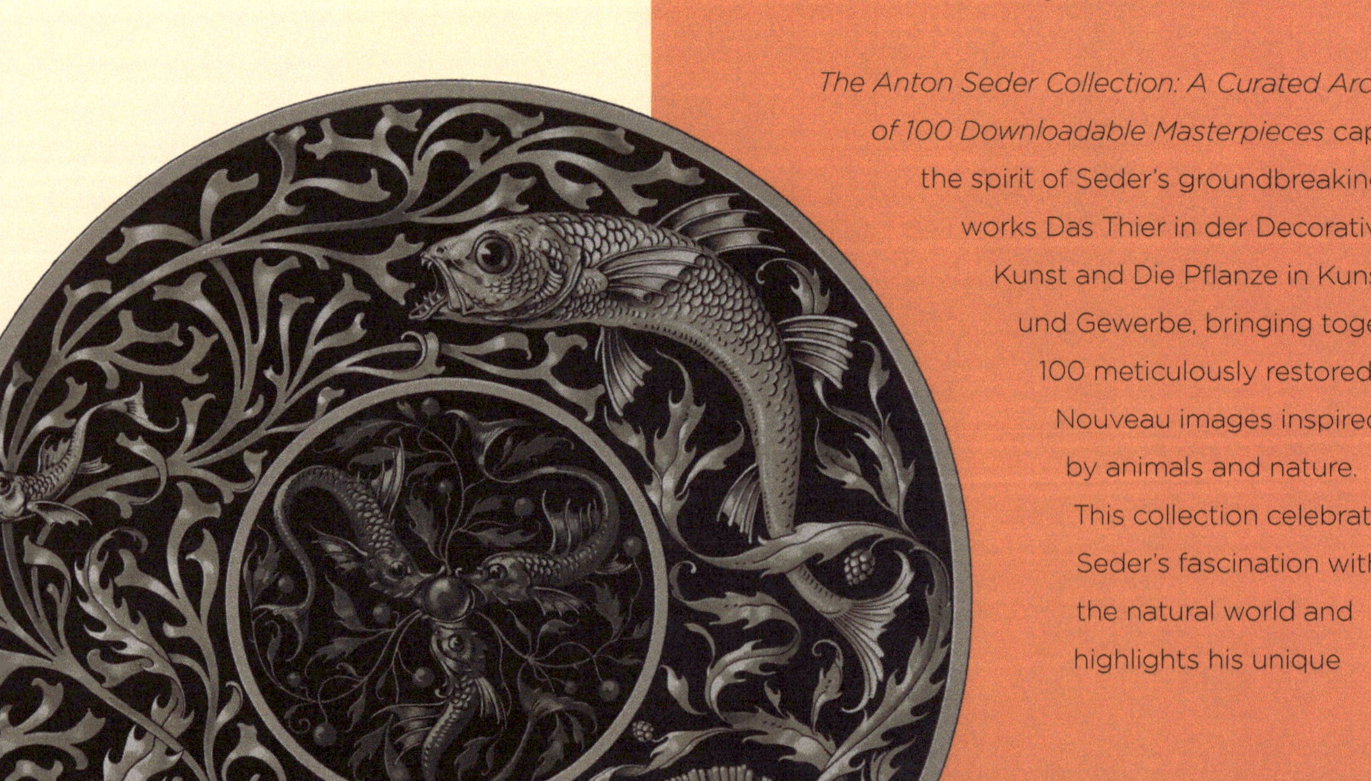

ability to transform flora and fauna into ornate, decorative forms. Each copy includes high-resolution digital downloads of every illustration, accessible via a download link at the back of the book. This addition allows artists and designers to explore Seder's intricate techniques or incorporate these stunning compositions into their creative projects.

The Anton Seder Collection: A Curated Archive of 100 Downloadable Masterpieces is an opportunity to explore Seder's visionary work. This book is perfect for art lovers, artists and designers. It is a timeless reference and a powerful tool to inspire, captivate, and transform your artistic journey. Seder's work remains as relevant now as it was over a century ago, offering endless possibilities for interpretation, adaptation, and inspiration in modern design.

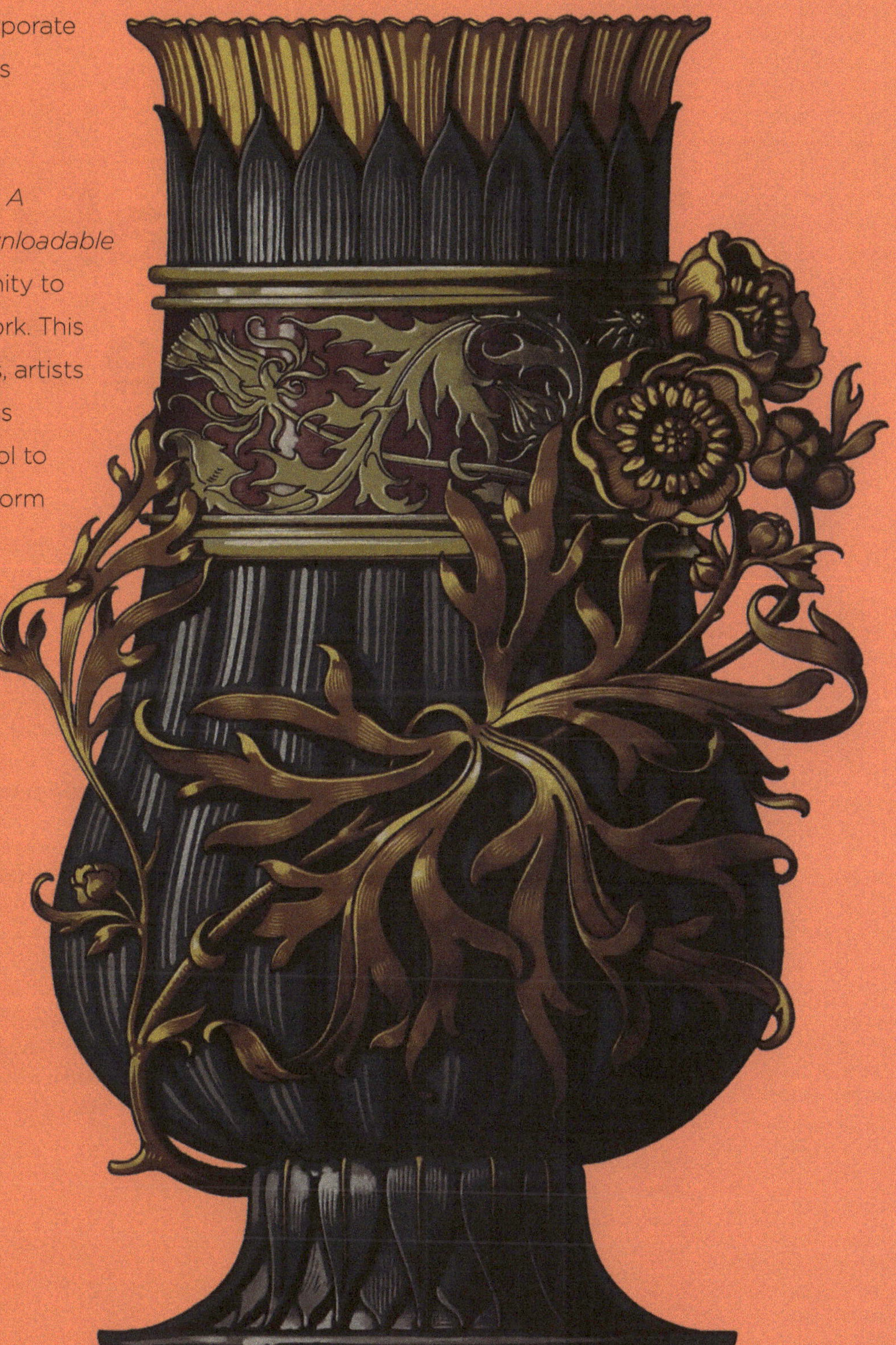

ANTON SEDER

02

The Animal in Decorative Art

ANTON SEDER

Anton Seder's *Das Thier in der Decorativen Kunst* (The Animal in Decorative Art) is a landmark work demonstrating his extraordinary talent for reimagining the natural world as an endless inspiration for decorative design. First published in the late 19th century, this book embodies Seder's vision of transforming real and mythical creatures into intricate ornamental forms. Readers encounter a captivating collection of meticulously rendered animals, from the graceful curves of birds and fish to the powerful forms of mammals, insects, and fantastical dragons. These illustrations reveal Seder's mastery of line and form, showcasing his ability to blend naturalistic detail with artistic stylisation.

Das Thier in der Decorativen Kunst is a testament to Seder's belief that nature, in all its diversity, holds an inexhaustible potential for artistic creation. By stylising animals into decorative motifs, Seder bridges the organic world with human creativity, encouraging artists to view natural forms through a design-focused lens. His realistically depicted or imaginatively embellished animals provide a unique blend of elegance and visual complexity that inspires contemporary artists and designers.

More than 125 years after its initial publication, *Das Thier in der Decorativen Kunst* remains a foundational reference for those interested in the Art Nouveau movement, the decorative arts, and the intersection of nature and design. Its illustrations offer timeless lessons in adapting organic forms into compelling patterns and compositions, making it an invaluable resource for modern creators seeking to incorporate Seder's techniques and aesthetic principles into their work.

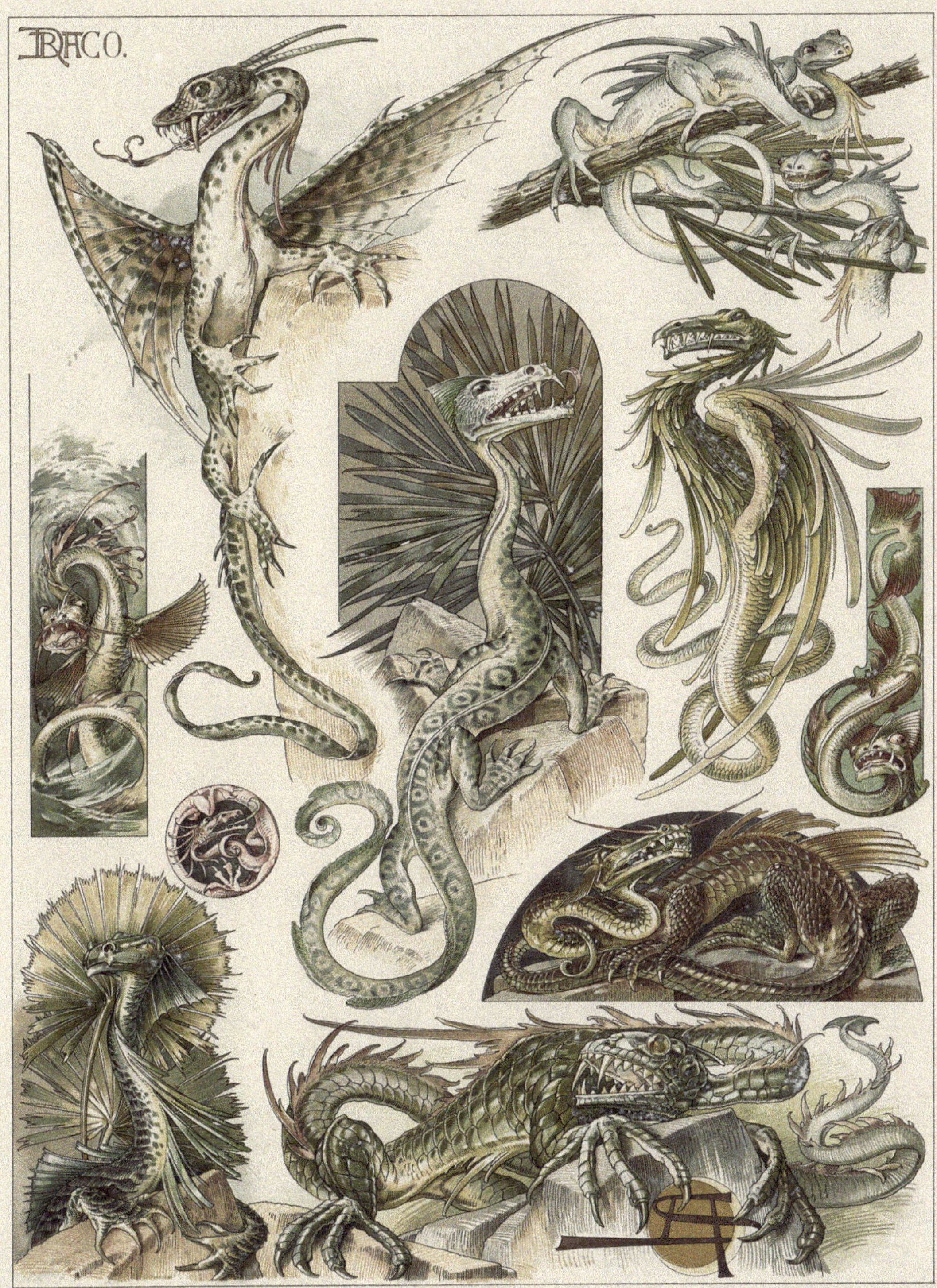
„ANIMAL"
DAS THIER
„THE ANIMAL"
DRACO.
ANTON SEDER

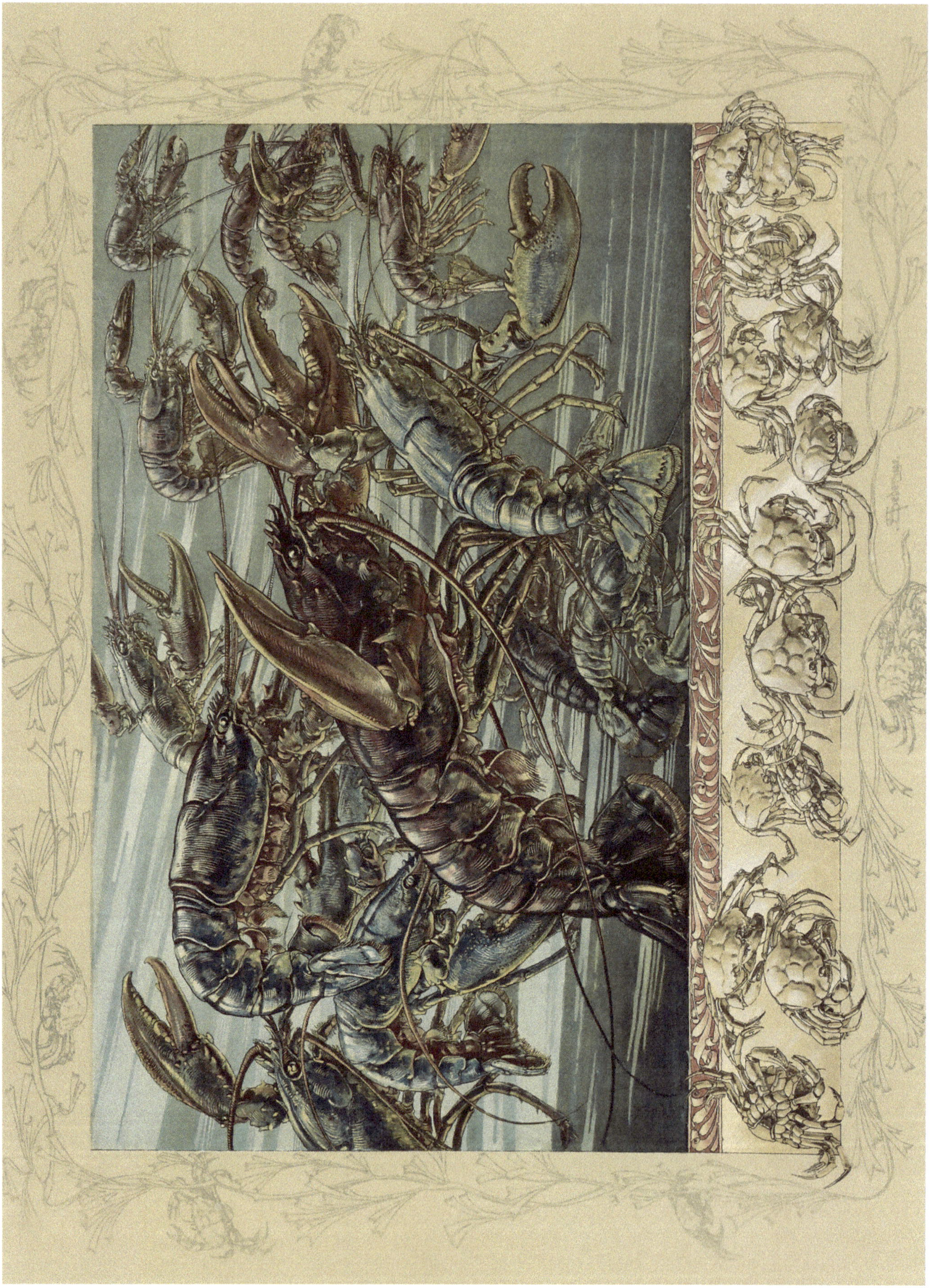

2. Plate Number 2, Das Thier in der Decorativen
Kunst, by A. Seder, 1896

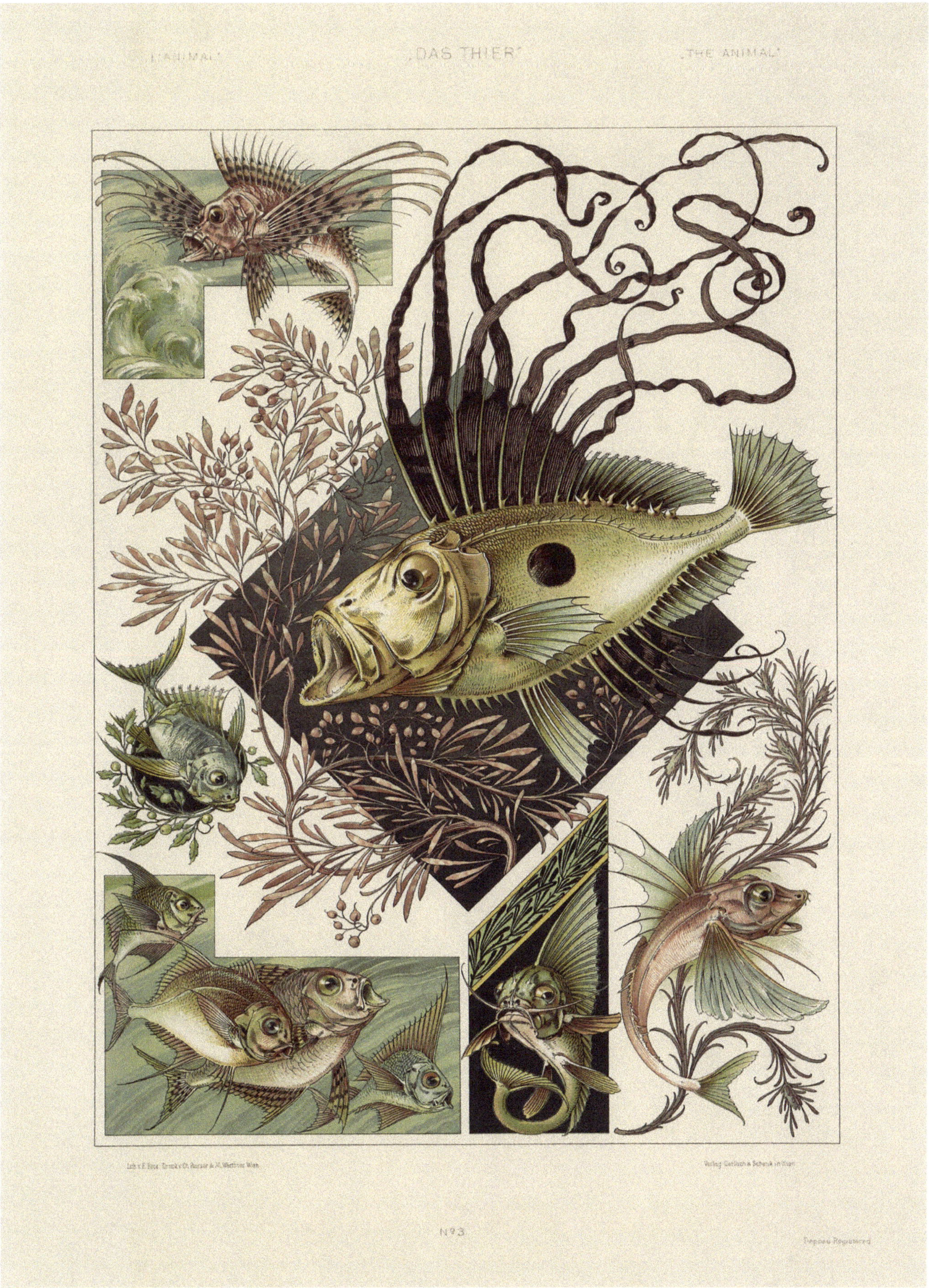

ANTON SEDER

3. Plate Number 3. Das Thier in der Decorativen
Kunst. by A. Seder. 1896

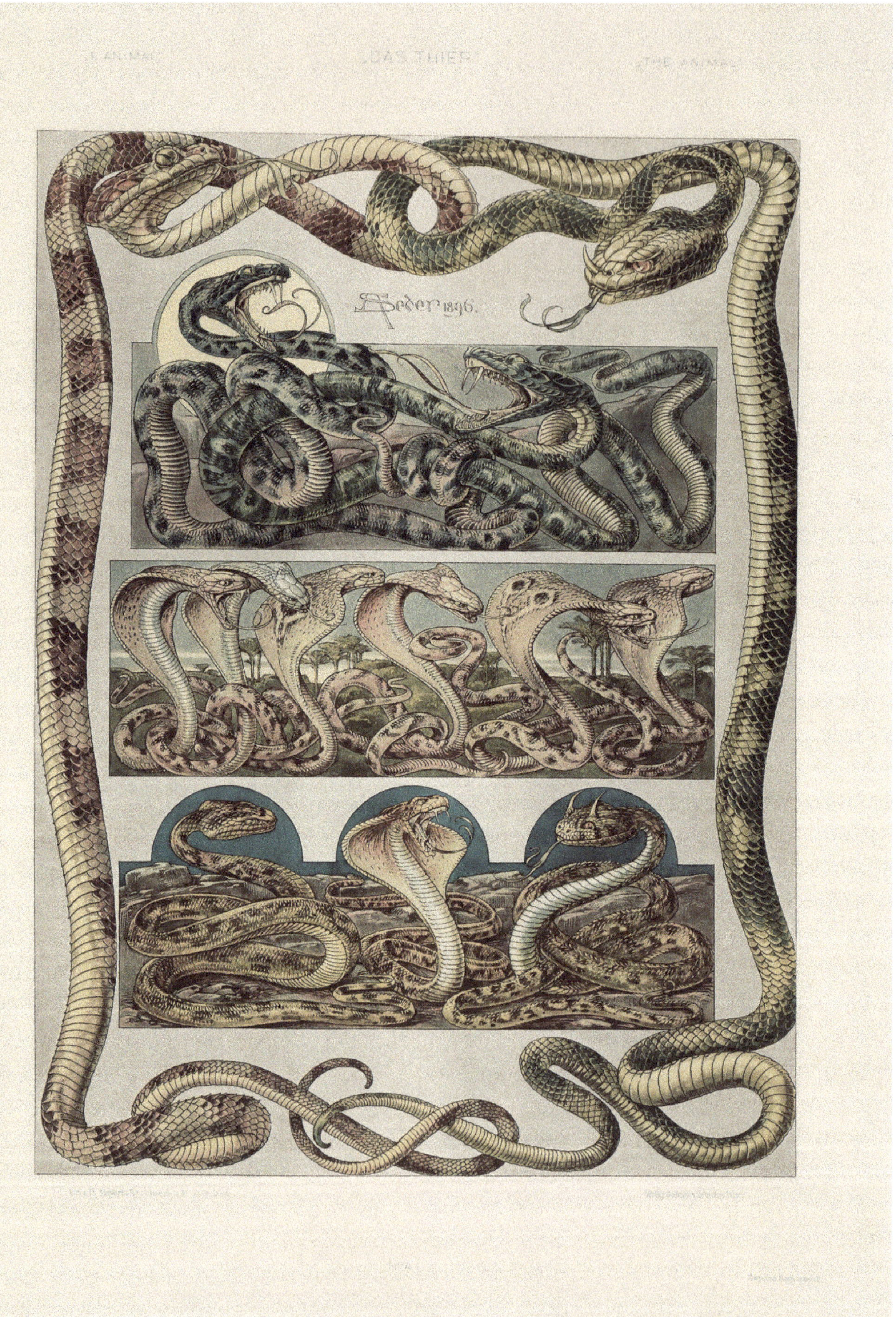

4. Plate Number 4 Das Thier in der Decorativen
Kunst, by A. Seder, 1896

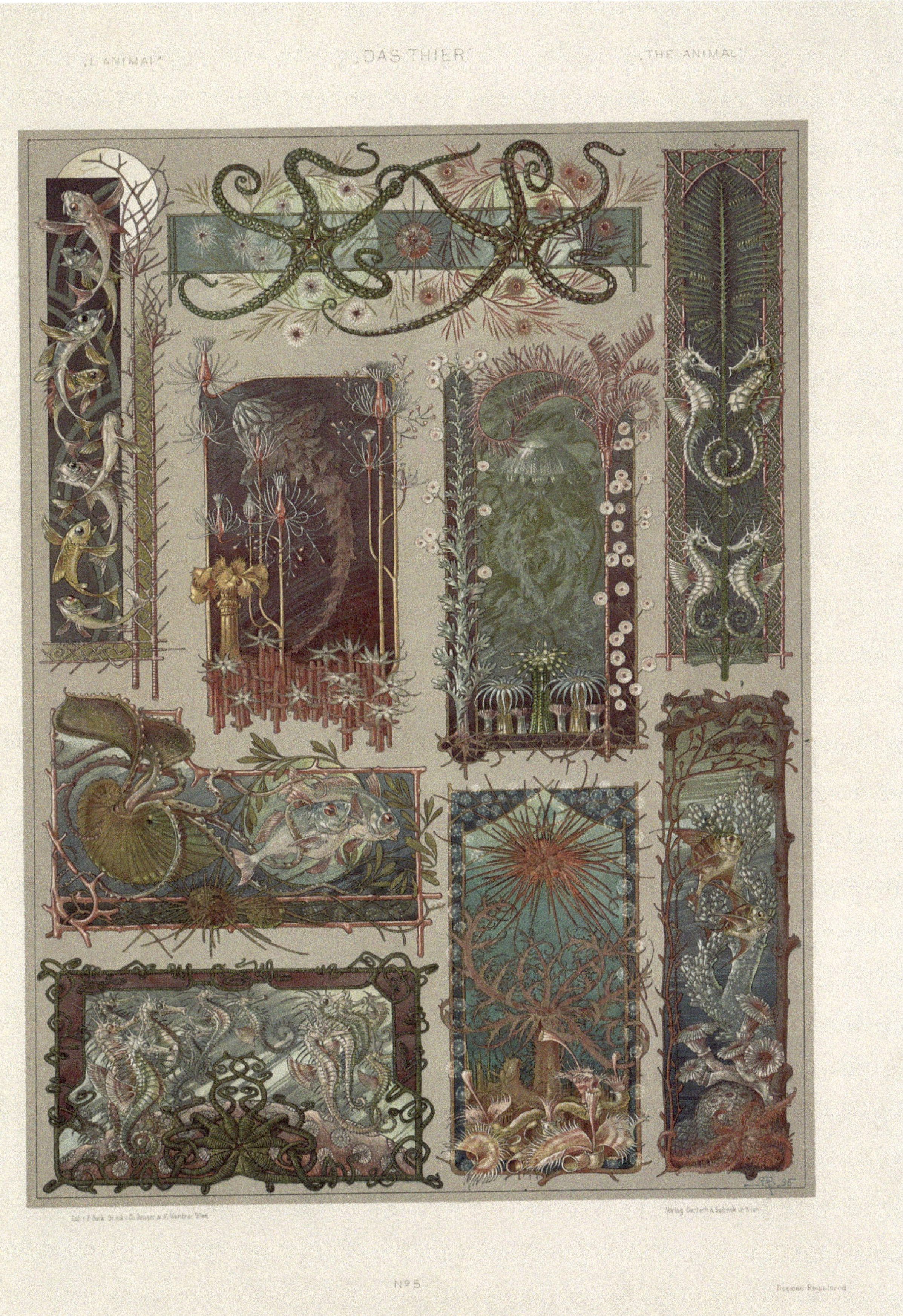

5. Plate Number 5, Das Thier in der Decorativen
Kunst, by A. Seder, 1896

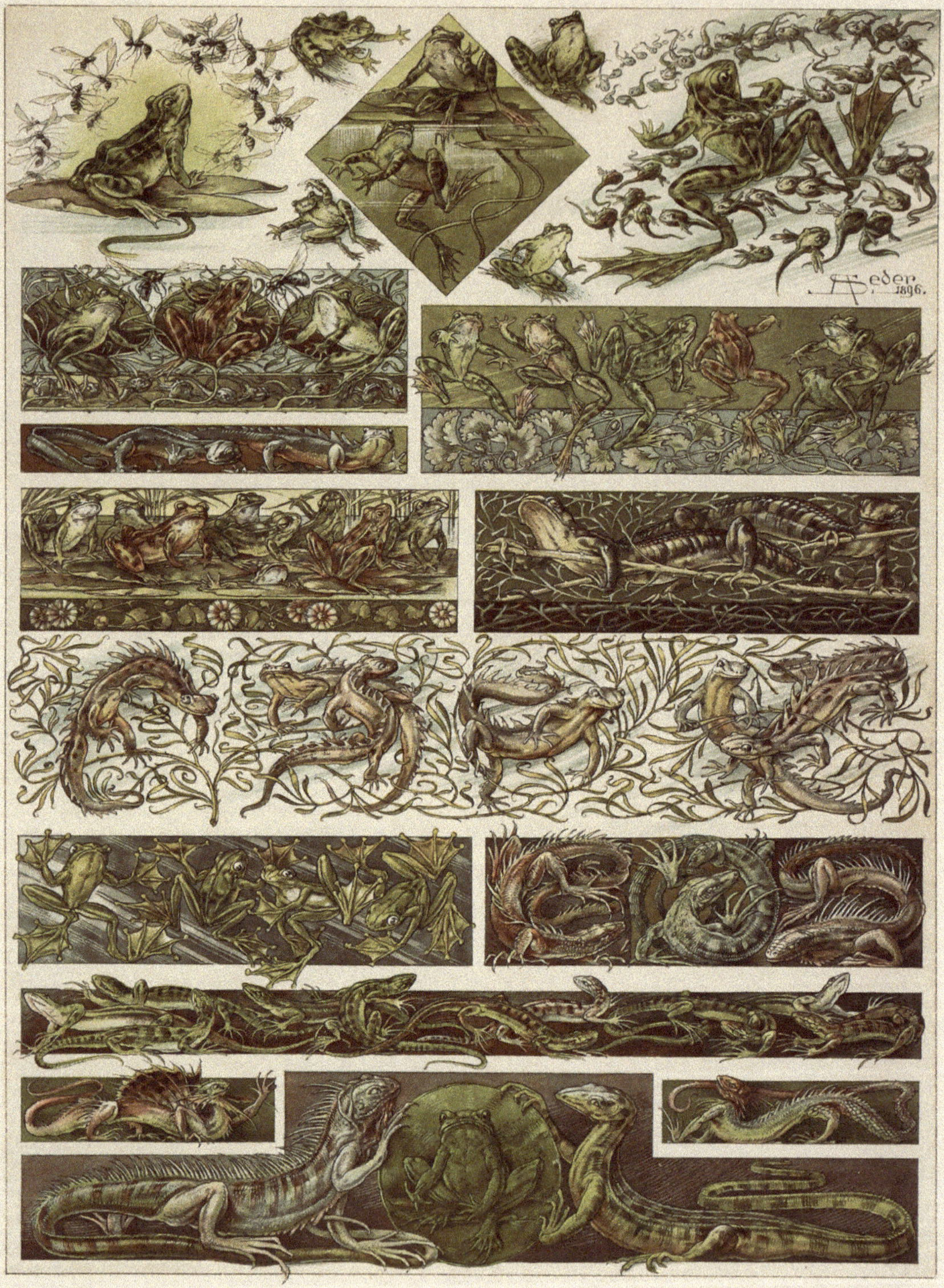

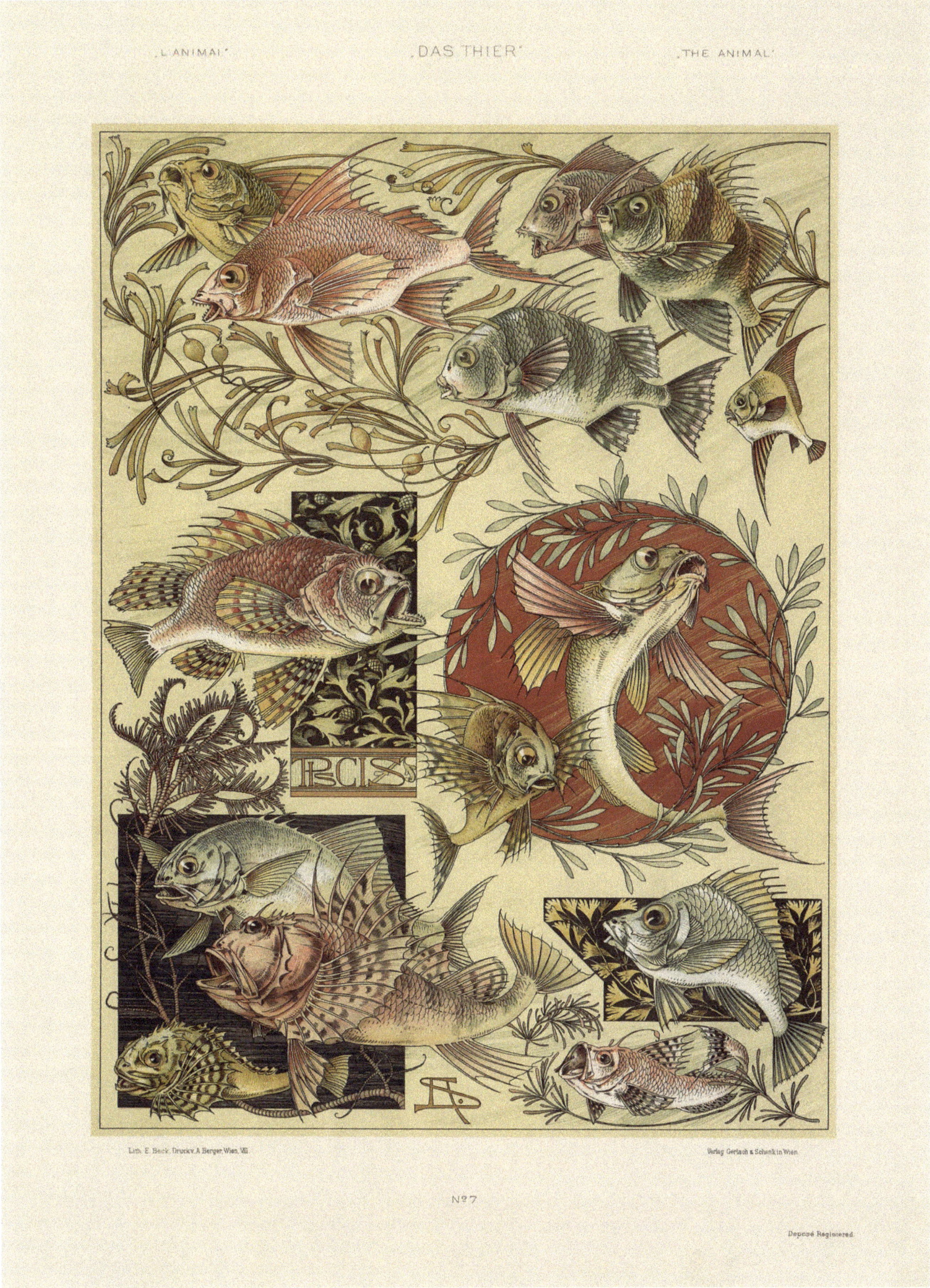

ANTON SEDER

7. Plate Number 7. Das Thier in der Decorativen
Kunst, by A. Seder, 1896

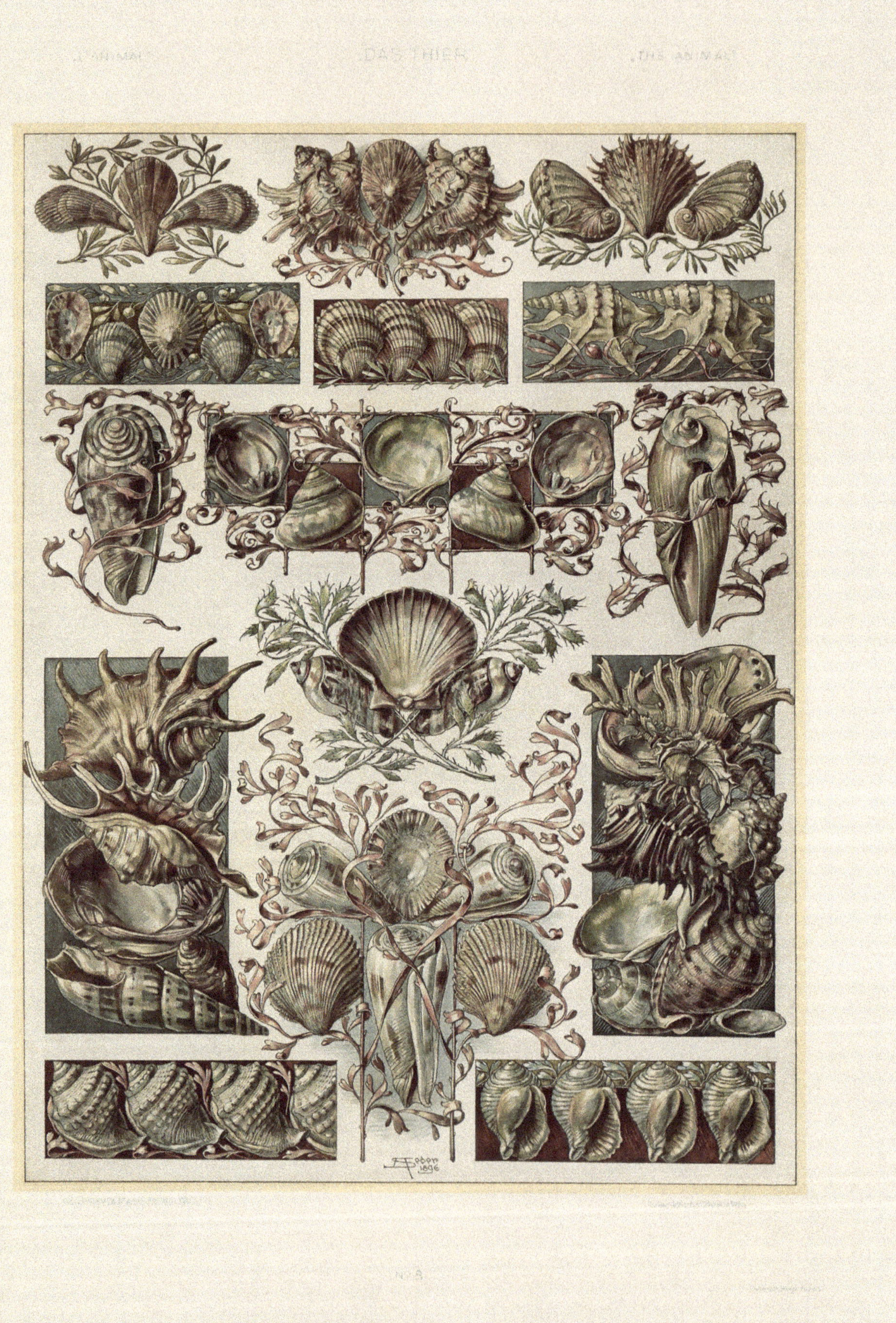

8. Plate Number 8, Das Thier in der Decorativen
Kunst, by A. Seder, 1896

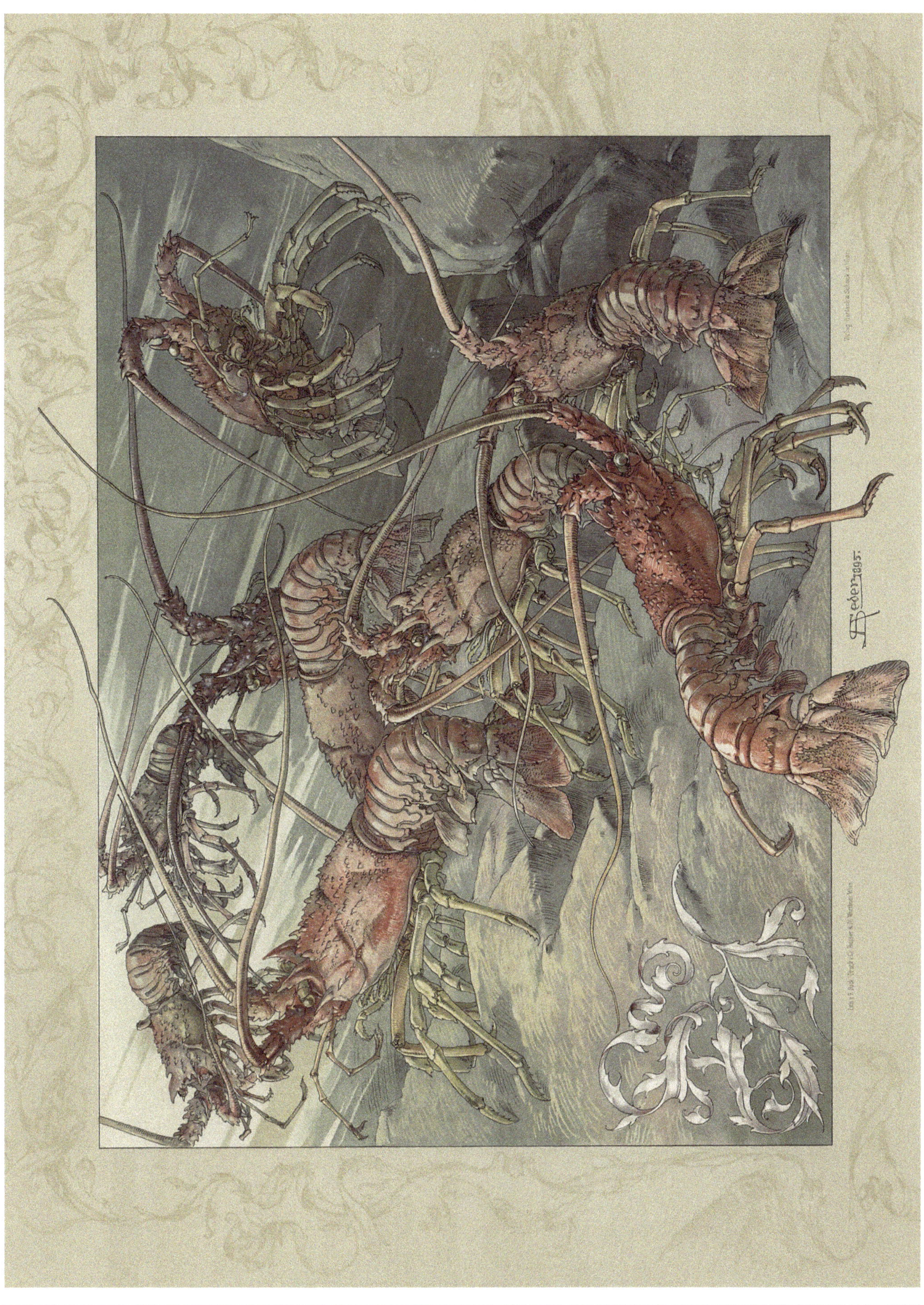

ANTON SEDER

9. Plate Number 9, Das Thier in der Decorativen
Kunst, by A. Seder, 1896

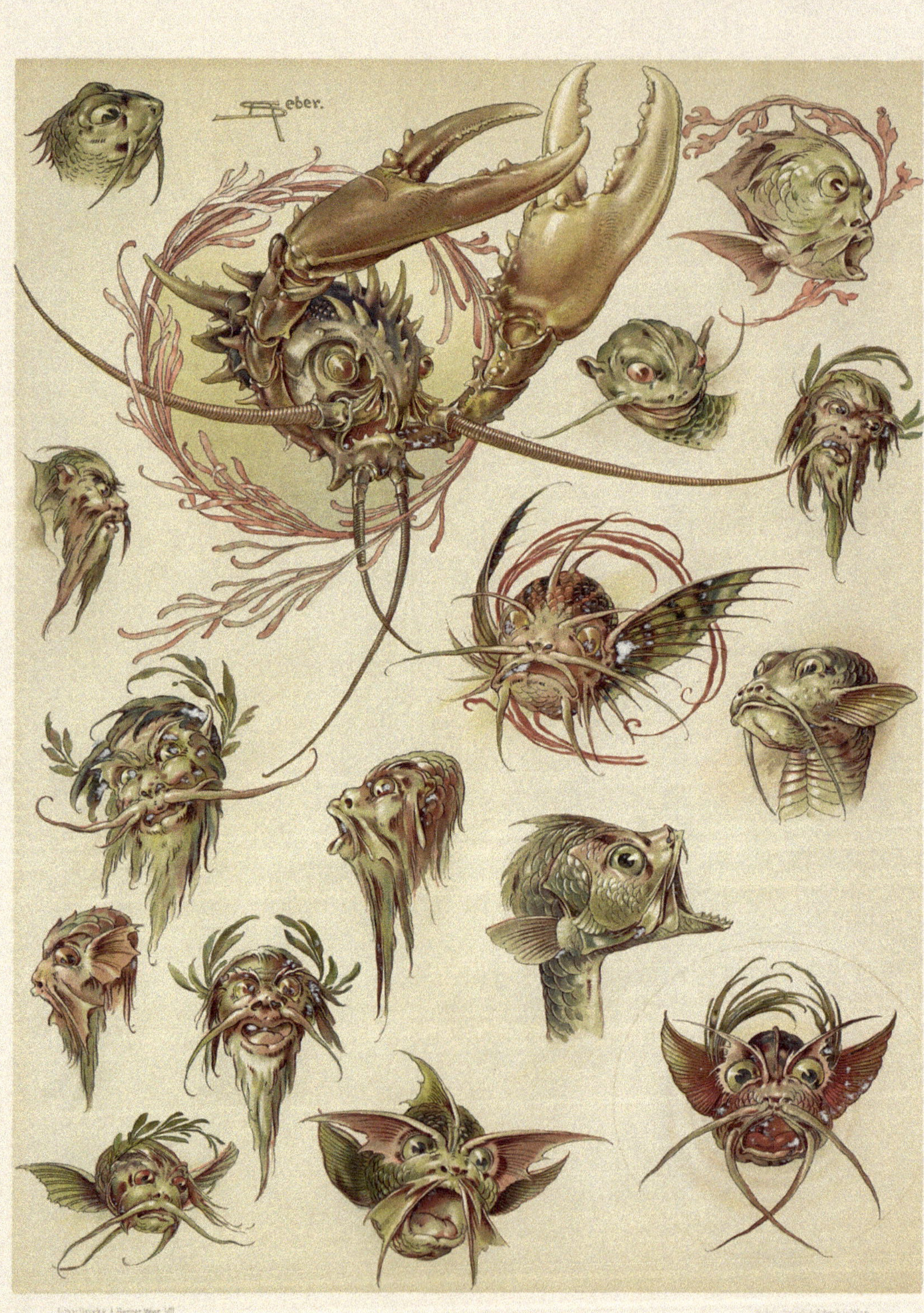

10. Plate Number 10. Das Thier in der
Decorativen Kunst, by A. Seder, 1896

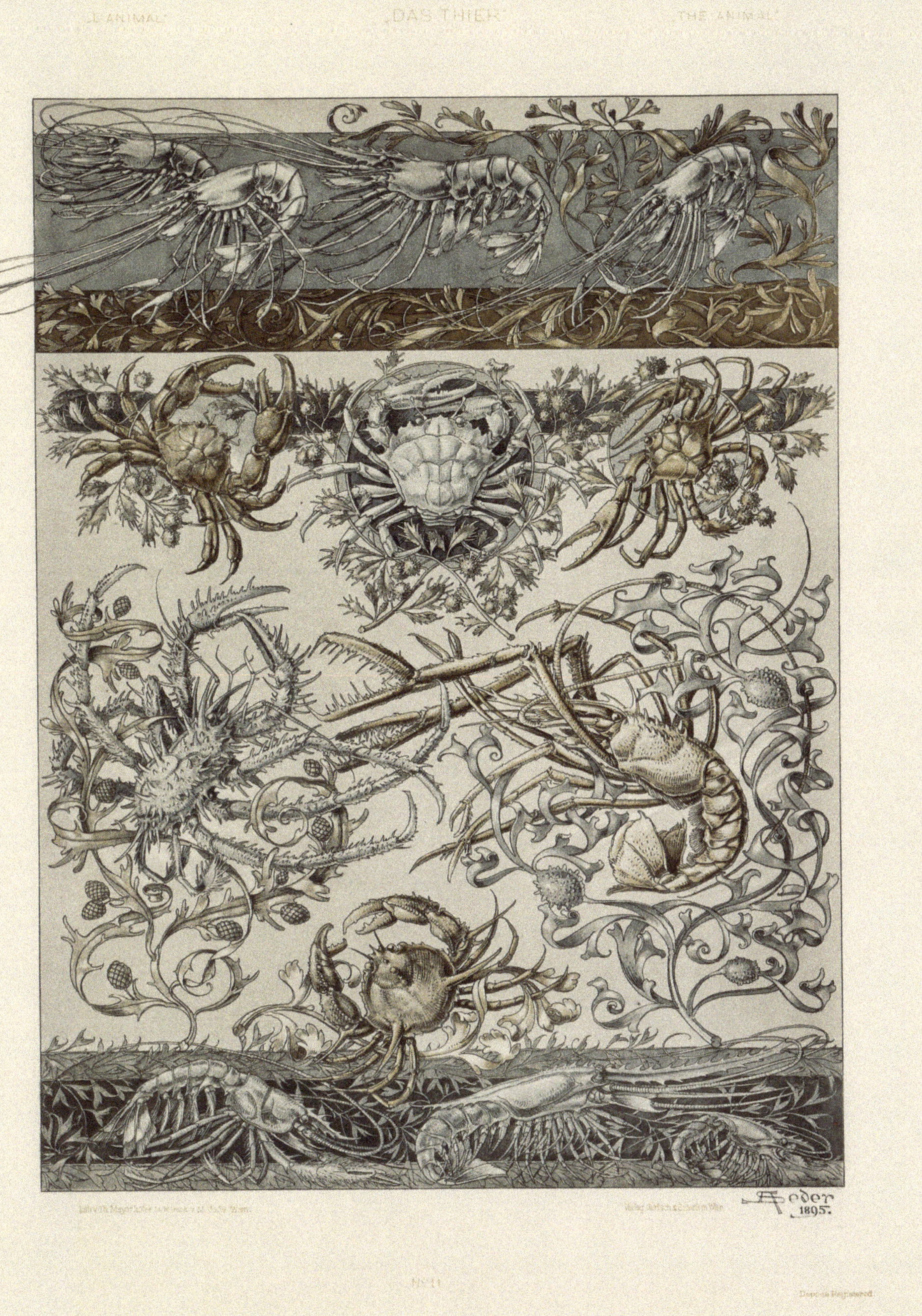

11. Plate Number 11, Das Thier in der Decorativen
Kunst, by A. Seder, 1896

12. Plate Number 12. Das Thier in der
Decorativen Kunst, by A. Seder, 1896.

ANTON SEDER

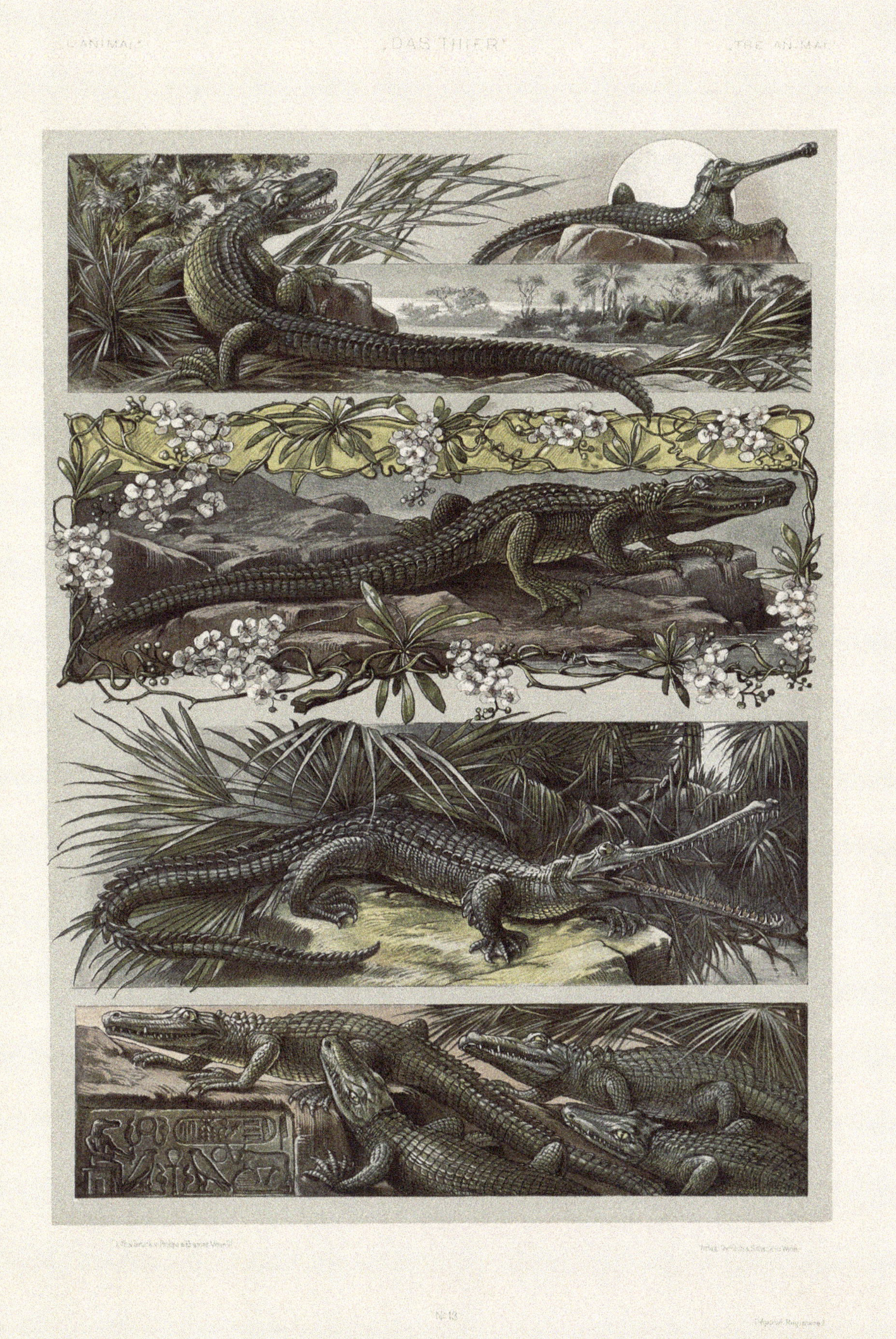

13. Plate Number 13. Das Thier in der
Decorativen Kunst, by A. Seder, 1896

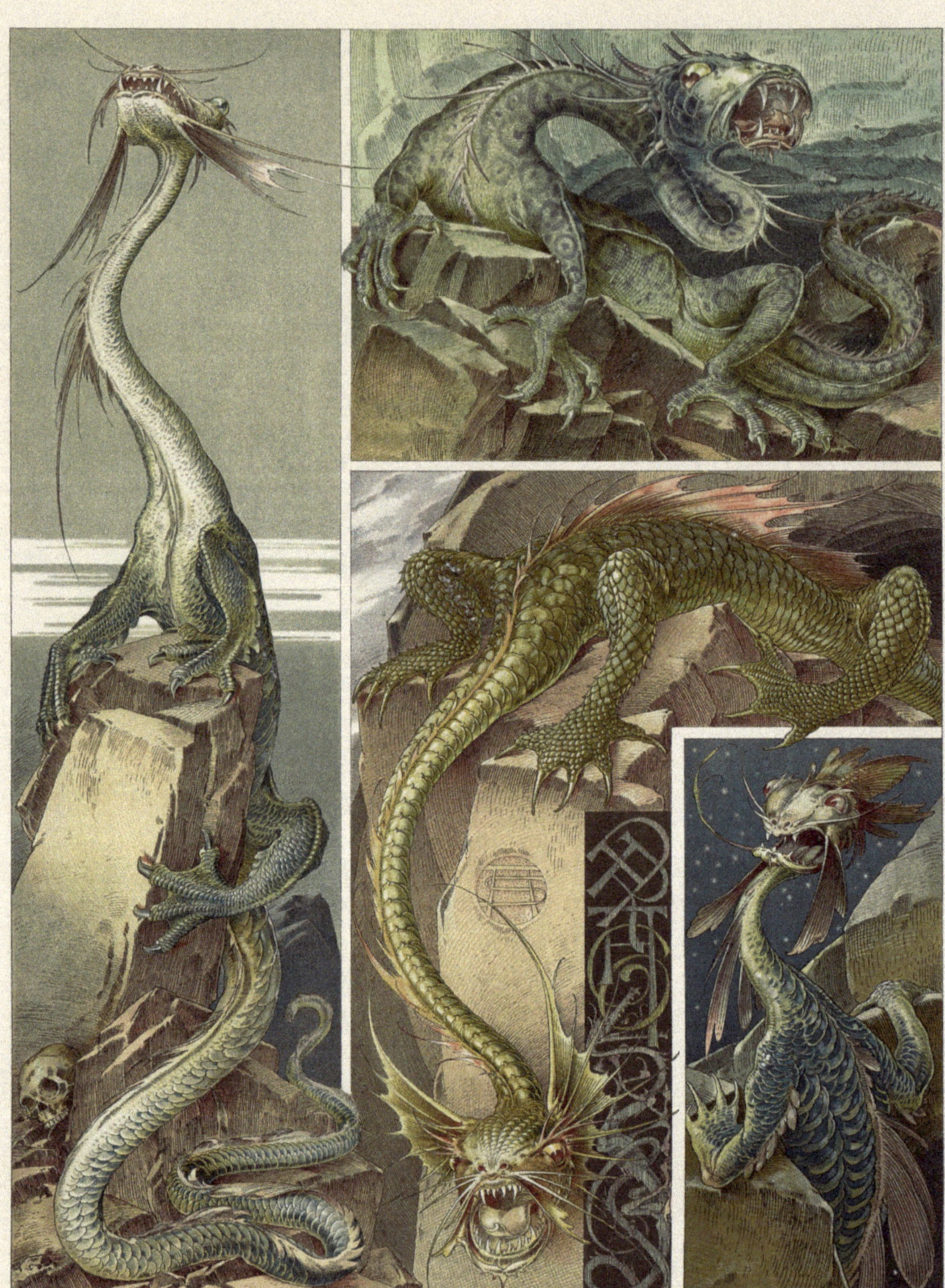

14 Plate Number 14, Das Thier in der
Decorativen Kunst, by A. Seder, 1896

.,L'ANIMAL`     .DAS TIER`.   THE ,ANIMAL`

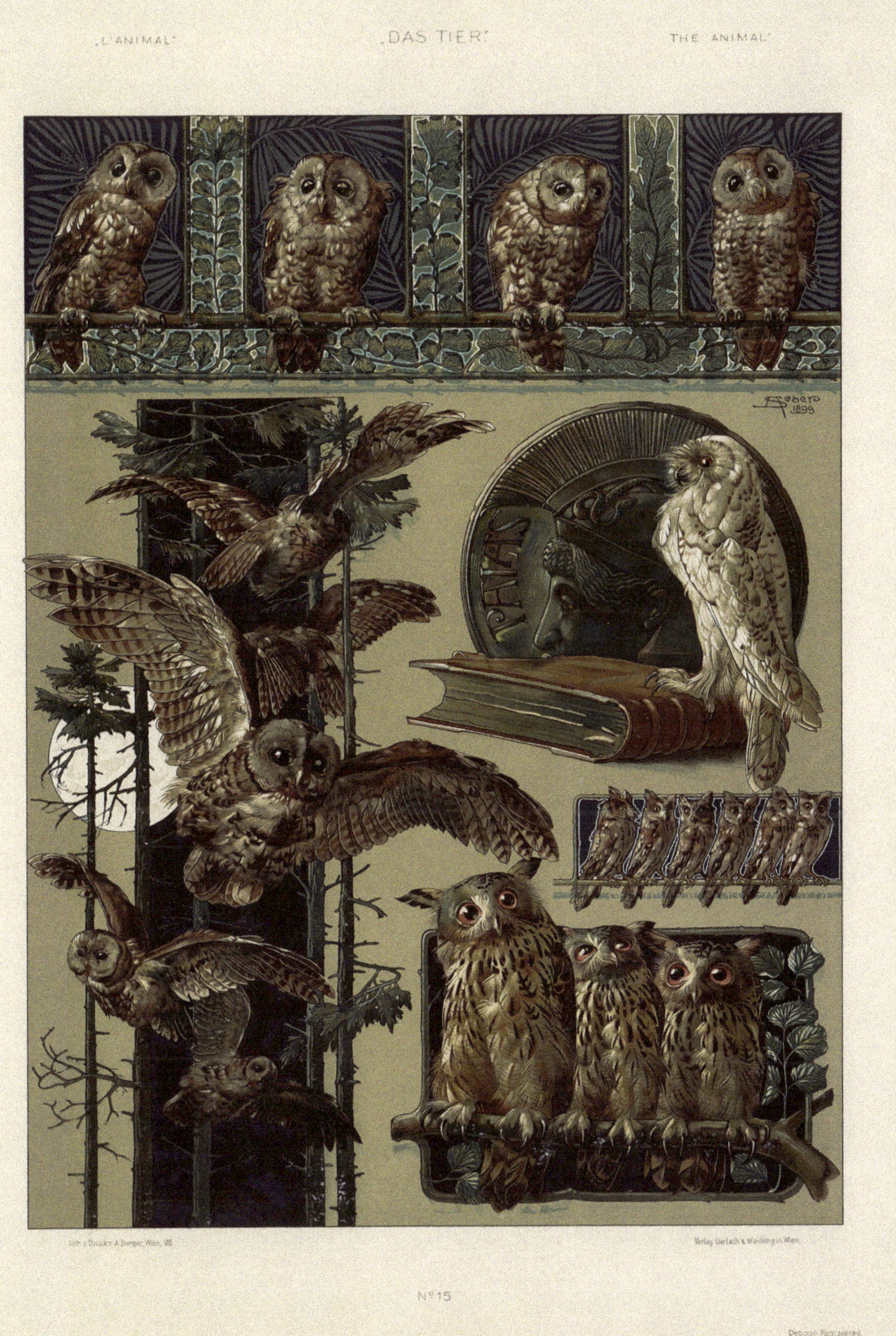

ANTON SEDER

Lith u Druck v A Berger, Wien, VII.   Verlag Gerlach & Wiedling in Wien.

Nº 15

Dépose Registered

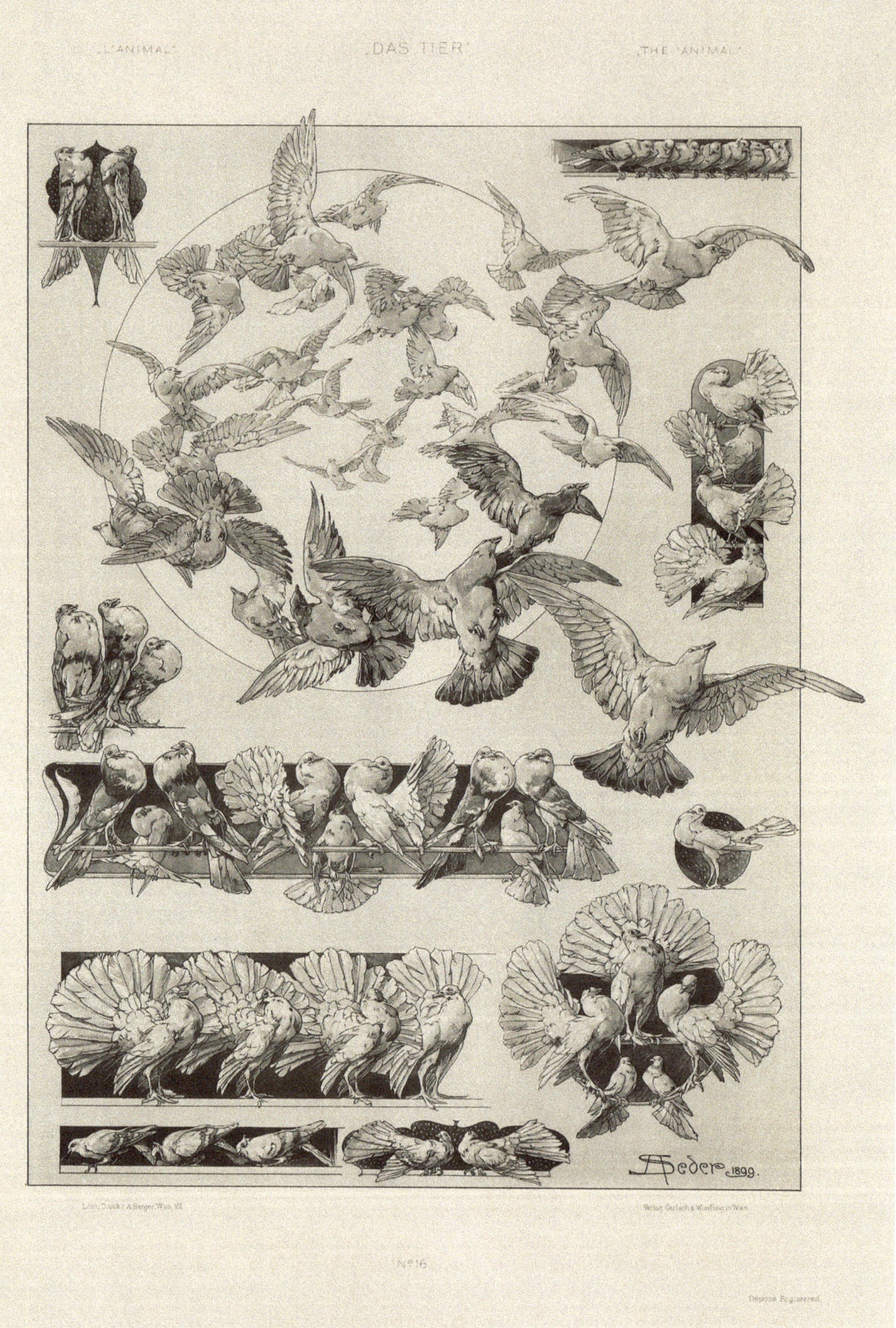

16. Plate Number 16, Das Thier in der
Decorativen Kunst, by A. Seder, 1896

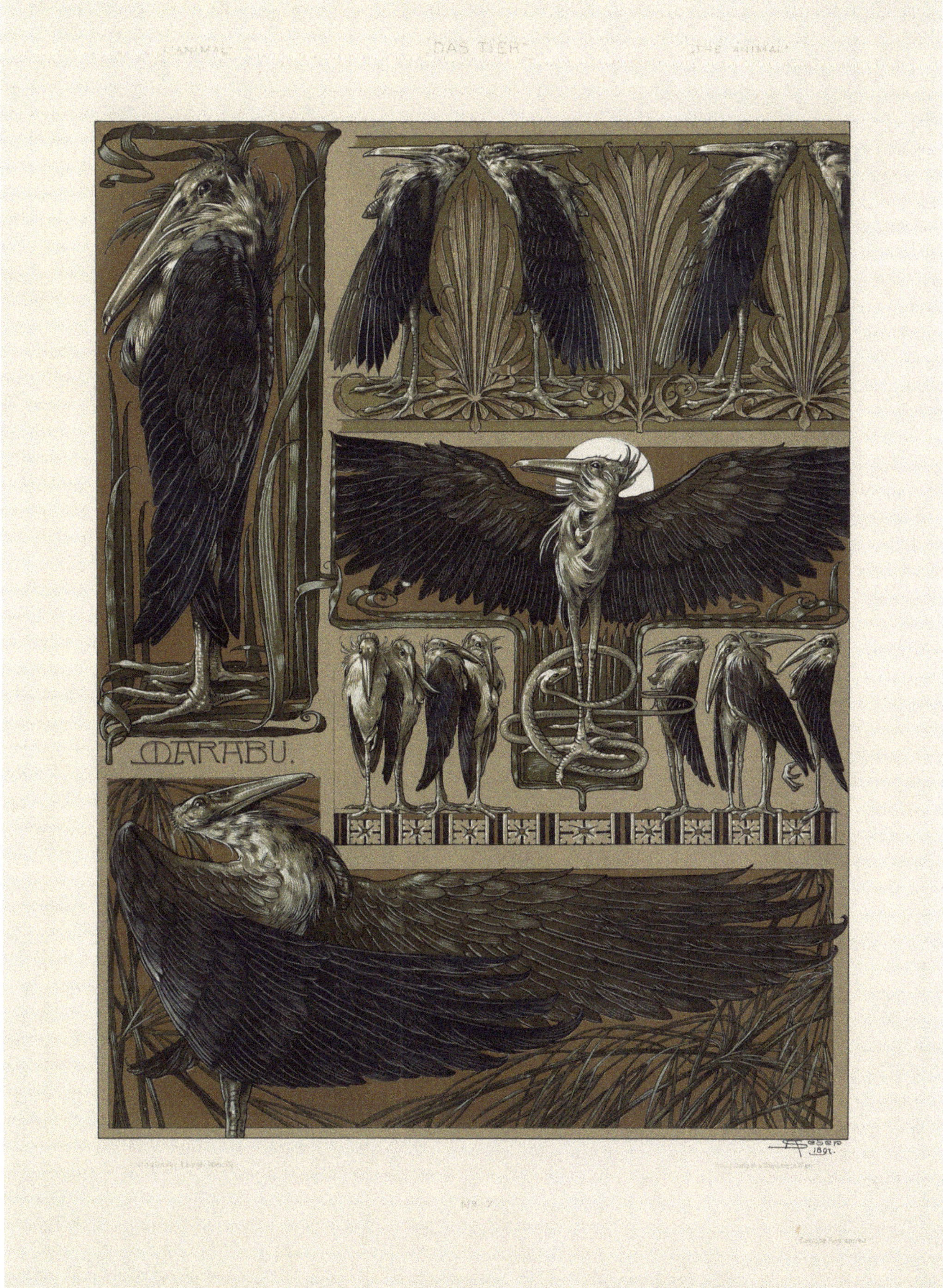

"ANIMAL"
"DAS TIER"
"THE ANIMAL"
MARABU.

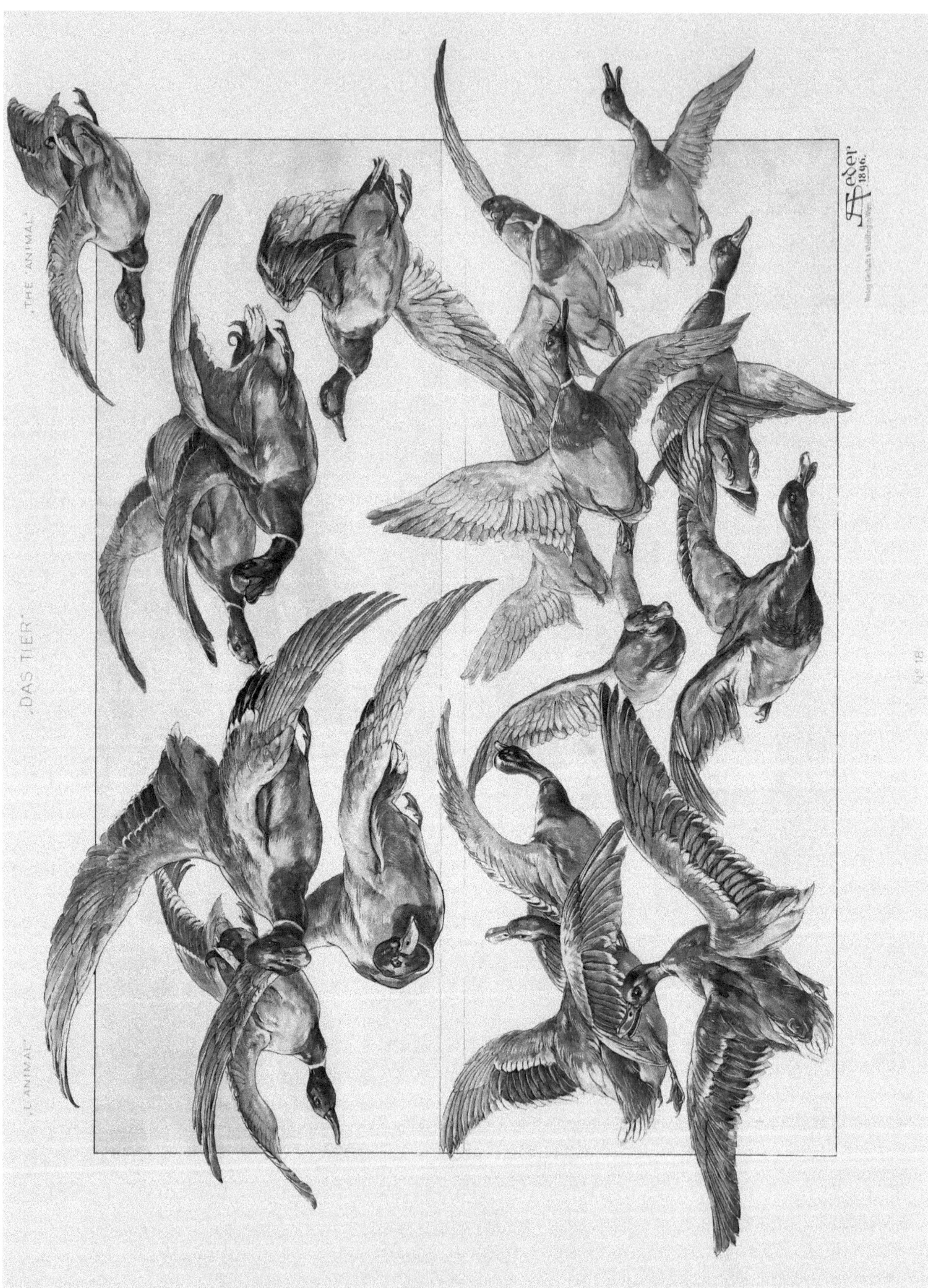

18. Plate Number 18. Das Thier in der
Decorativen Kunst, by A. Seder, 1896

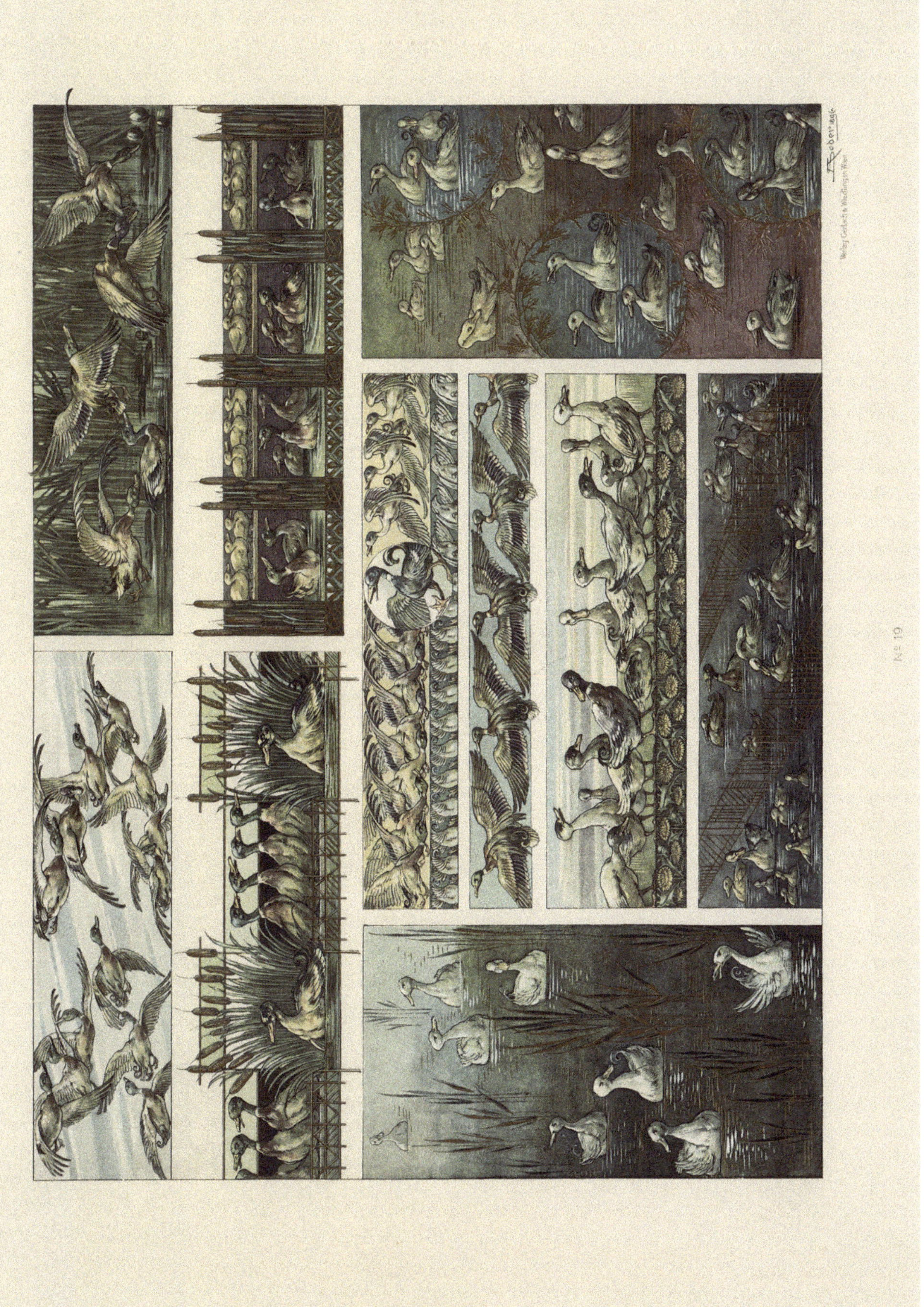

ANTON SEDER

19. Plate Number 19. Das Thier in der
Decorativen Kunst, by A. Seder, 1896

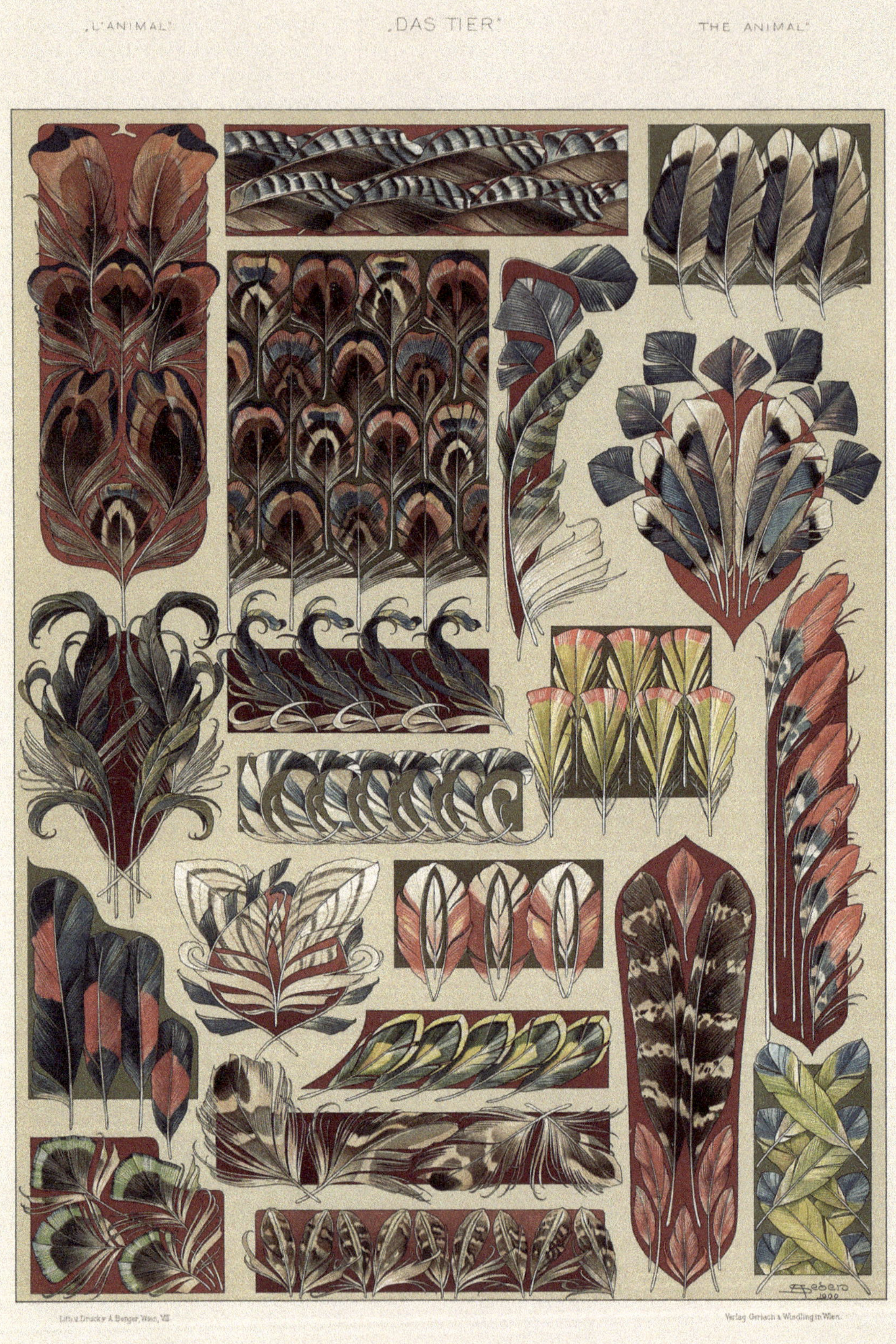

20. Plate Number 20, Das Thier in der
Decorativen Kunst, by A. Seder, 1896

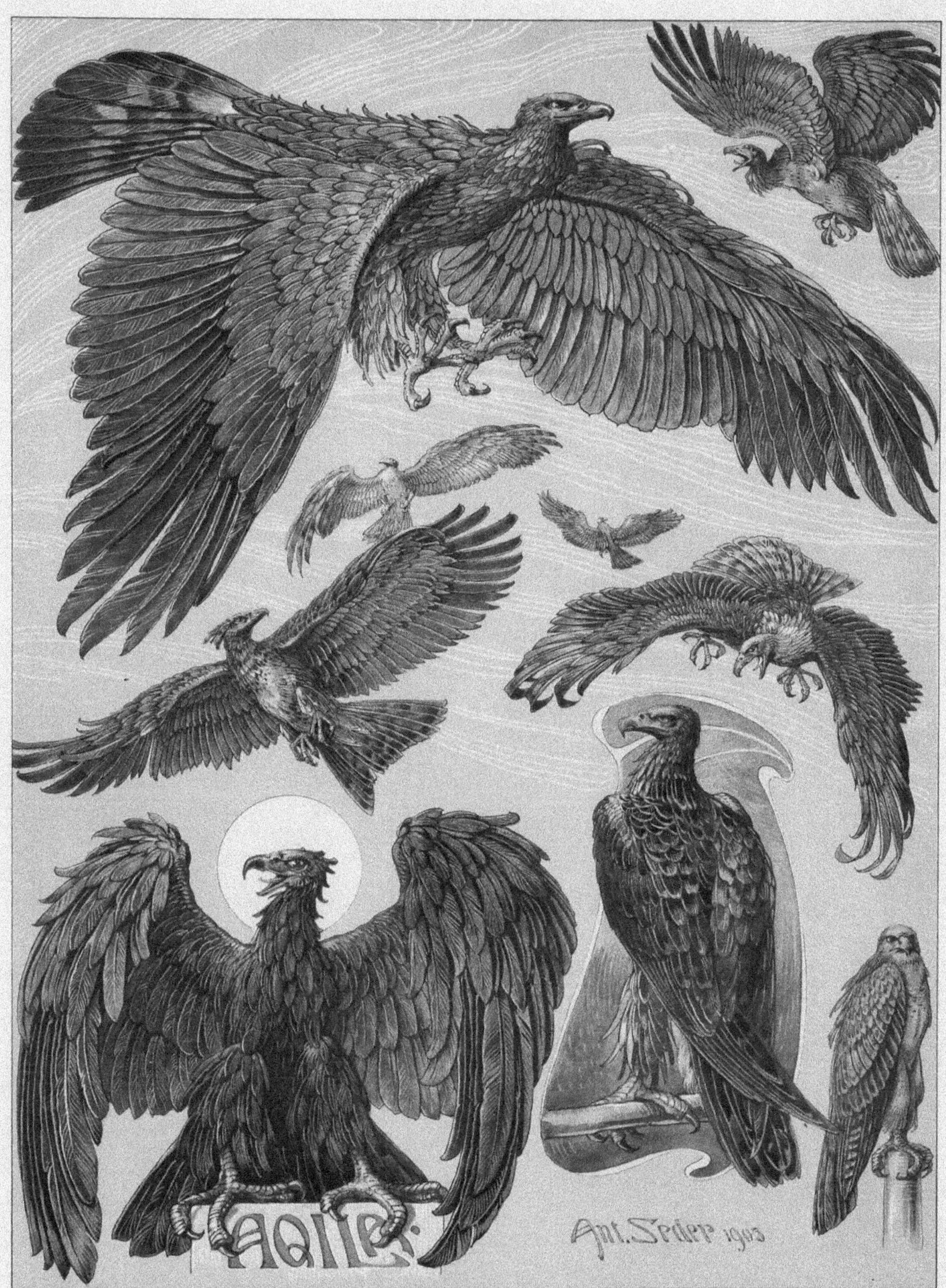

21. Plate Number 21, Das Thier in der
Decorativen Kunst, by A. Seder, 1896

ANTON SEDER

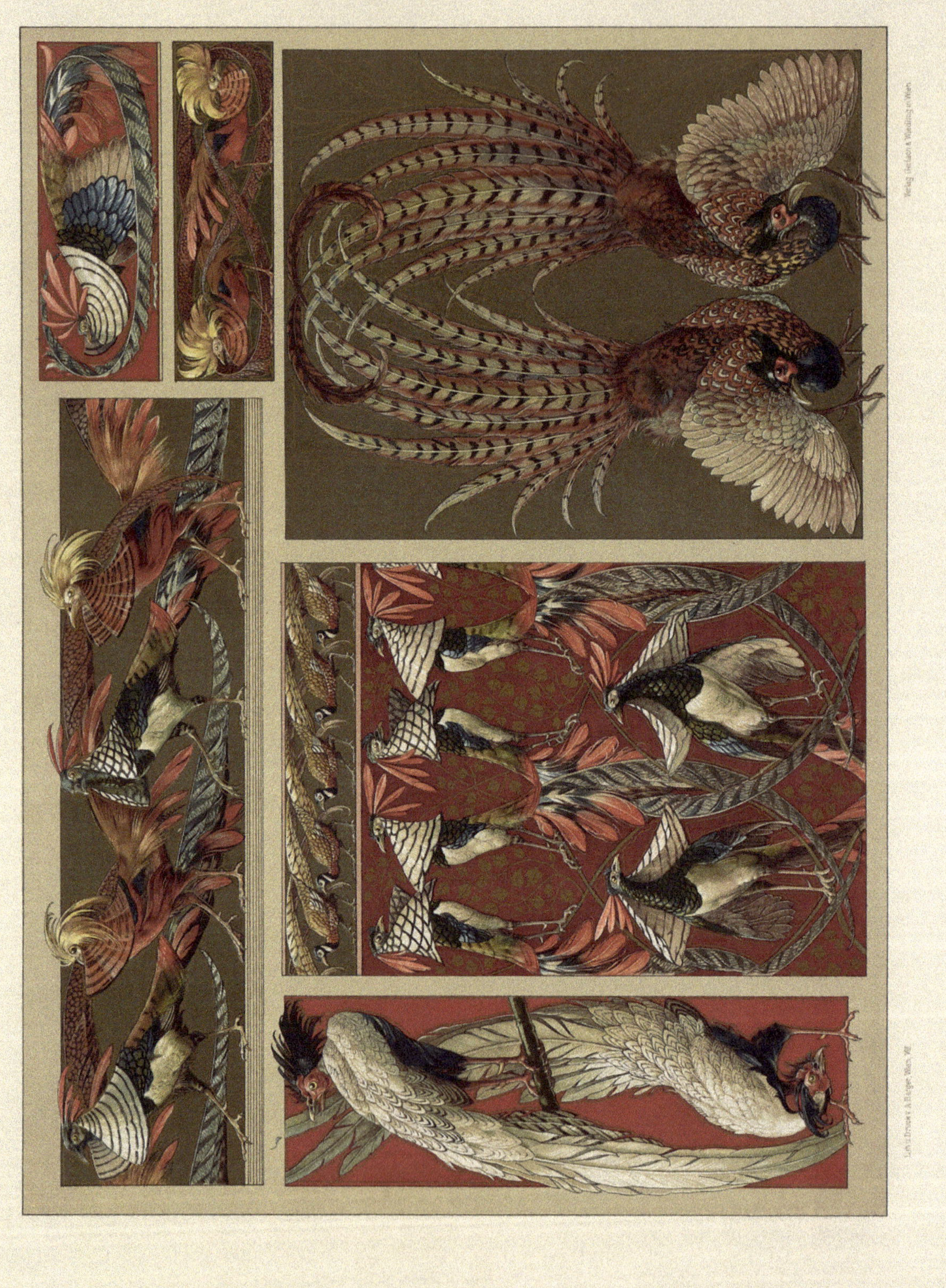

22 Plate Number 22 Das Thier in der
Decorativen Kunst, by A. Seder, 1896

23. Plate Number 23, Das Thier in der
Decorativen Kunst, by A. Seder, 1896

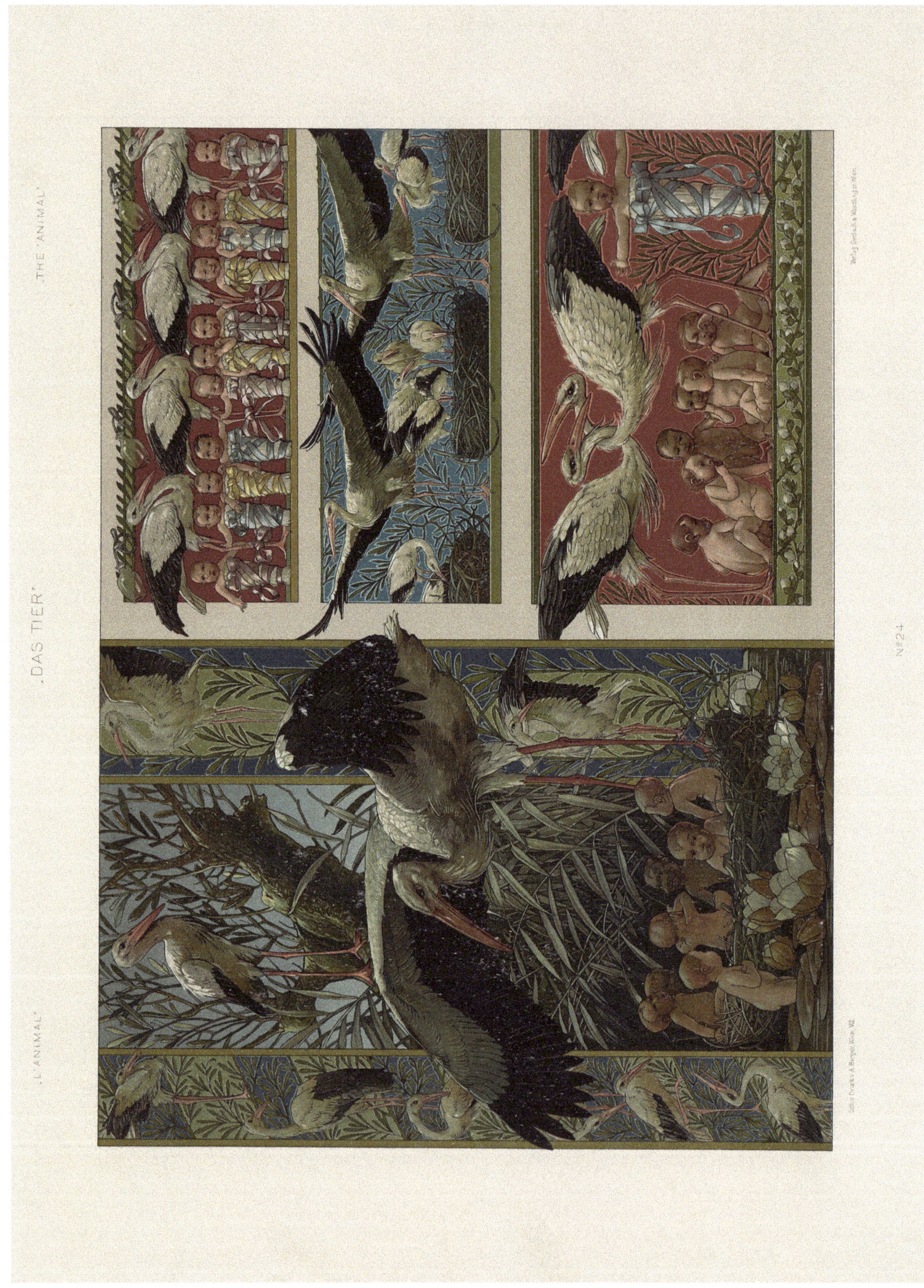

24. Plate Number 24, Das Thier in der
Decorativen Kunst, by A. Seder, 1896

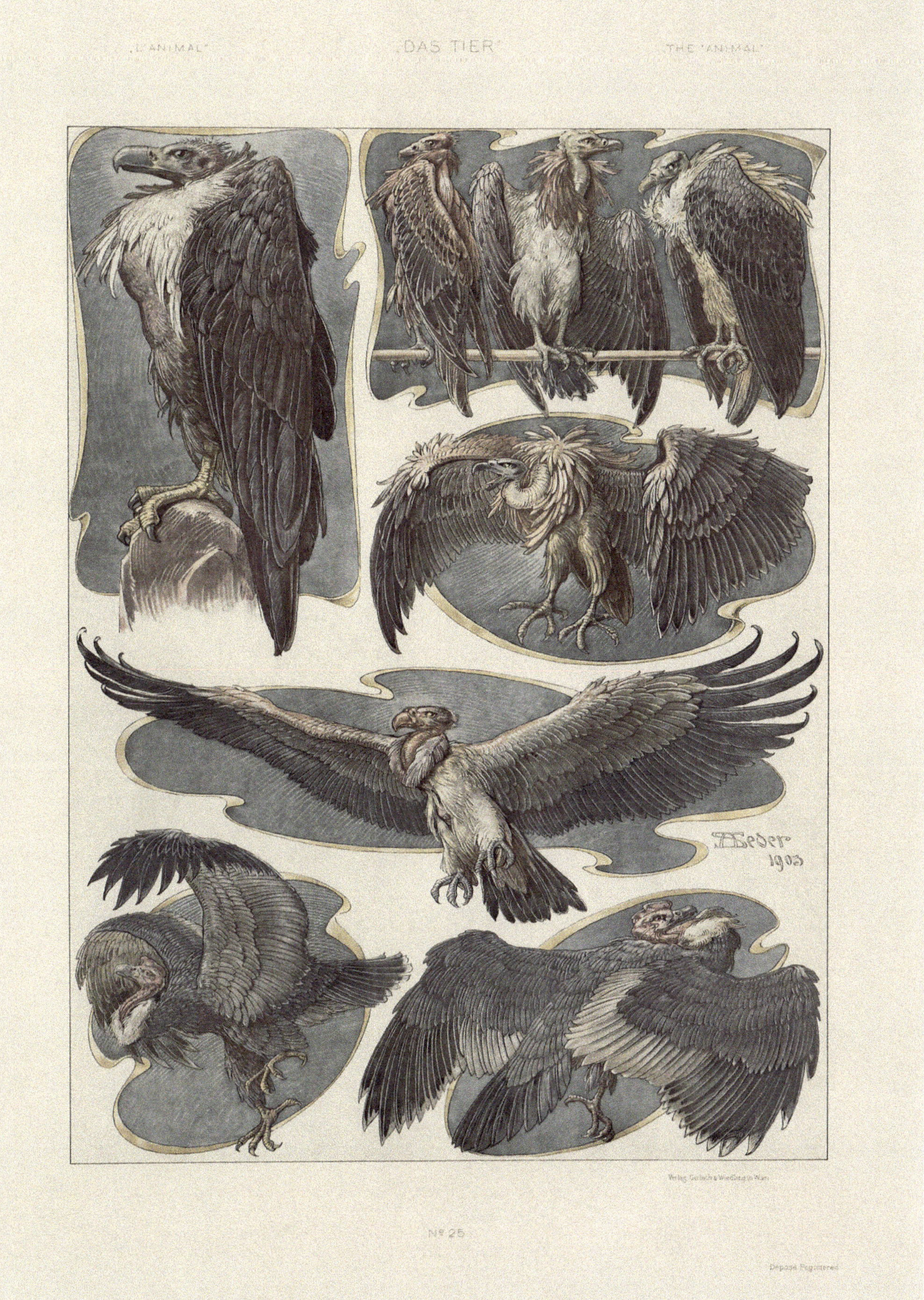

25. Plate Number 25. Das Thier in der
Decorativen Kunst, by A. Seder, 1896

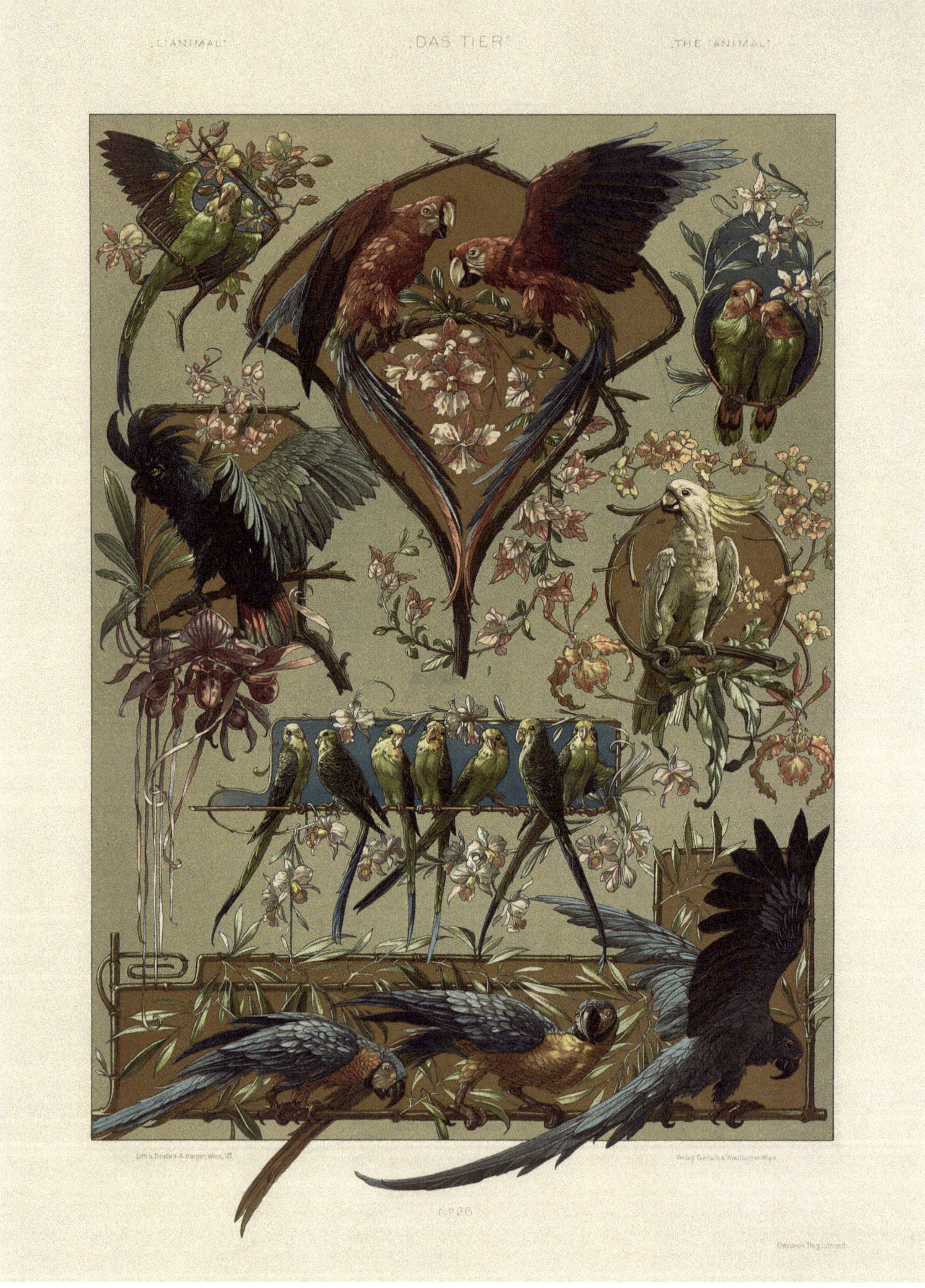

26. Plate Number 26, Das Thier in der
Decorativen Kunst, by A. Seder, 1896.

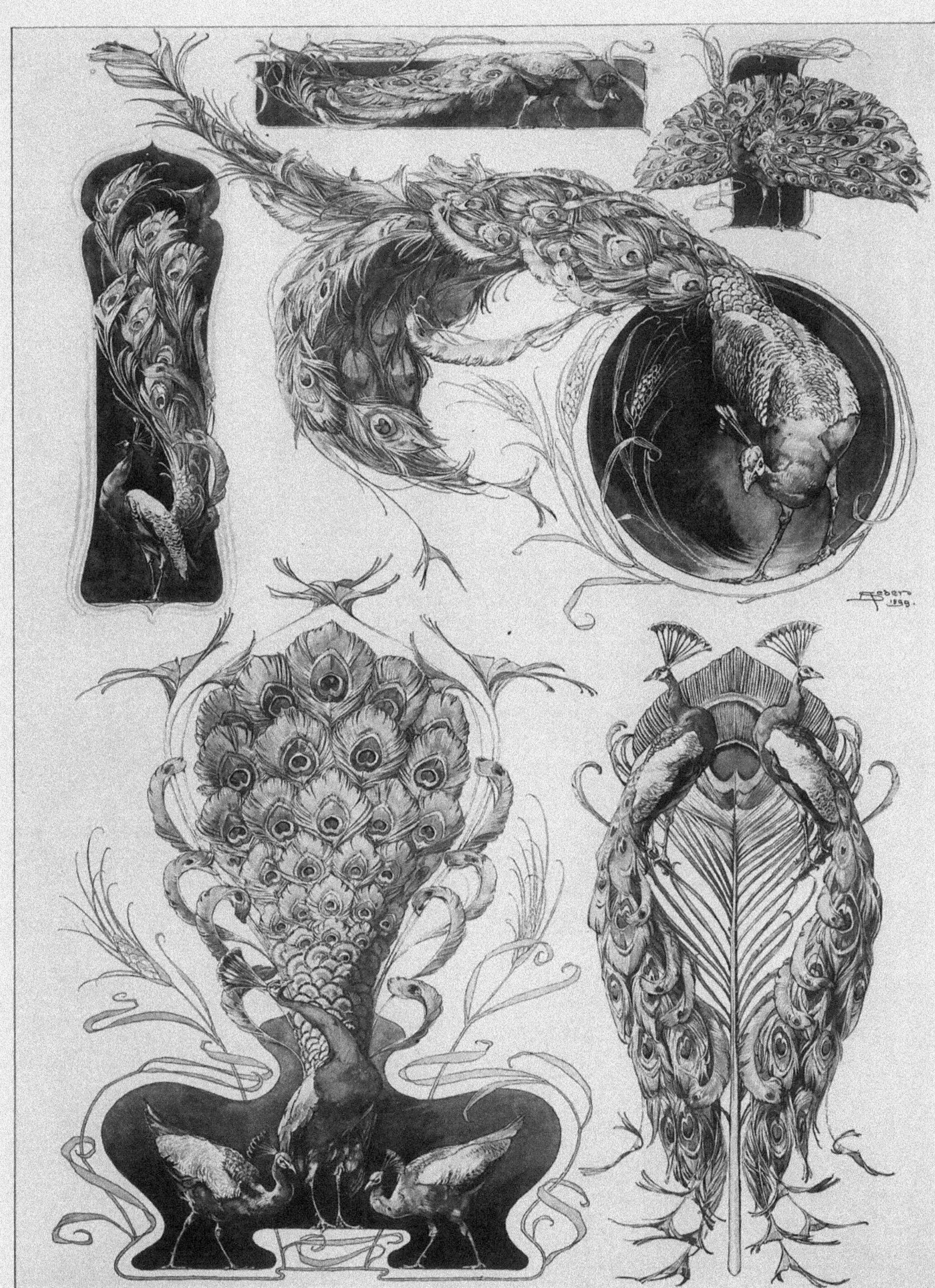

27. Plate Number 27, Das Thier in der
Decorativen Kunst, by A. Seder, 1896

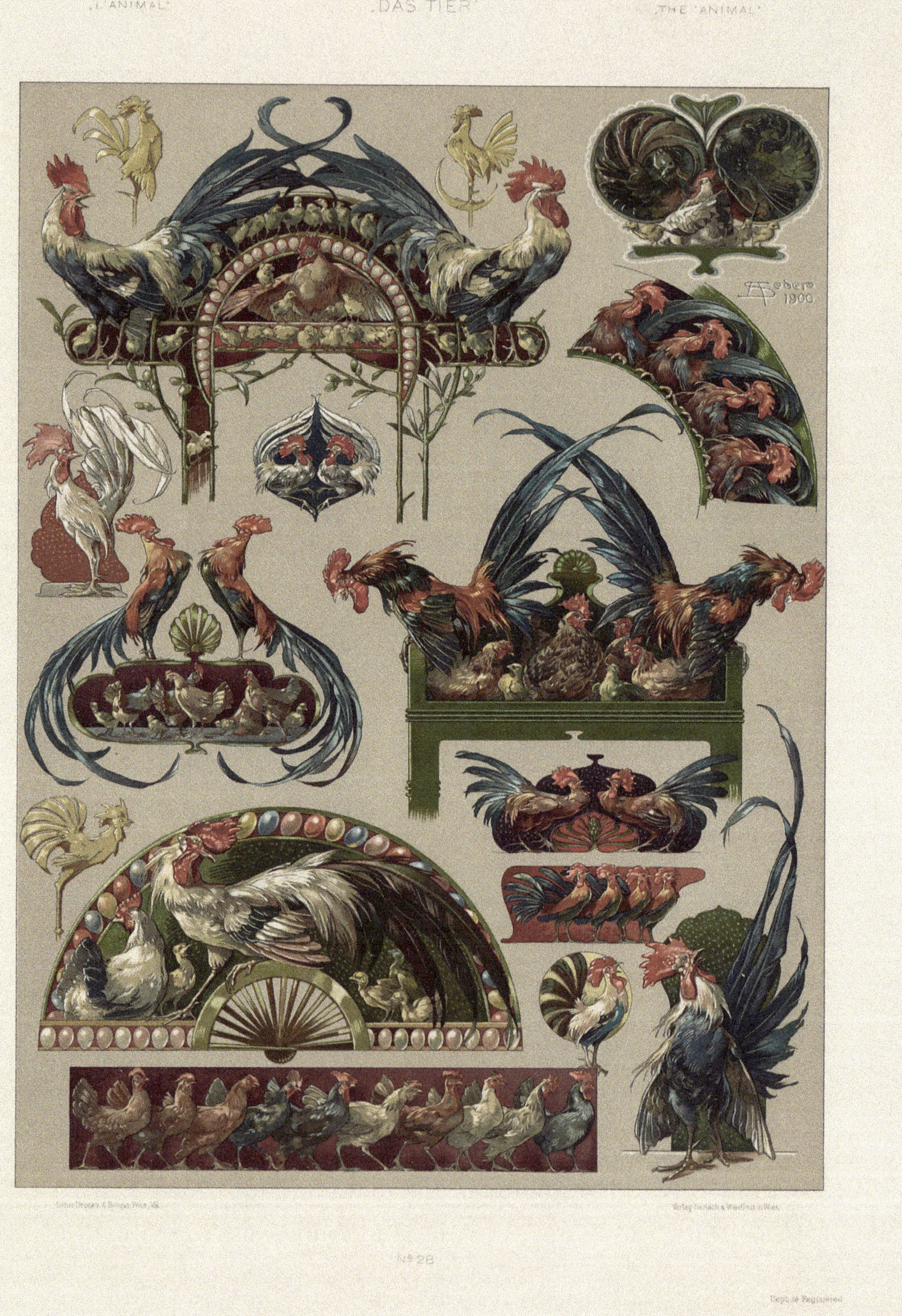

28. Plate Number 28. Das Thier in der
Decorativen Kunst, by A. Seder, 1896.

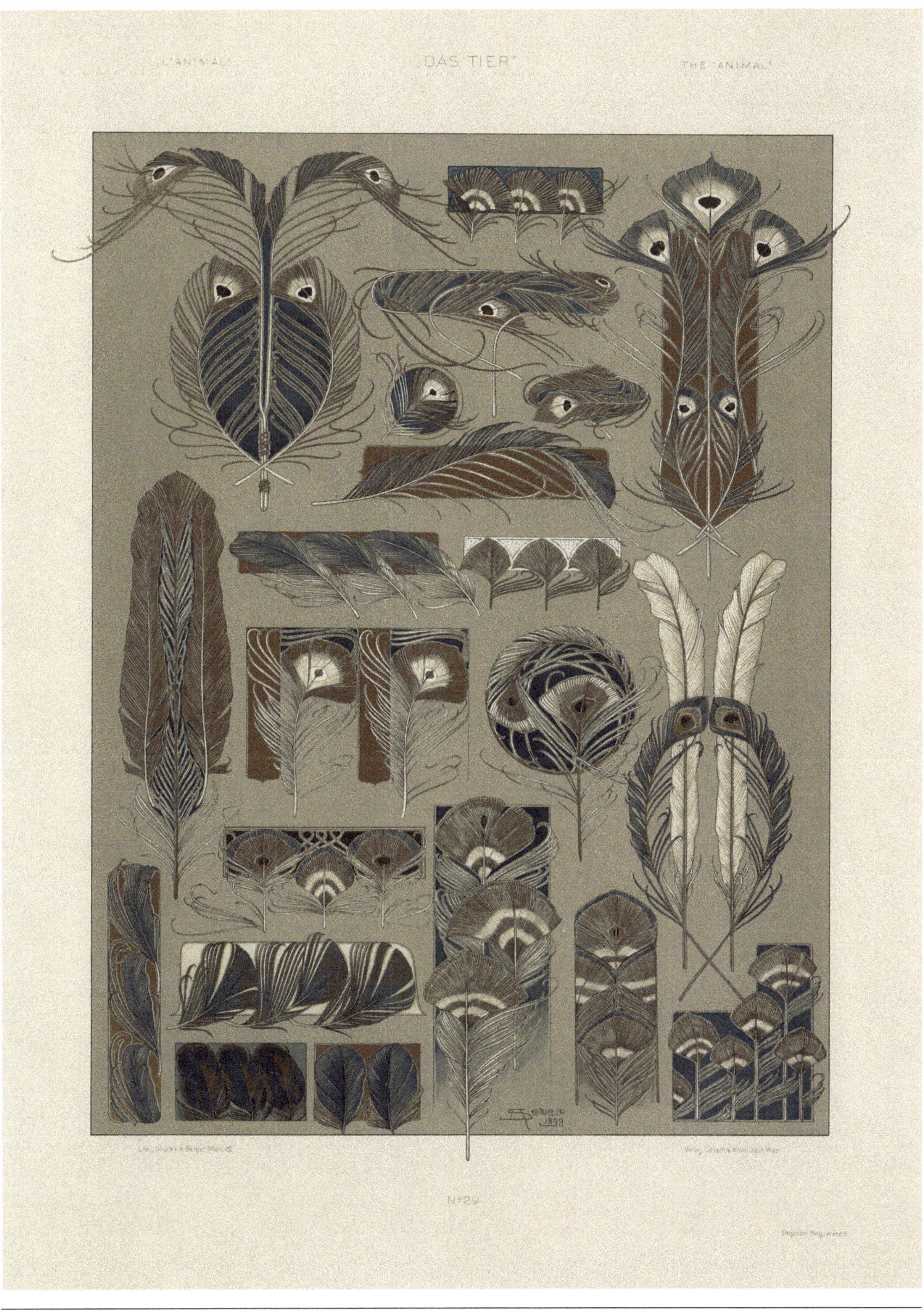

29 Plate Number 29. Das Thier in der
Decorativen Kunst. by A. Seder. 1896

03

The Plant in Art and Craft

Anton Seder's *Die Pflanze in Kunst und Gewerbe* (The Plant in Art and Craft) is a stunning exploration of the botanical world as a foundation for decorative art. This influential work exemplifies Seder's belief that the forms and structures of plants—leaves, flowers, vines, and stems—possess a unique elegance that can inspire a limitless range of artistic applications. Each illustration is meticulously crafted and coloured, revealing the intricate details of plant life and demonstrating how these natural shapes can be adapted into ornamental designs. Seder's work showcases a variety of artistic possibilities, from delicate floral motifs to bold, sweeping vine patterns that capture the rhythmic flow of nature.

Die Pflanze in Kunst und Gewerbe influenced the Art Nouveau movement, which drew heavily on nature for its aesthetic and structural inspiration. Seder's designs highlight how plant motifs can be stylised to enhance architecture, furniture,

textiles, and other applied arts, bridging the gap between organic forms and human-made beauty. His botanical illustrations offer timeless lessons in translating the grace and complexity of nature into design elements that feel both refined and dynamic.

More than a century after its publication, *Die Pflanze in Kunst und Gewerbe* remains a vital resource for contemporary artists and designers who seek to incorporate the elegance of natural forms into their work. Seder's ability to distil nature's essence into visually captivating patterns continues to inspire and educate, making this book an essential resource for those looking to deepen their understanding of the relationship between the natural world and decorative arts.

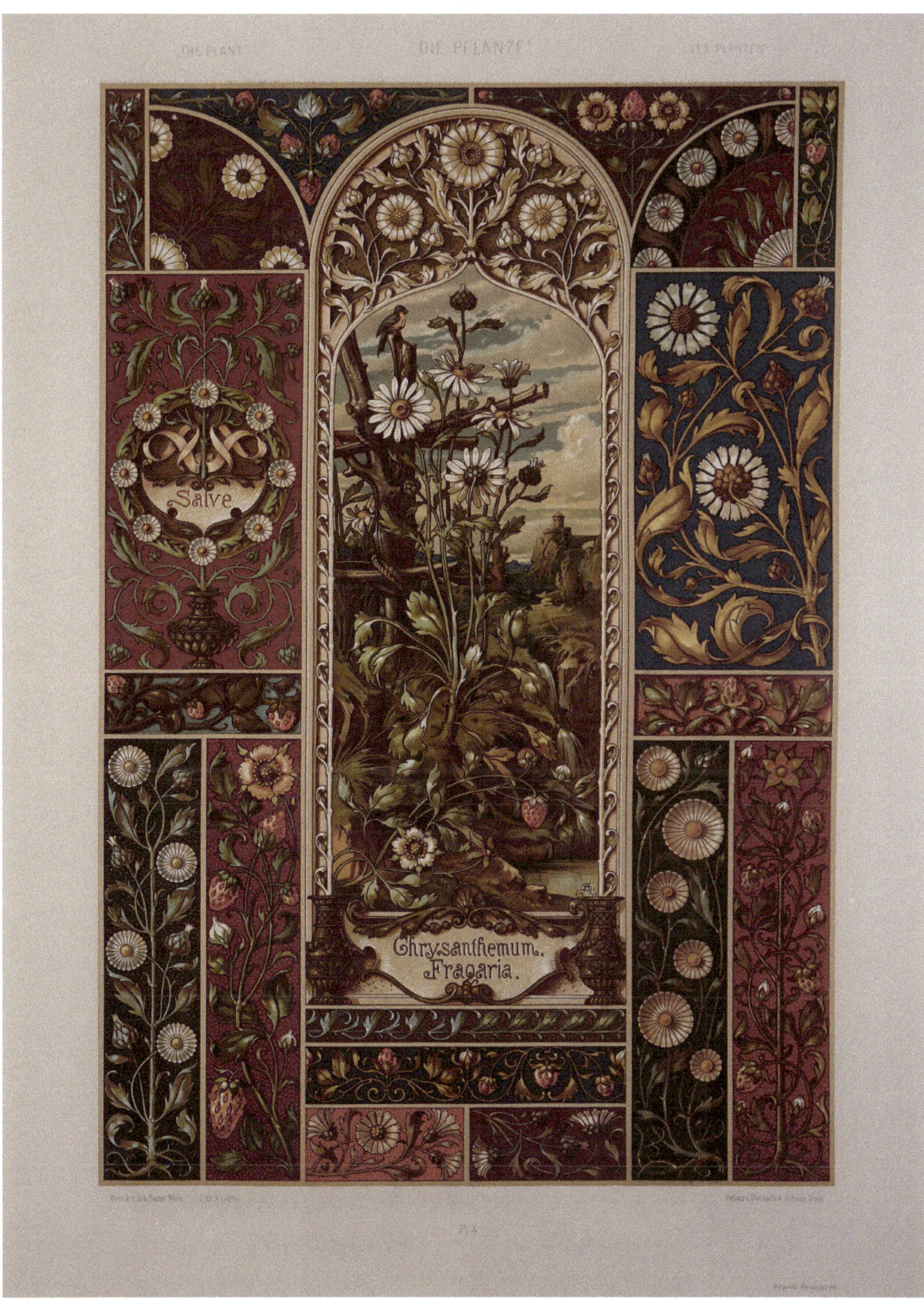
THE PLANT
DIE PFLANZE
LES PLANTES
Salve
Chrysanthemum.
Fragaria.
ANTON SEDER

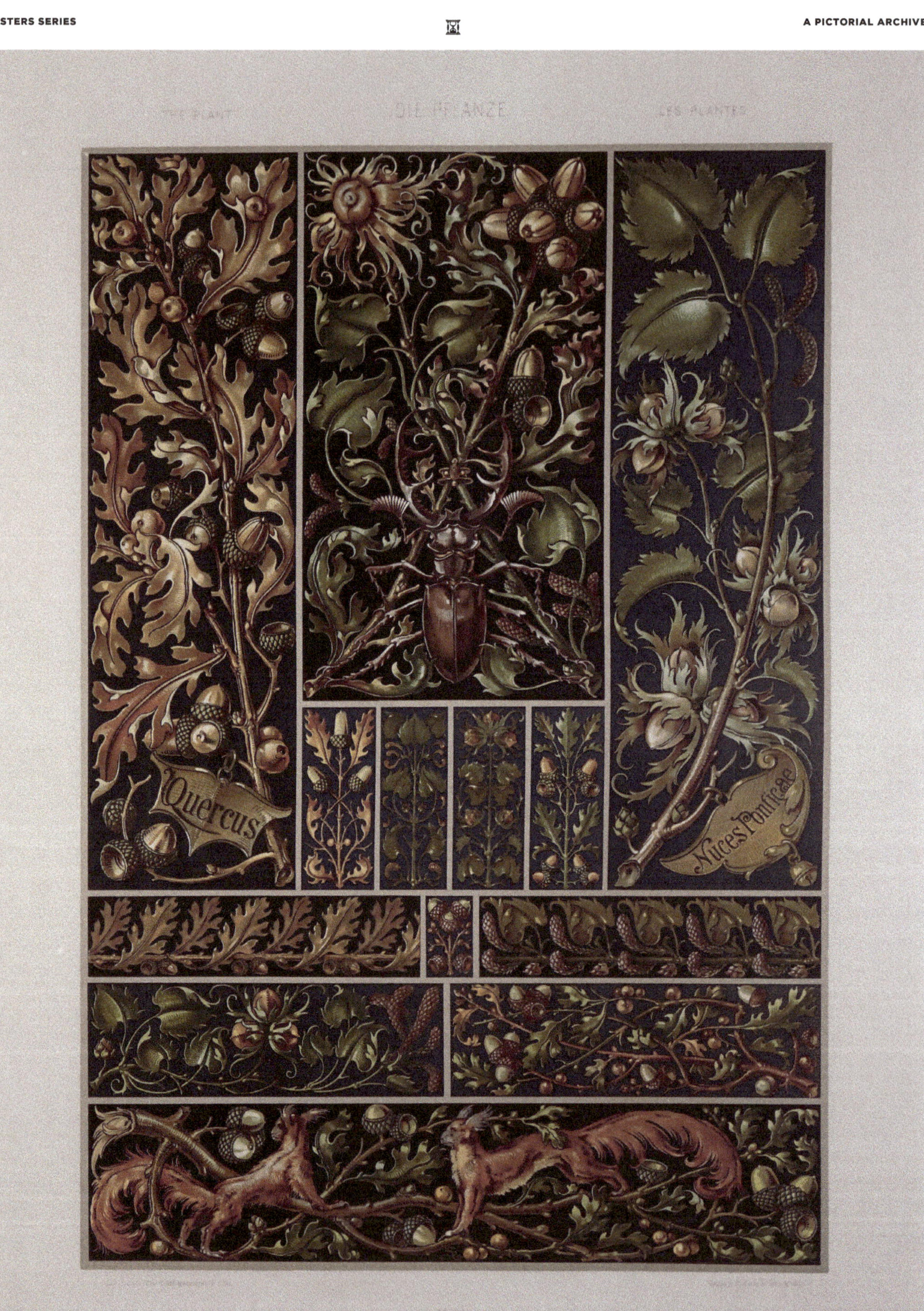

31. Plate 22. Die Pflanze in Kunst und Gewerbe
Volume 2, by A. Seder, c. 1886

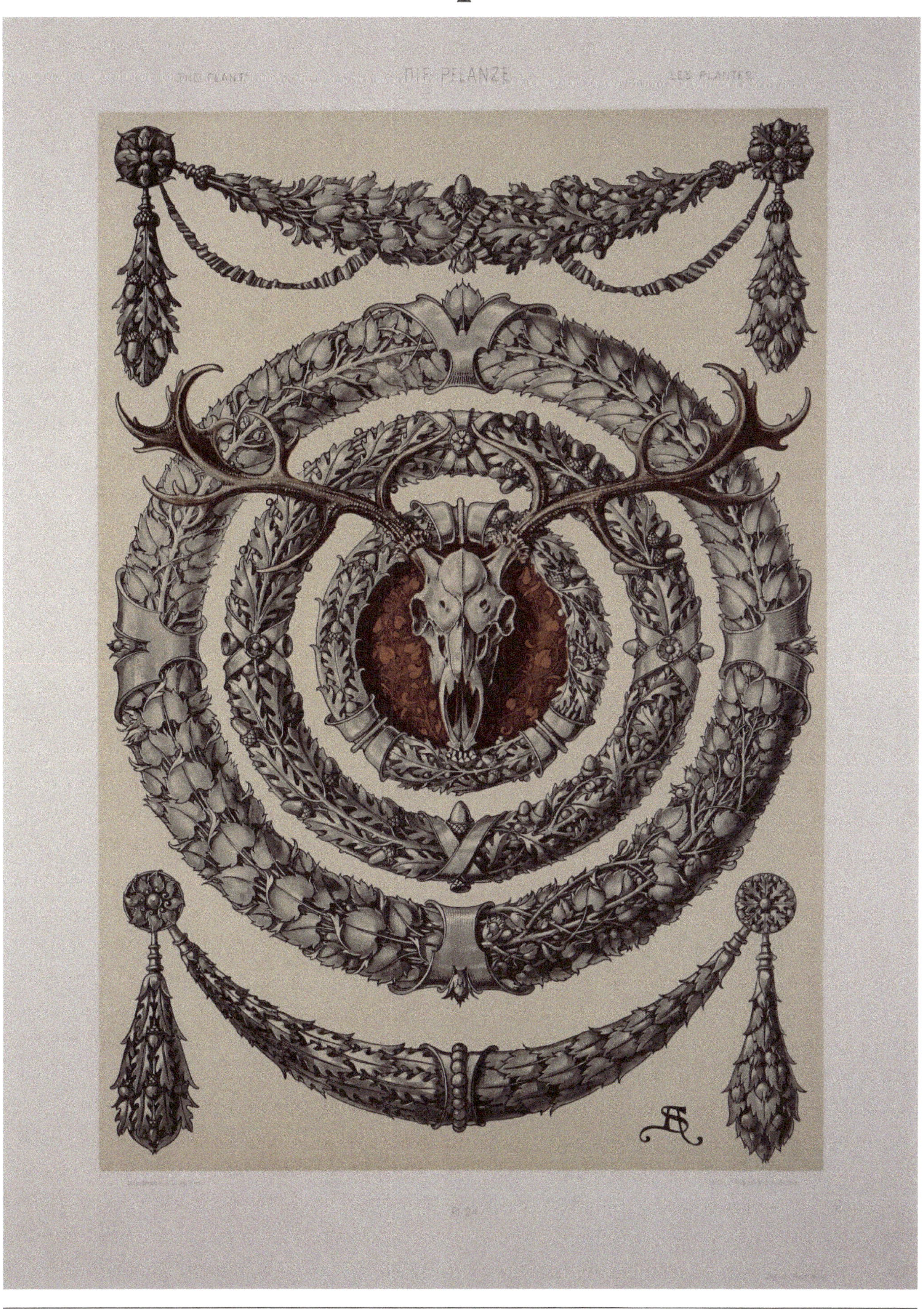

32. Plate 24, Die Pflanze in Kunst und Gewerbe
Volume 2 by A. Seder, c 1886

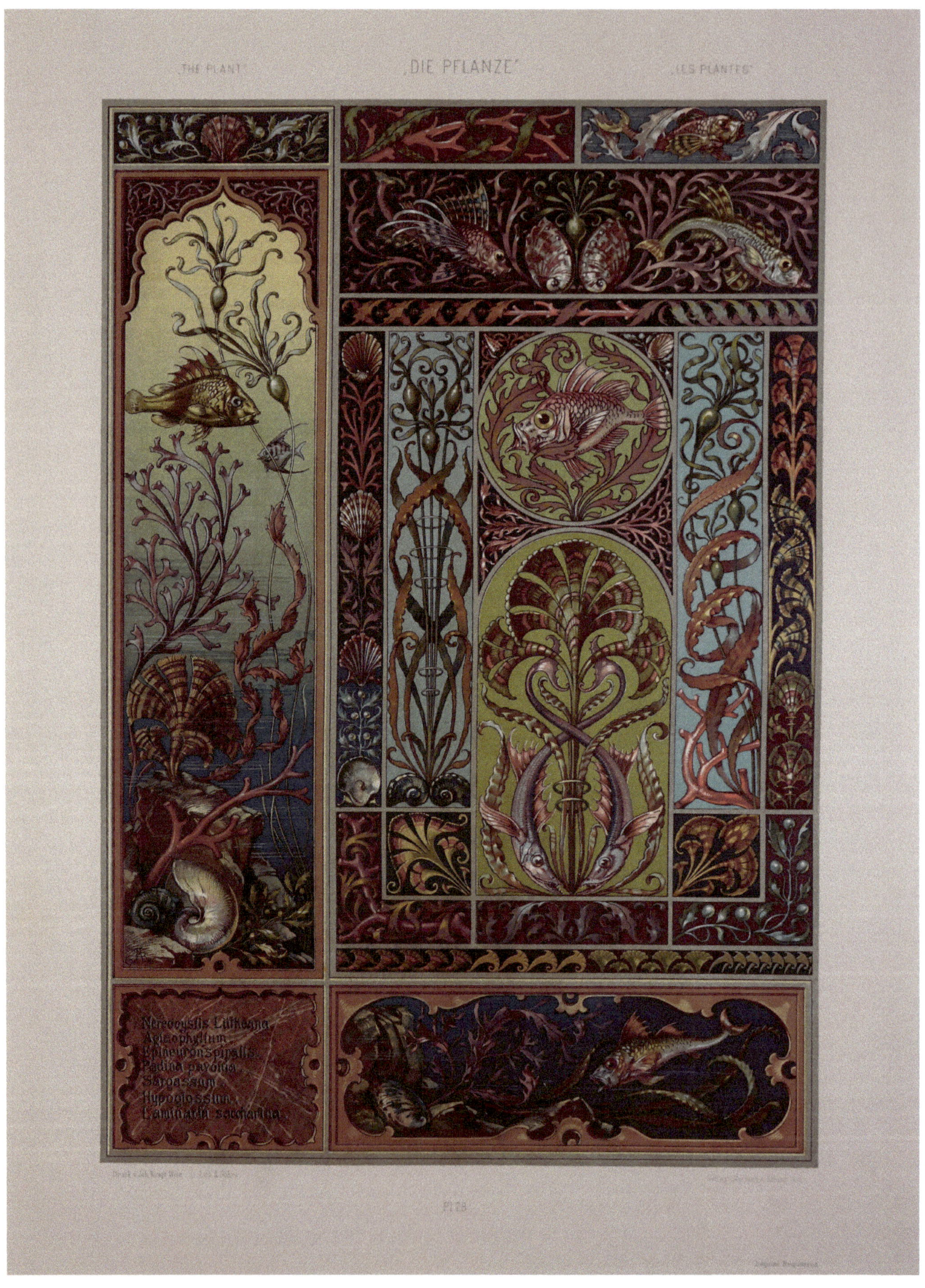

33. Plate 28. Die Pflanze in Kunst und Gewerbe
Volume 2, by A. Seder, c. 1886

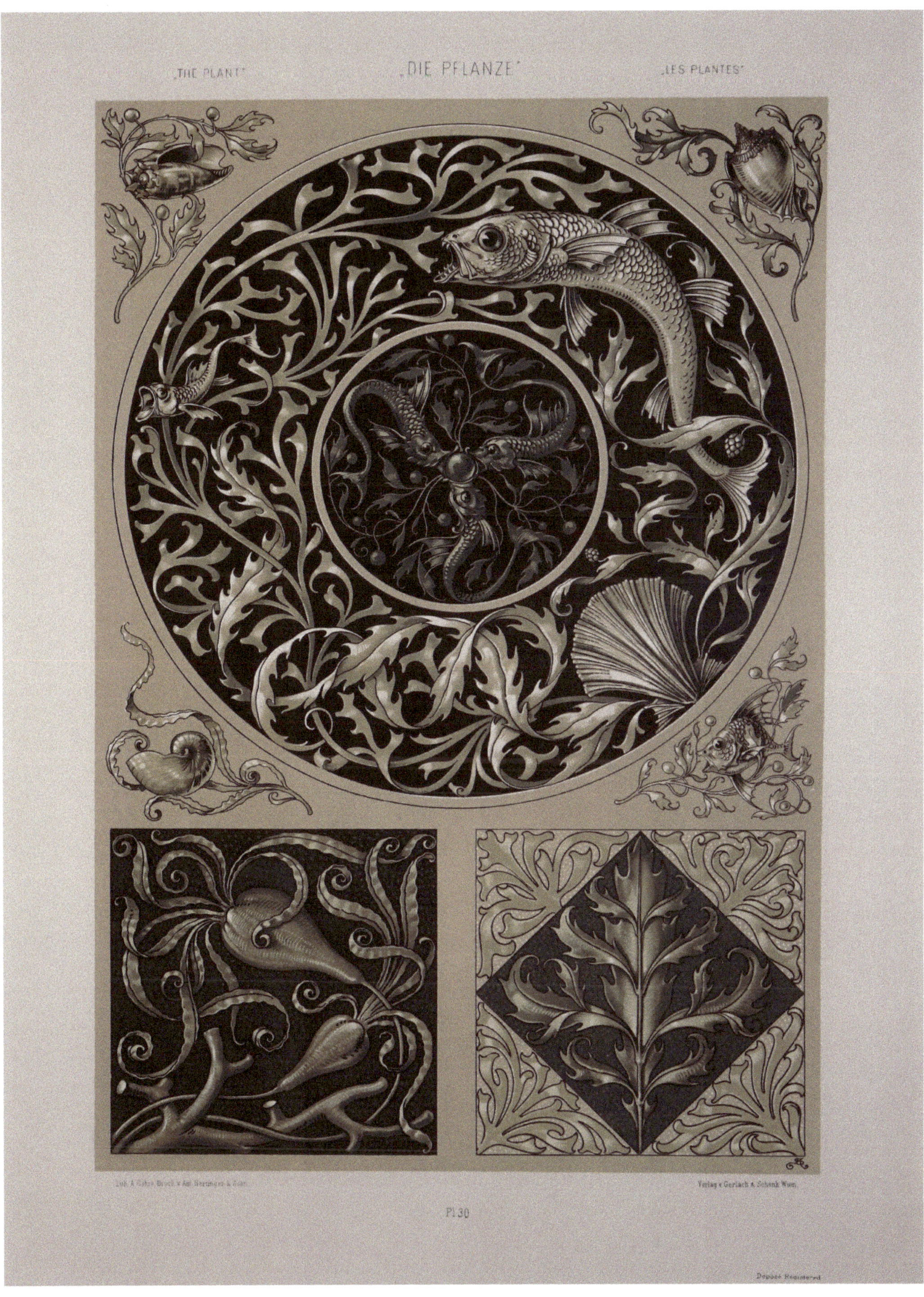

34. Plate 30, Die Pflanze in Kunst und Gewerbe
Volume 2, by A. Seder, c 1886

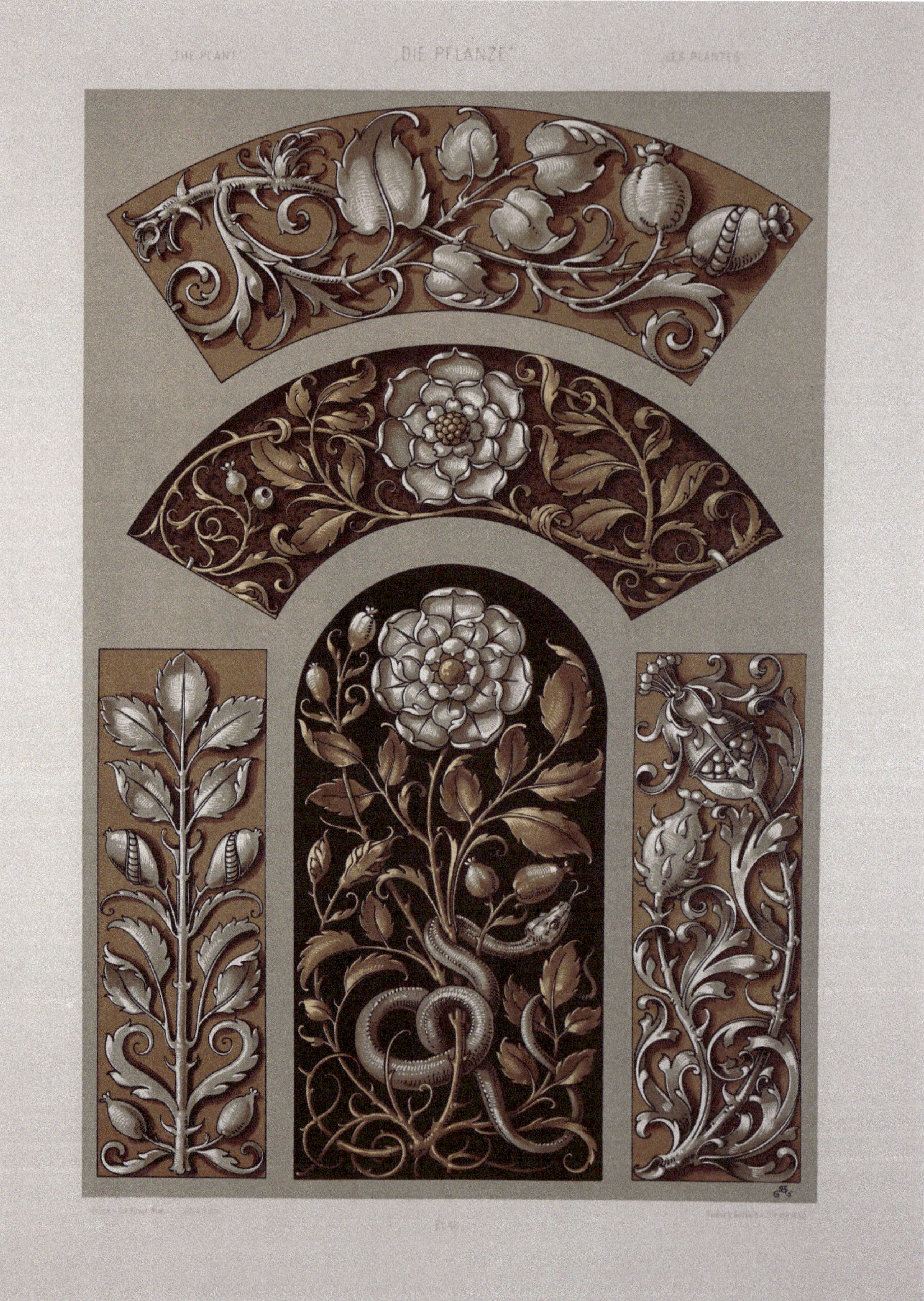

35. Plate 46, Die Pflanze in Kunst und Gewerbe
Volume 2, by A. Seder, c. 1886

THE PLANT
DIE PFLANZE
LES PLANTES

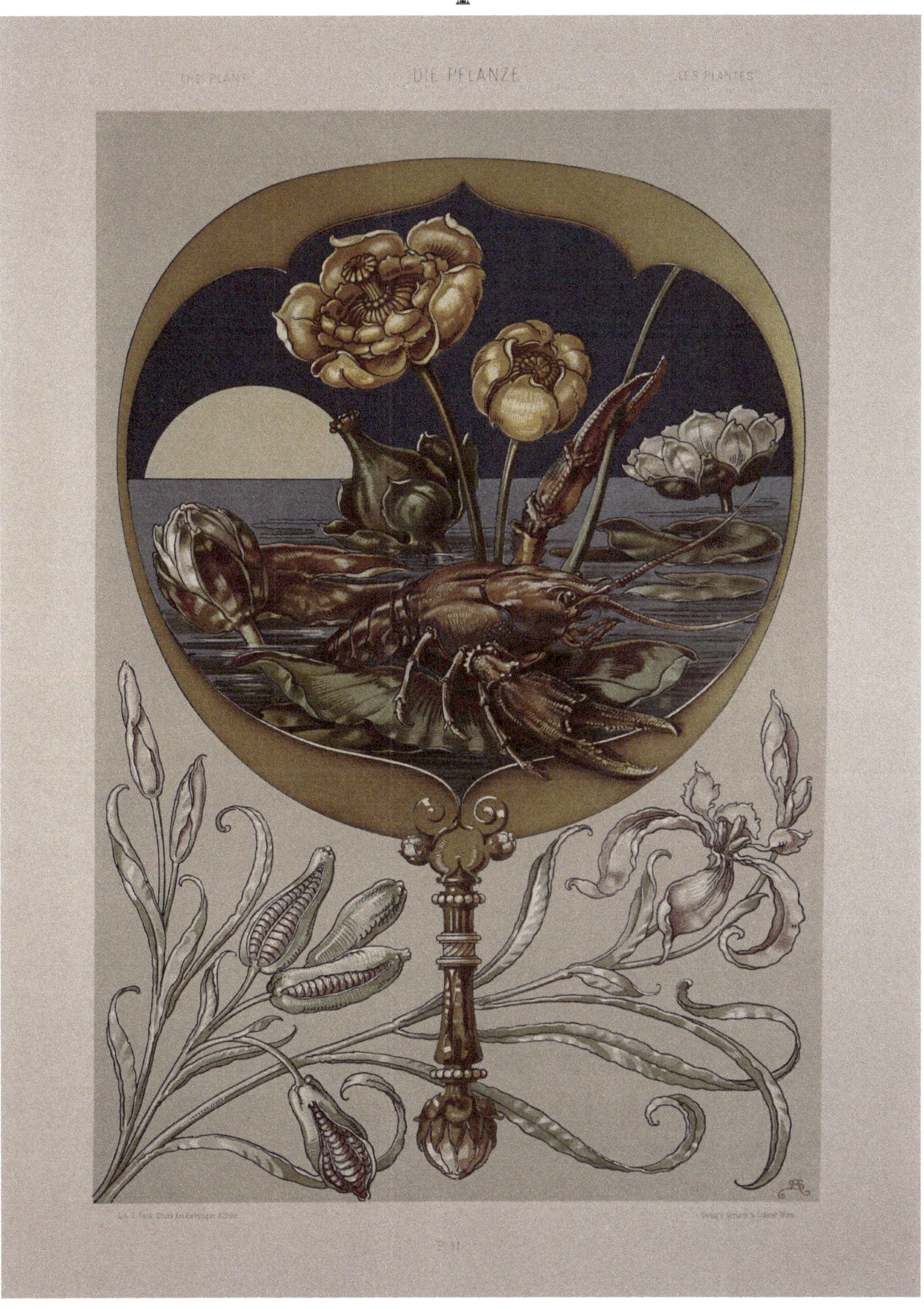

ANTON SEDER

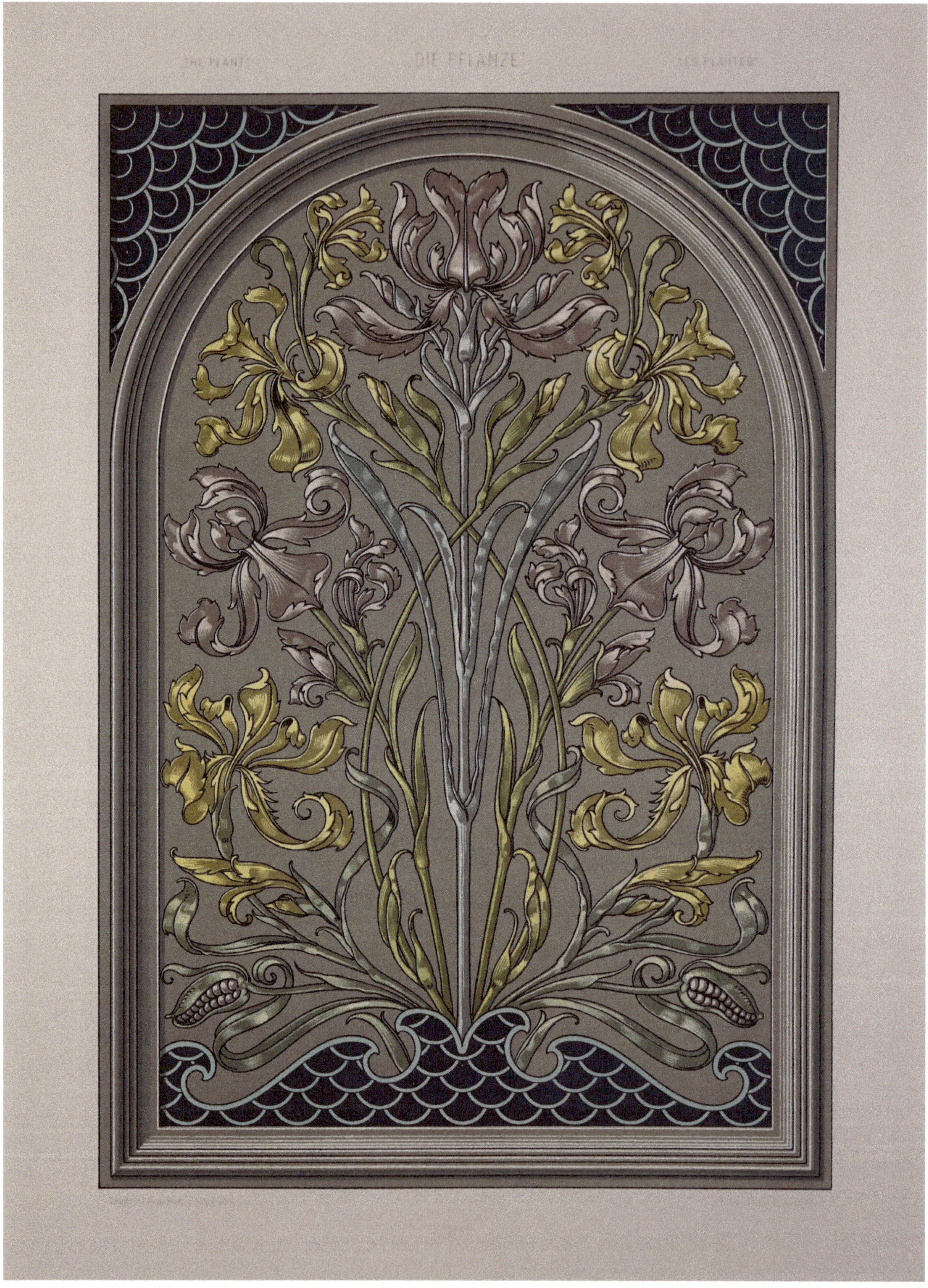

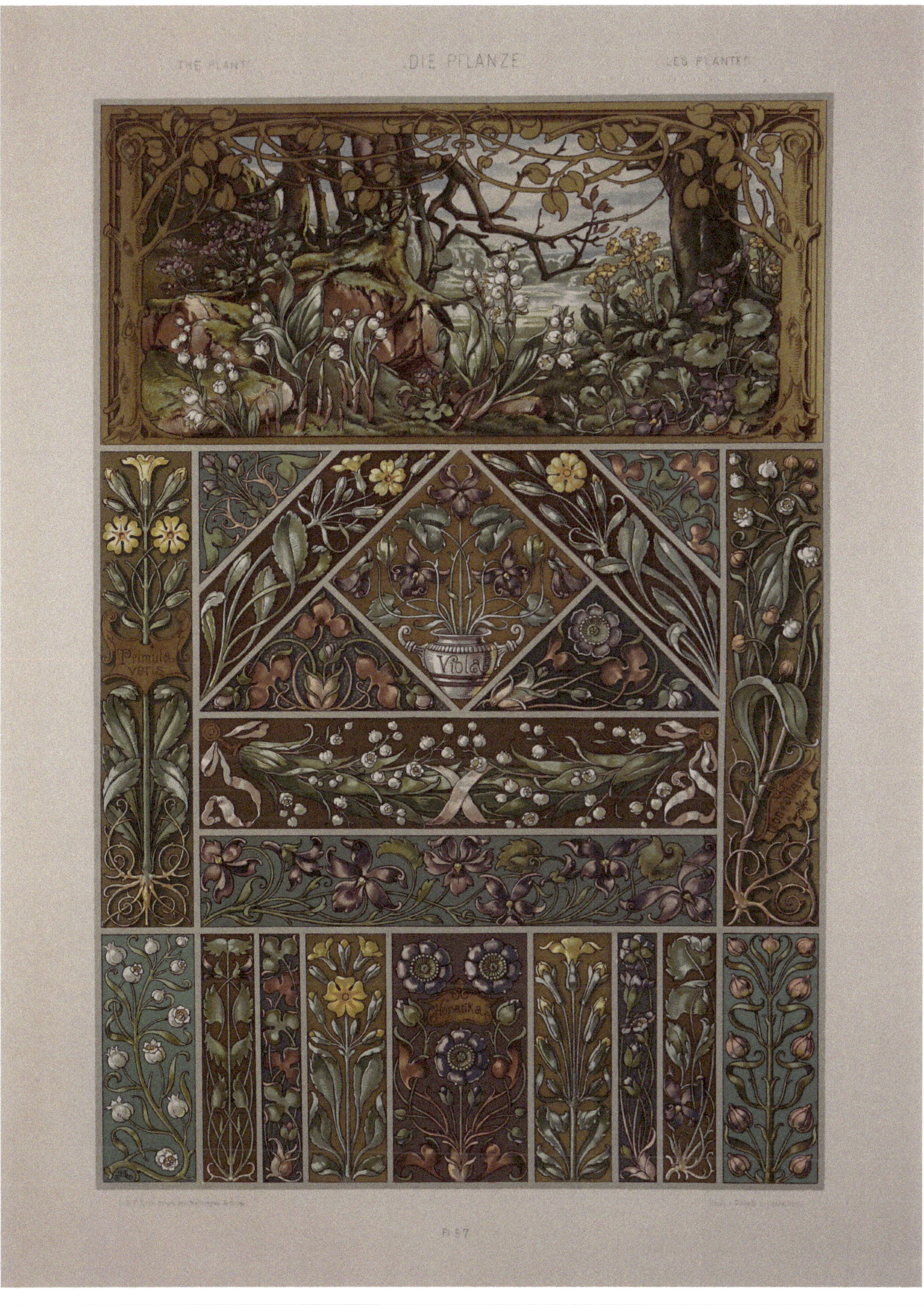

38. Plate 57. Die Pflanze in Kunst und Gewerbe
Volume 2, by A. Seder, c. 1886

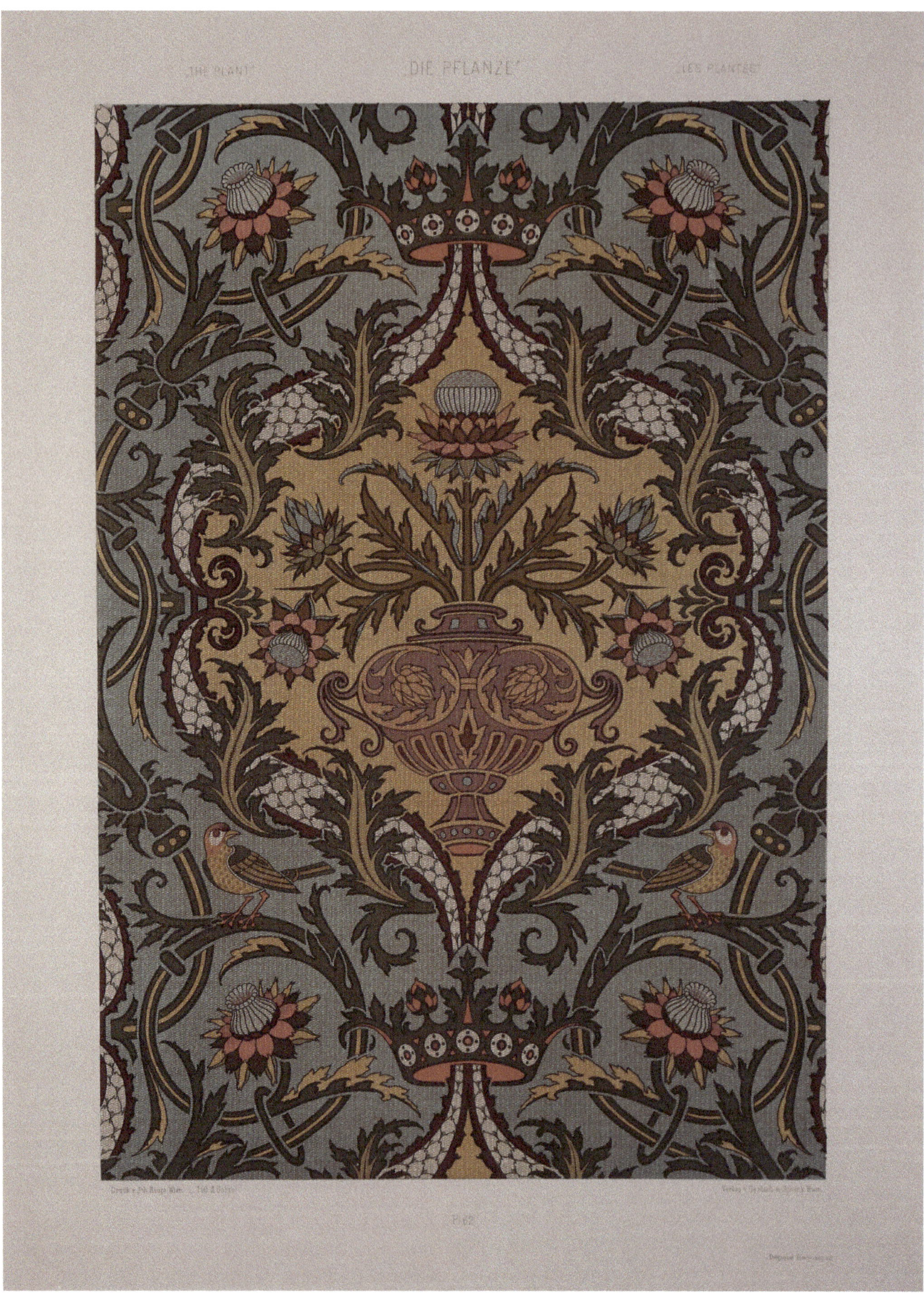

39. Plate 62, Die Pflanze in Kunst und Gewerbe
Volume 2, by A. Seder, c. 1886

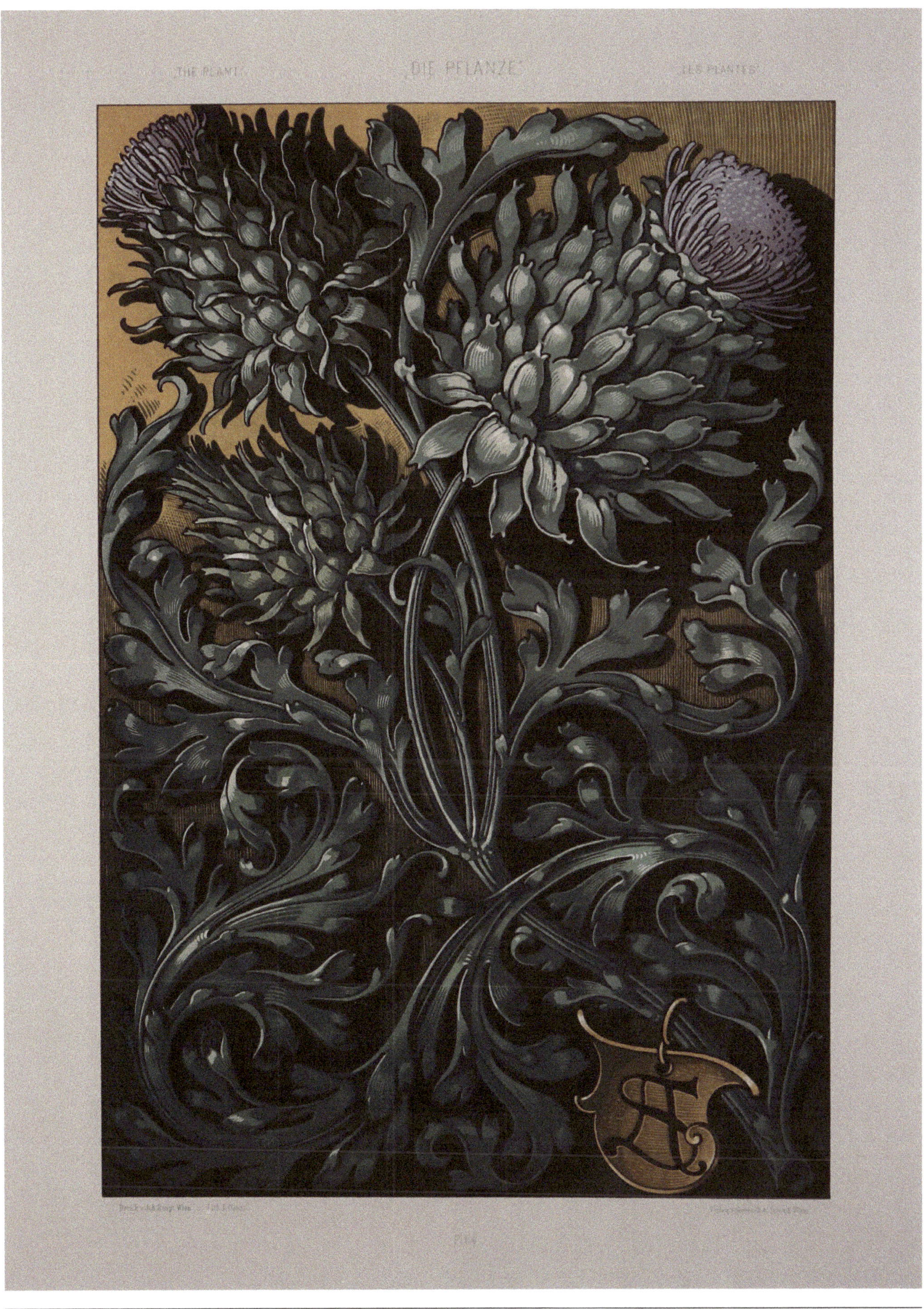

40. Plate 64 *Die Pflanze in Kunst und Gewerbe*
Volume 2, by A. Seder, c. 1886.

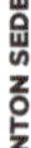

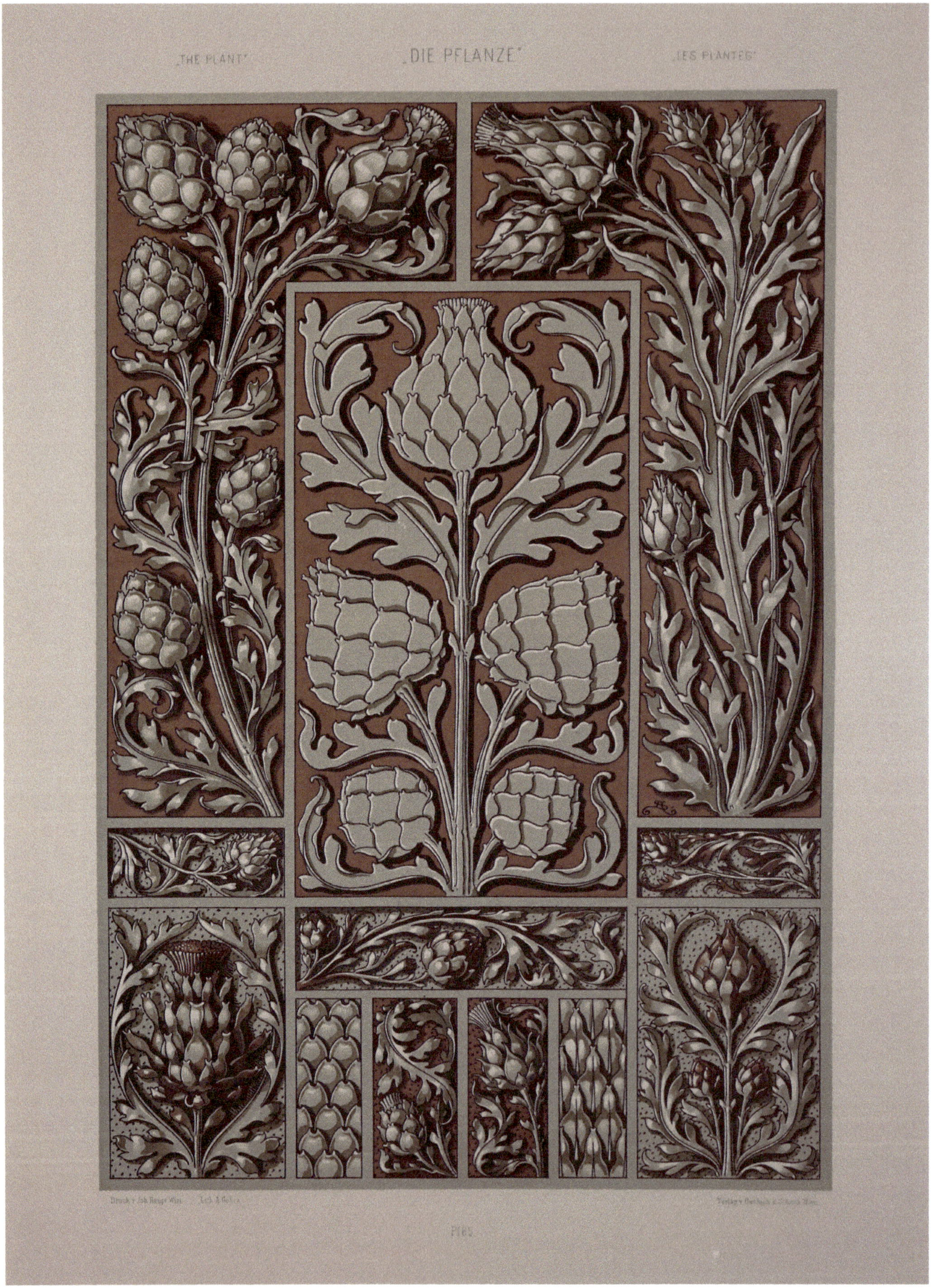

„THE PLANT"
„DIE PFLANZE"
„LES PLANTES"

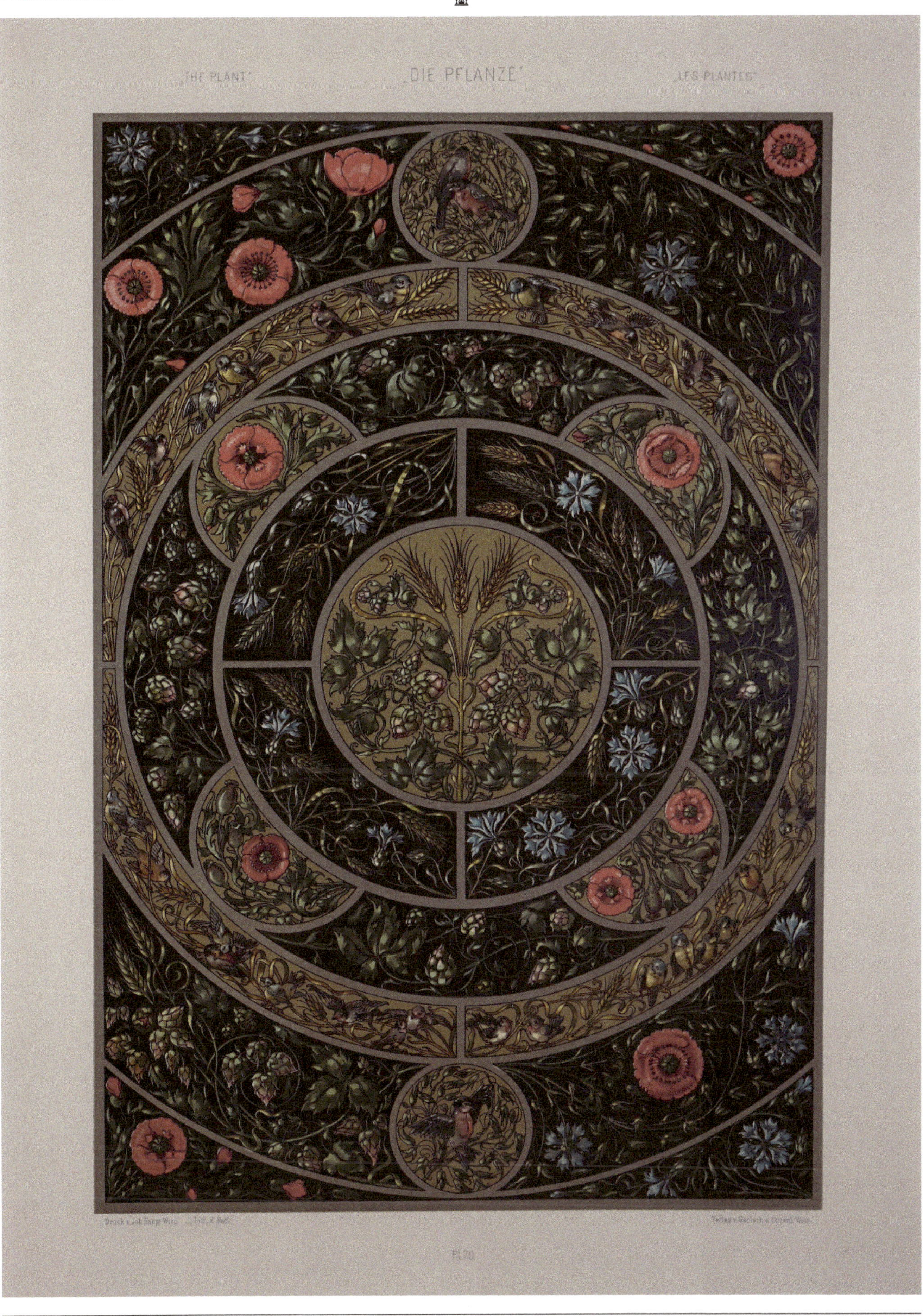

ANTON SEDER

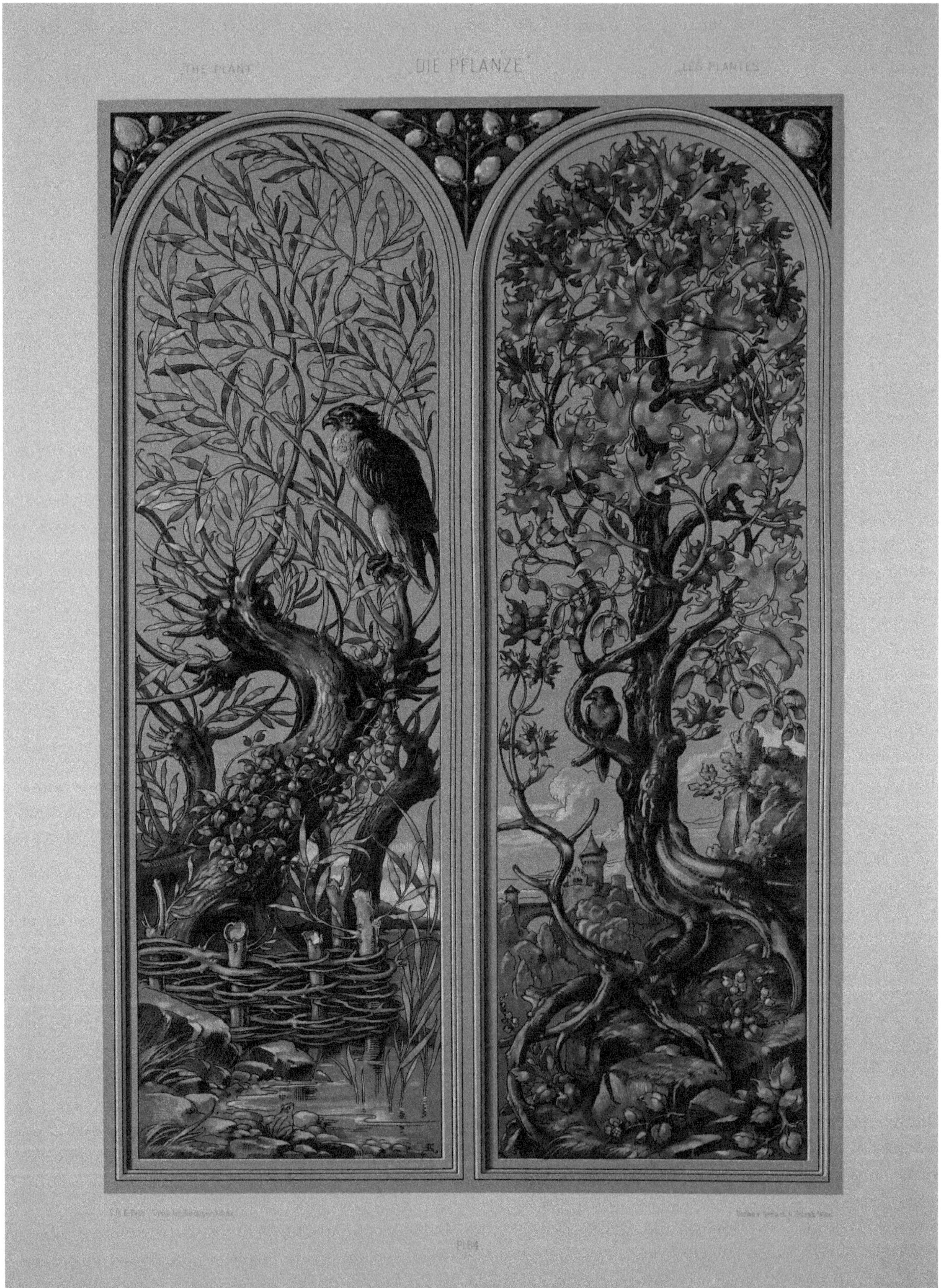

43. Plate 84. Die Pflanze in Kunst und Gewerbe
Volume 2, by A. Seder. c. 1886

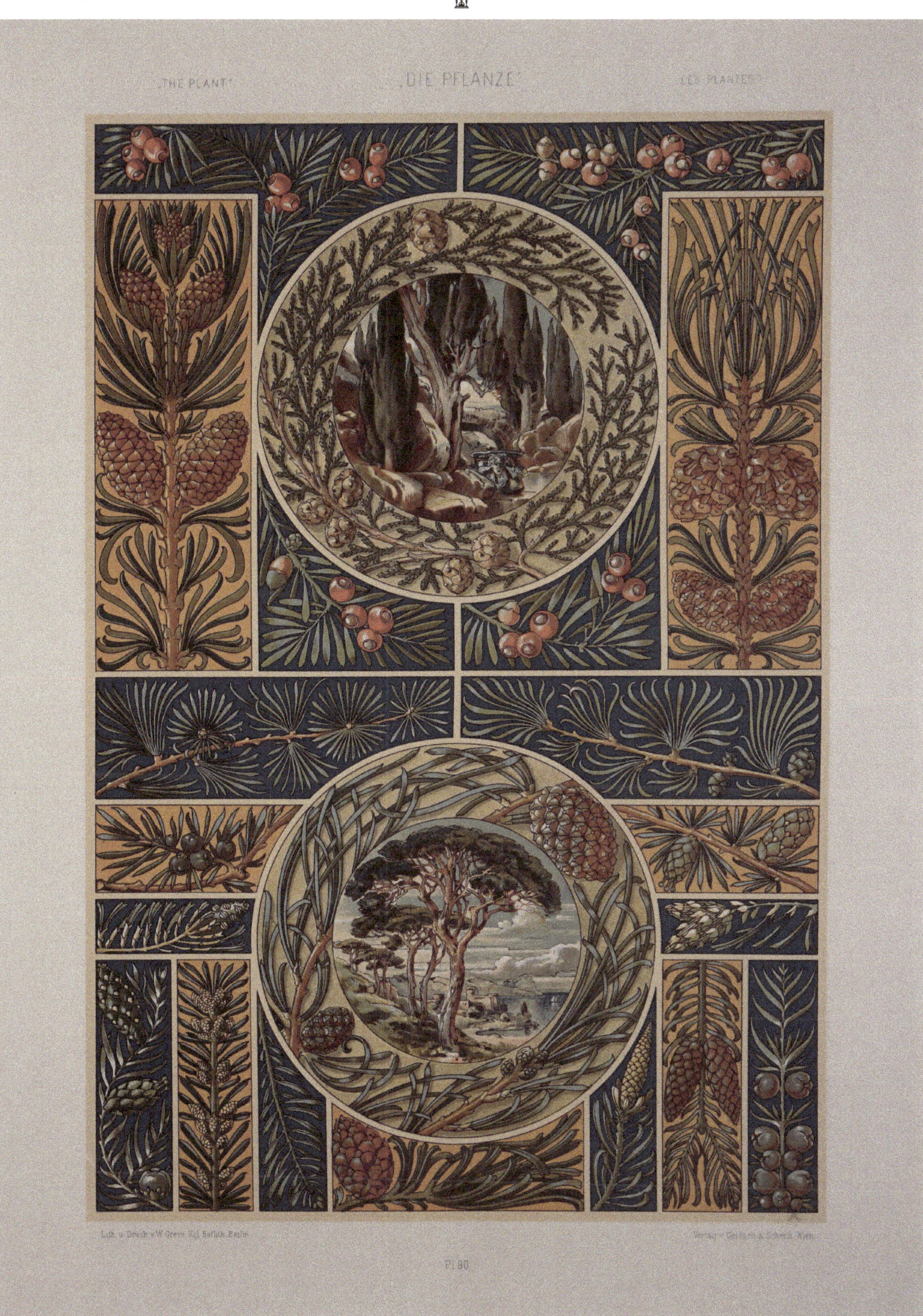
„THE PLANT"
„DIE PFLANZE"
„LES PLANTES"
ANTON SEDER
Pl. 90

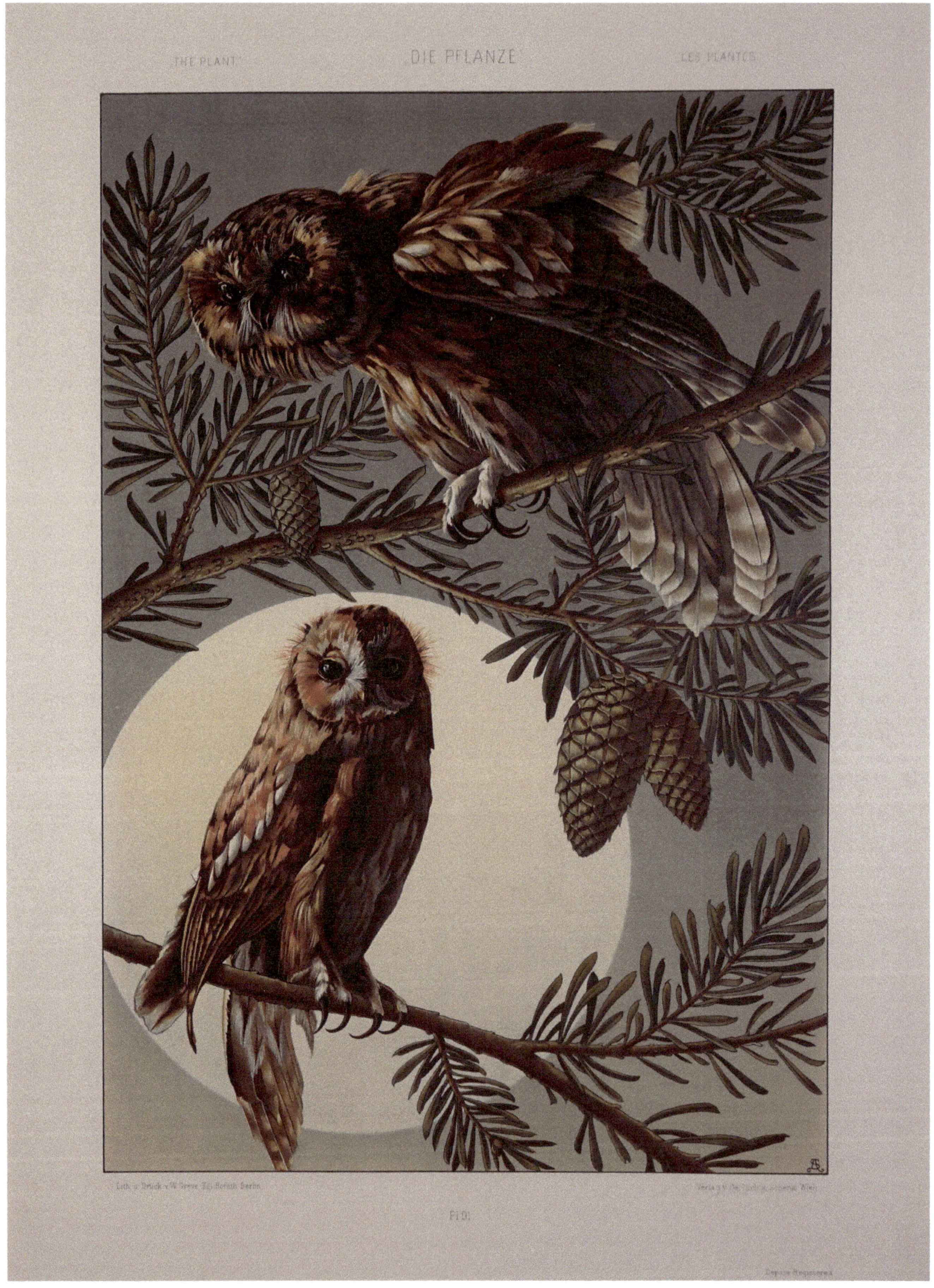

45. Plate 91. Die Pflanze in Kunst und Gewerbe.
Volume 2. by A. Seder. c. 1886.

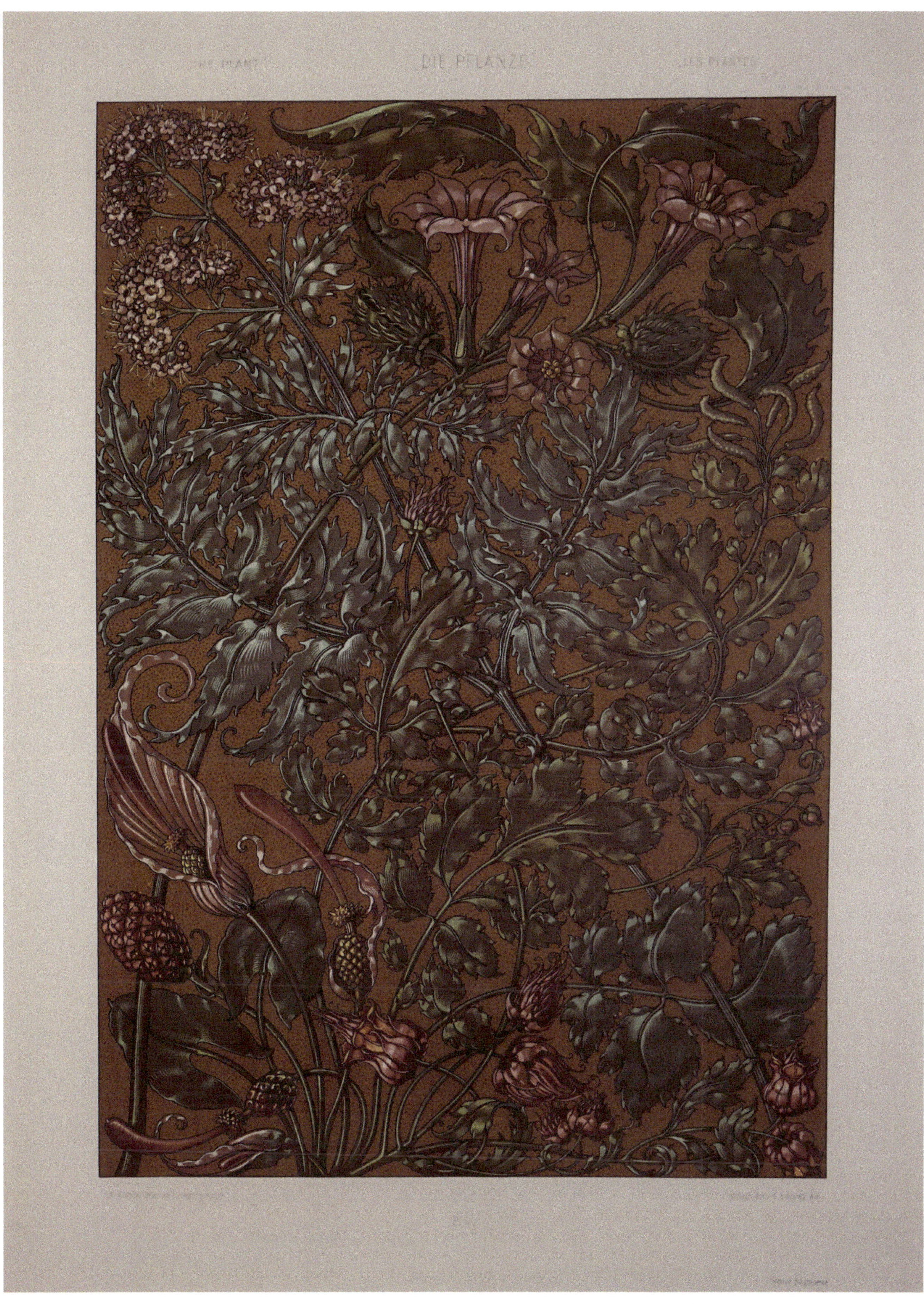

ANTON SEDER

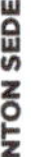

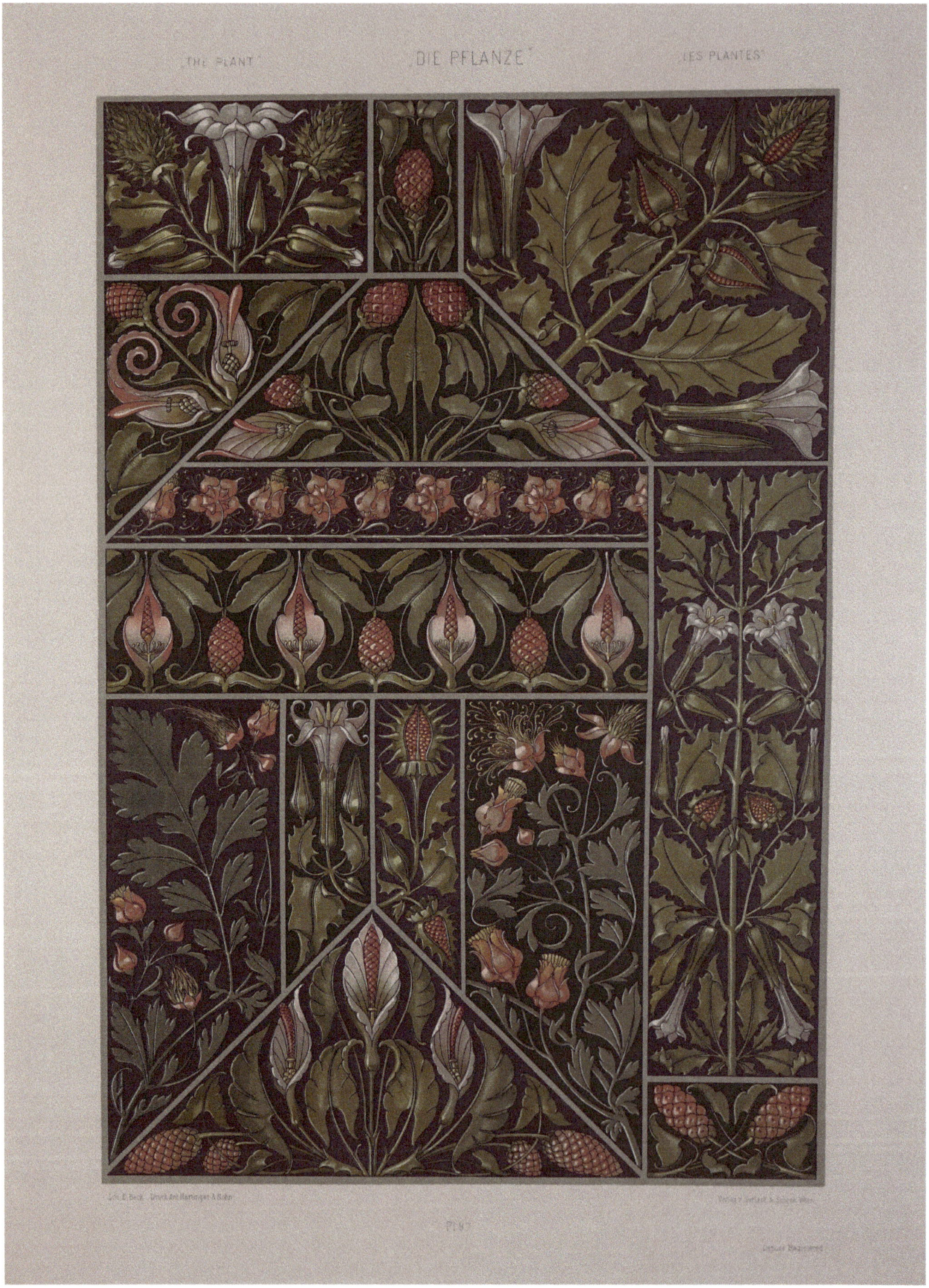

47. Plate 97. Die Pflanze in Kunst und Gewerbe
Volume 2, by A. Seder, c. 1886

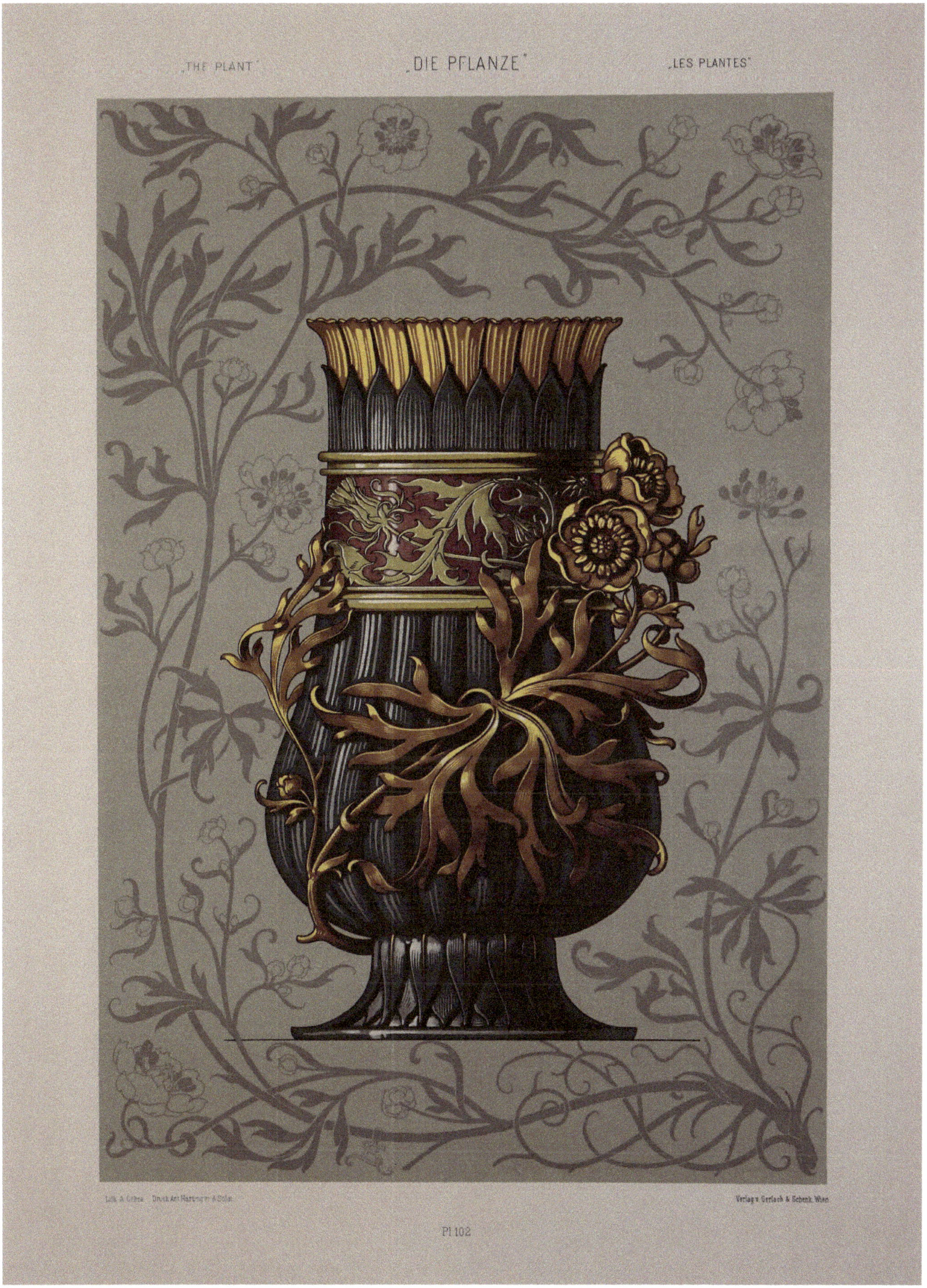

48. Plate 102. Die Pflanze in Kunst und Gewerbe
Volume 2, by A. Seder, c. 1886

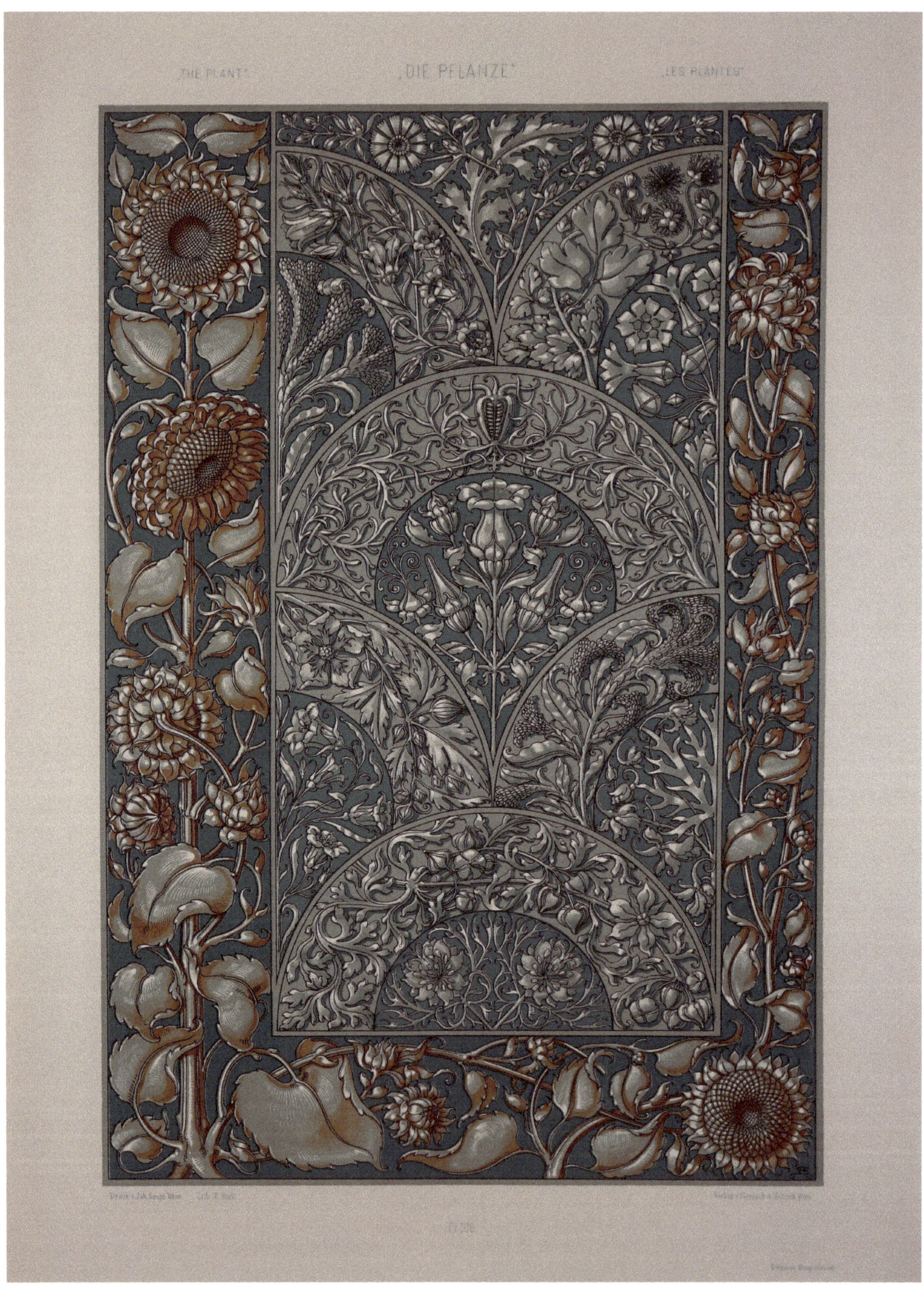

49. Plate 108. Die Pflanze in Kunst und Gewerbe
Volume 2, by A. Seder, c. 1886

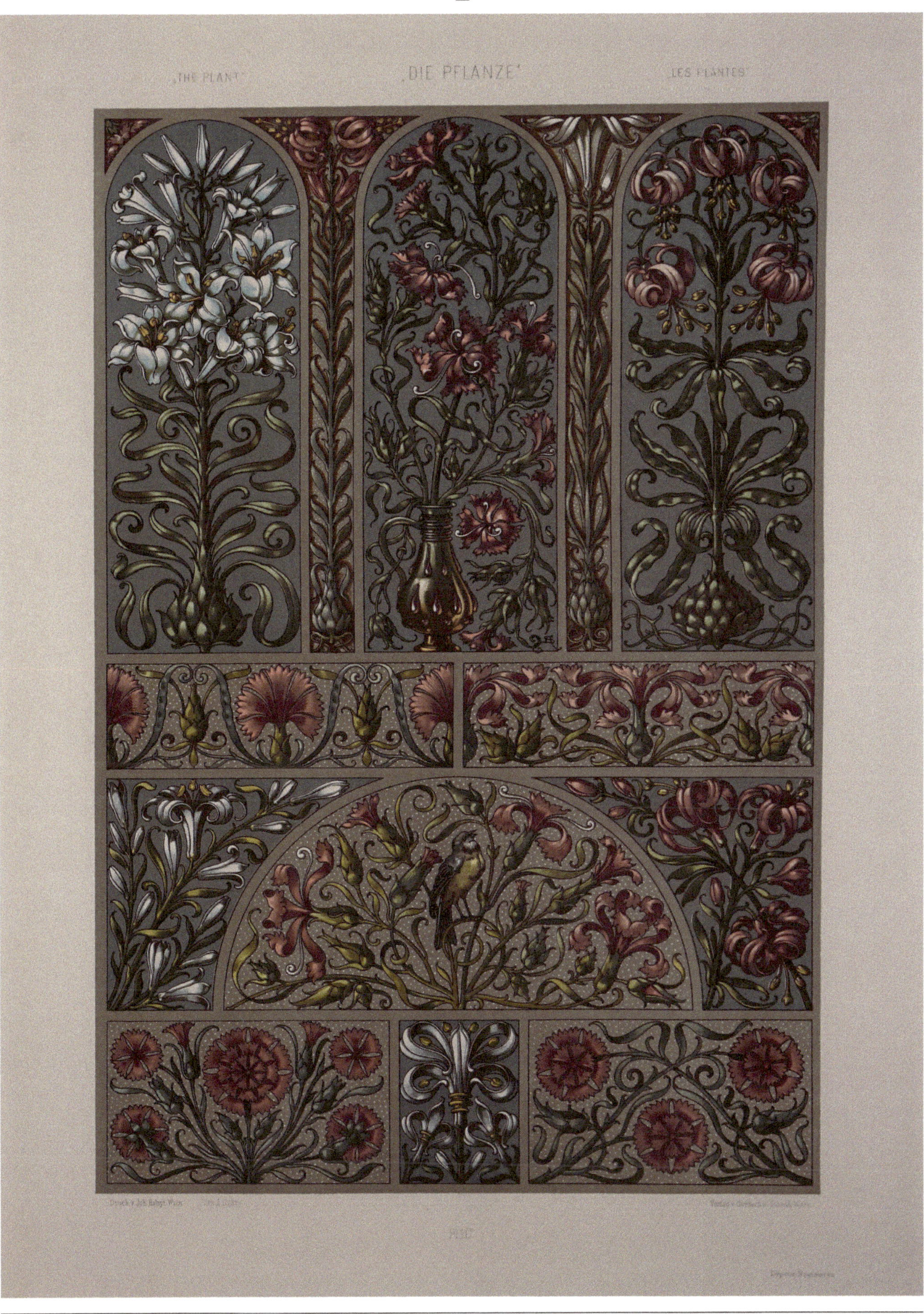
„THE PLANT"
„DIE PFLANZE"
„LES PLANTES"

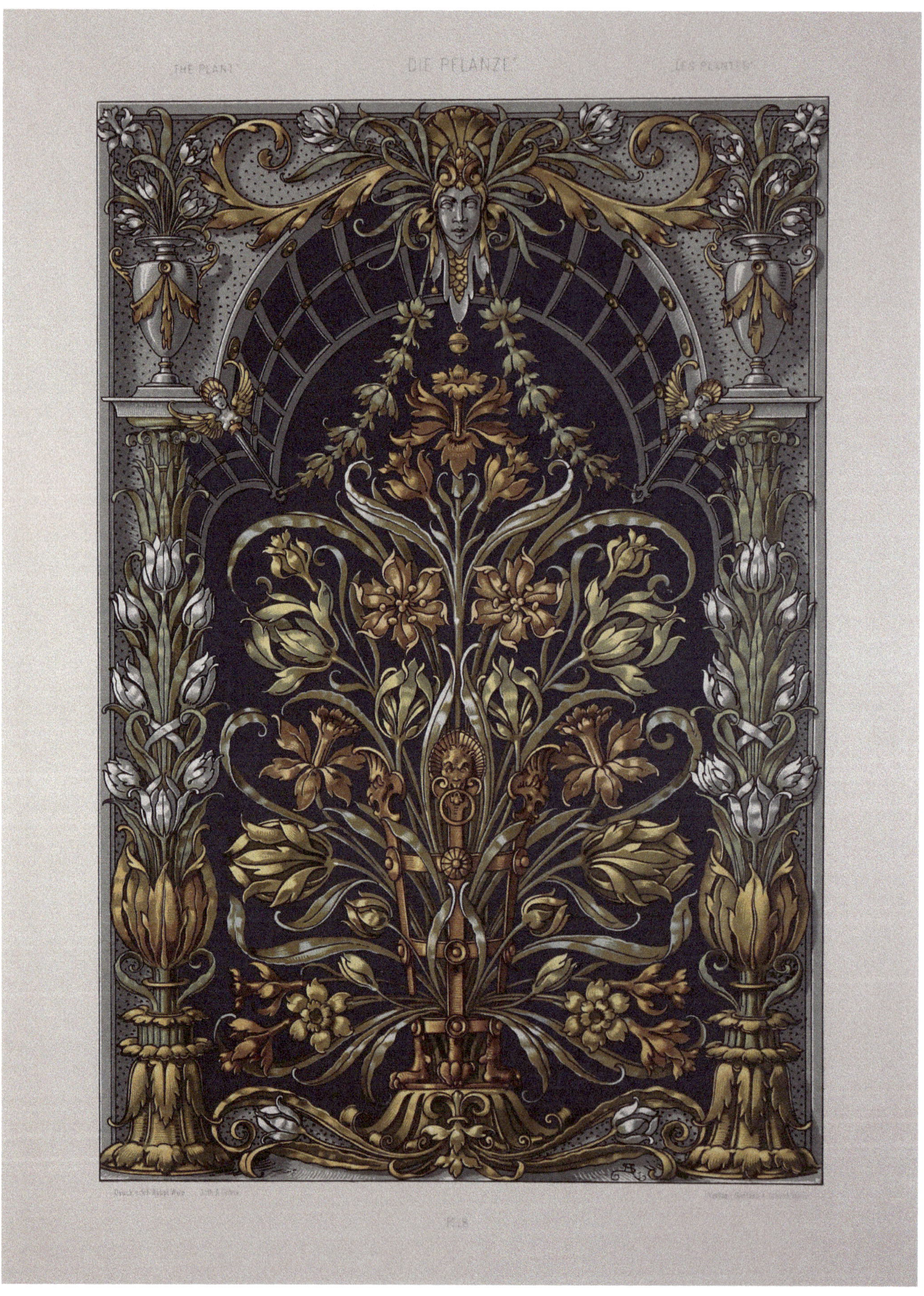

51. Plate 118, Die Pflanze in Kunst und Gewerbe
Volume 2, by A. Seder, c. 1886

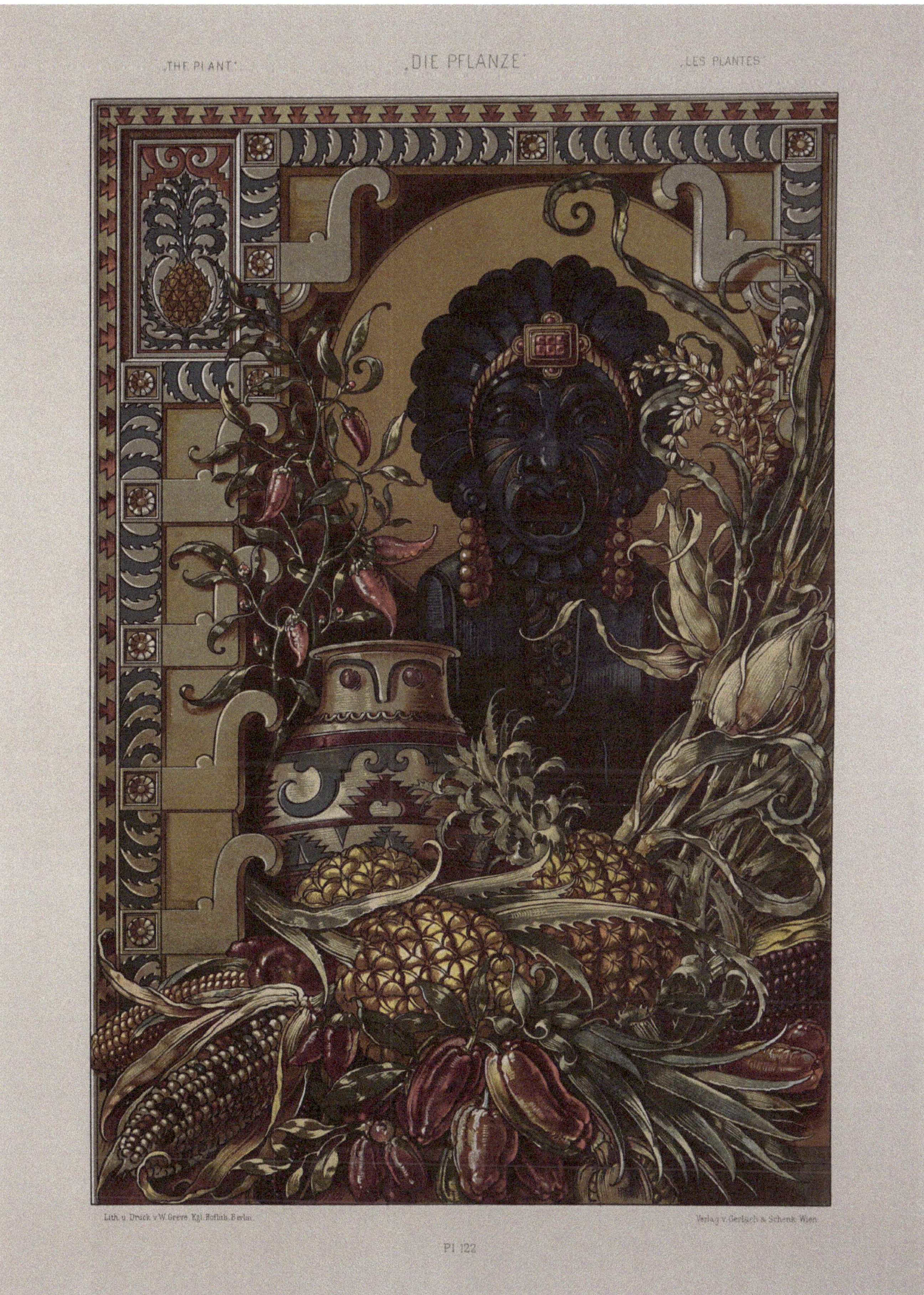

ANTON SEDER

52. Plate 122. Die Pflanze in Kunst und Gewerbe
Volume 2, by A. Seder, c. 1886

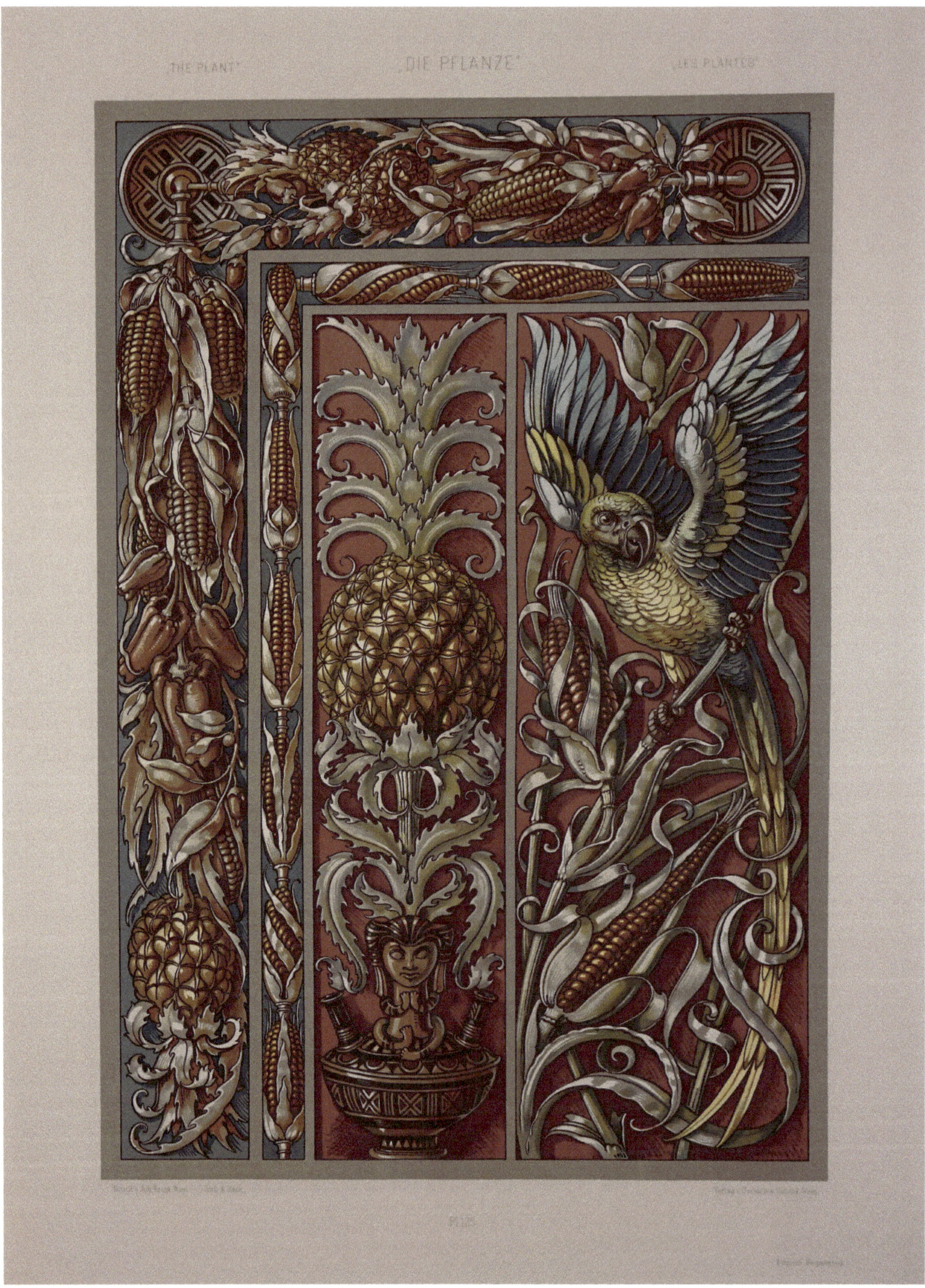

53. Plate 125, Die Pflanze in Kunst und Gewerbe
Volume 2, by A. Seder, c. 1886

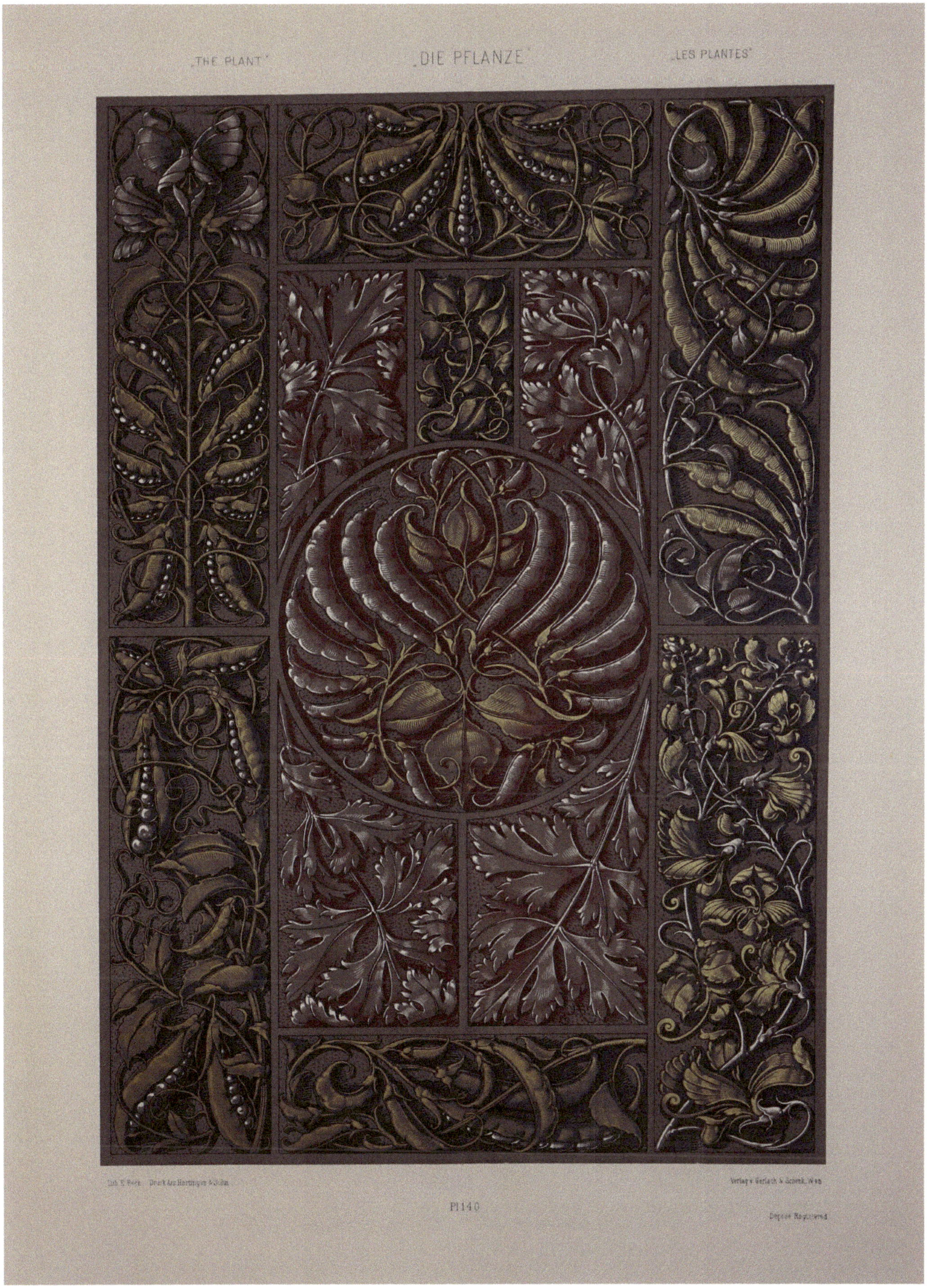

ANTON SEDER

54. Plate 140, Die Pflanze in Kunst und Gewerbe
Volume 2, by A. Seder, c 1886

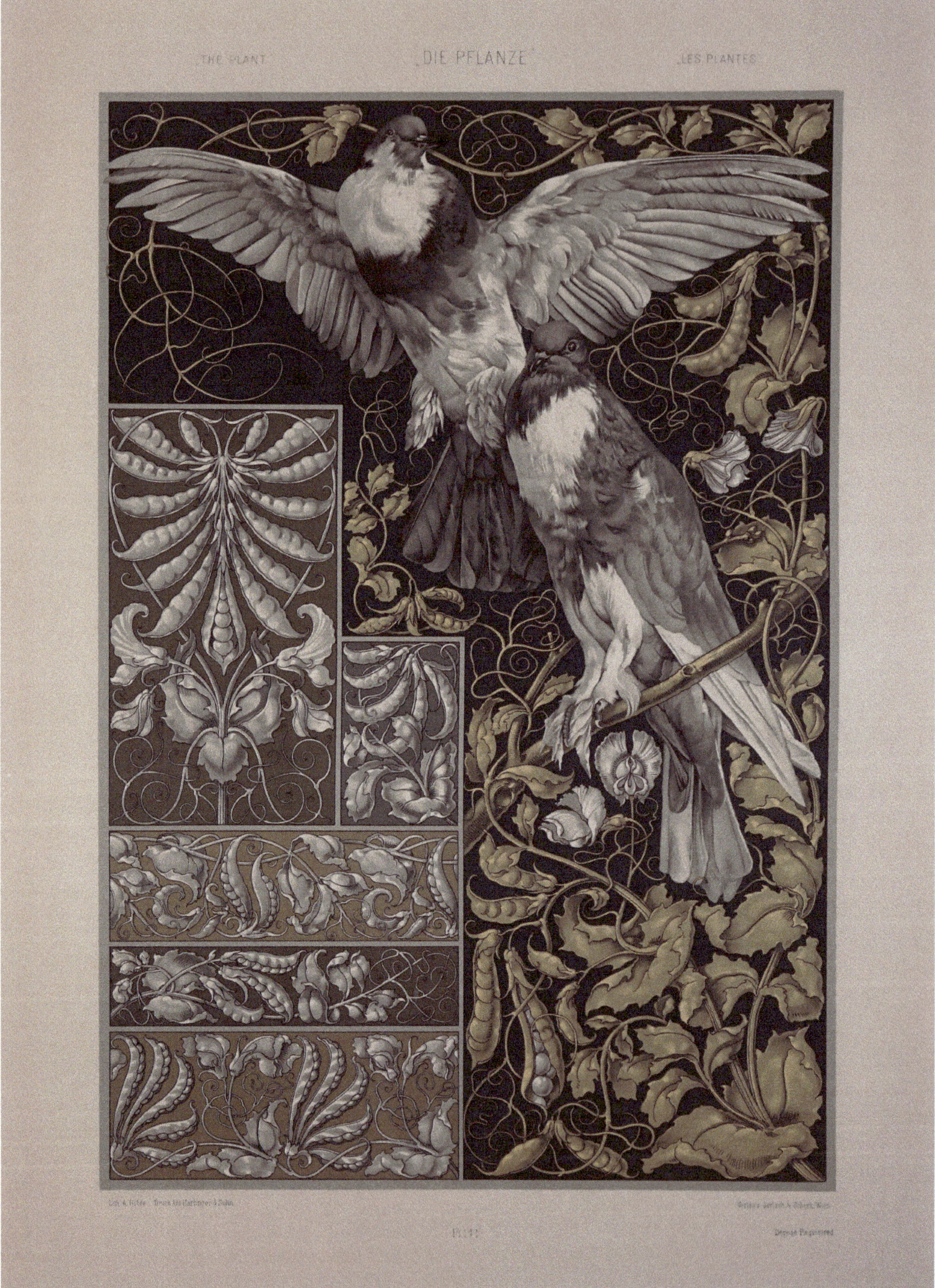

55. Plate 141, Die Pflanze in Kunst und Gewerbe
Volume 2, by A. Seder, c. 1886

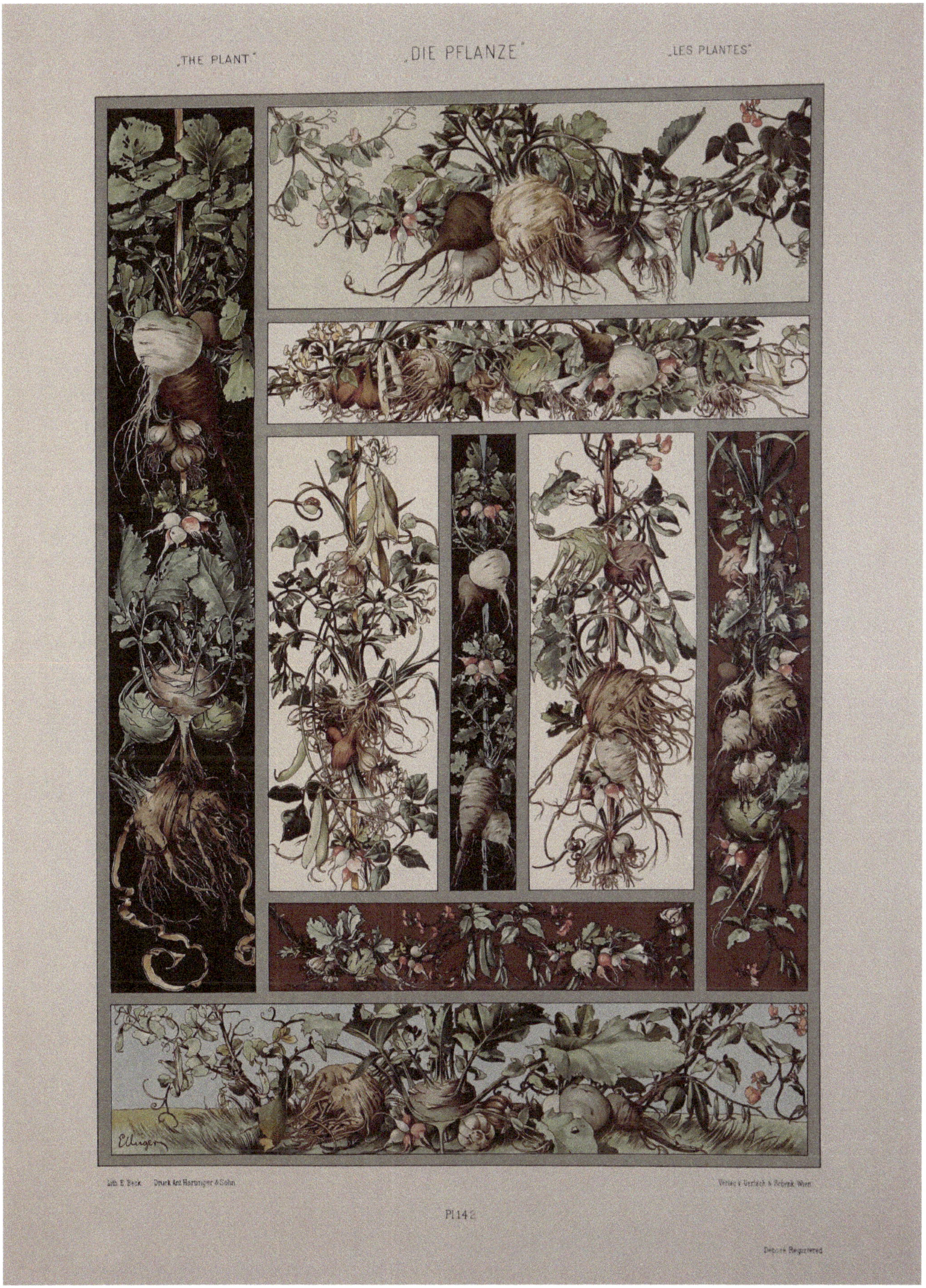

56. Plate 142. Die Pflanze in Kunst und Gewerbe
Volume 2, by A. Seder, c. 1886

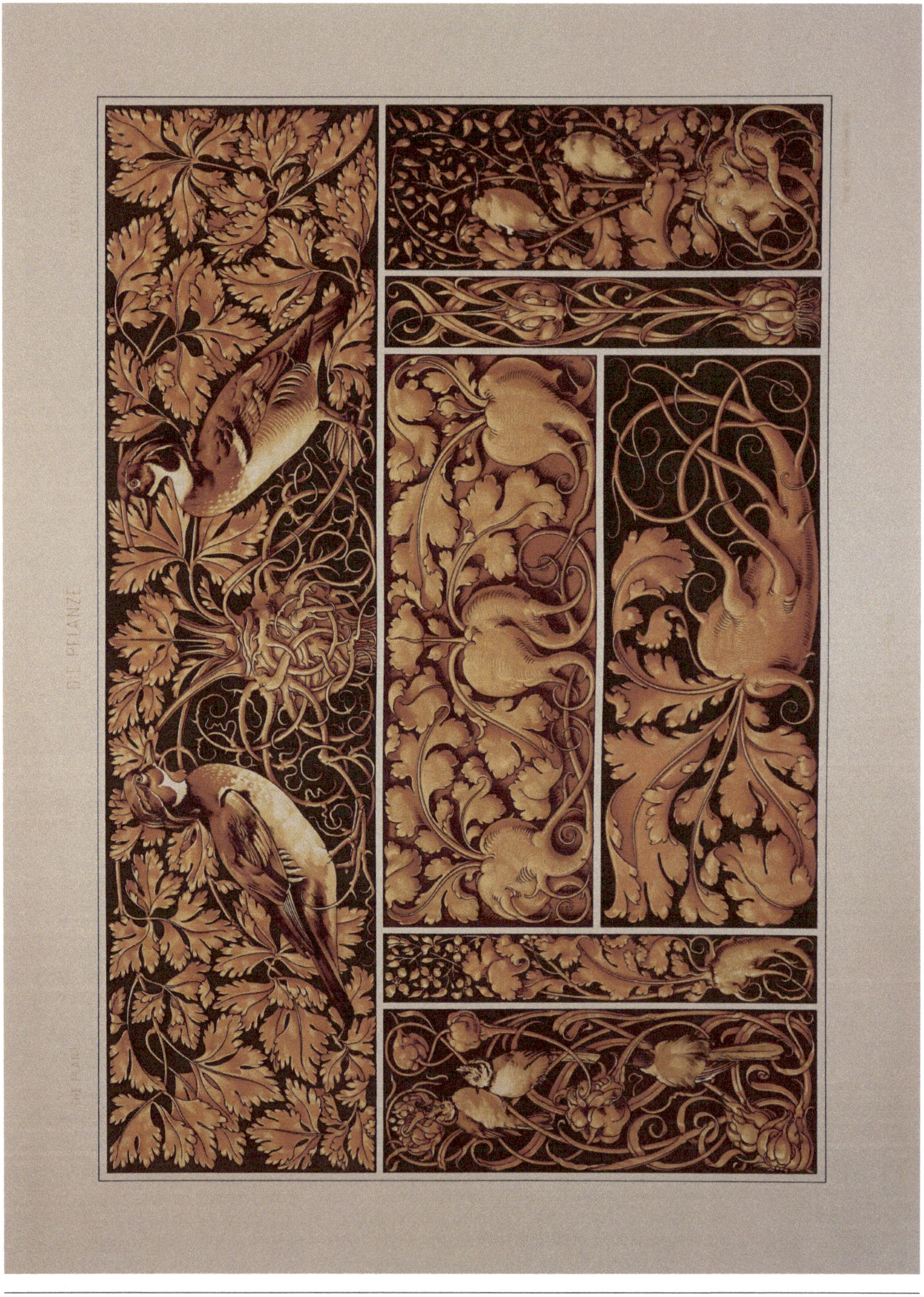

57. Plate 143, Die Pflanze in Kunst und Gewerbe
Volume 2, by A. Seder, c. 1886

„THE PLANT"   „DIE PFLANZE"   „LES PLANTES"

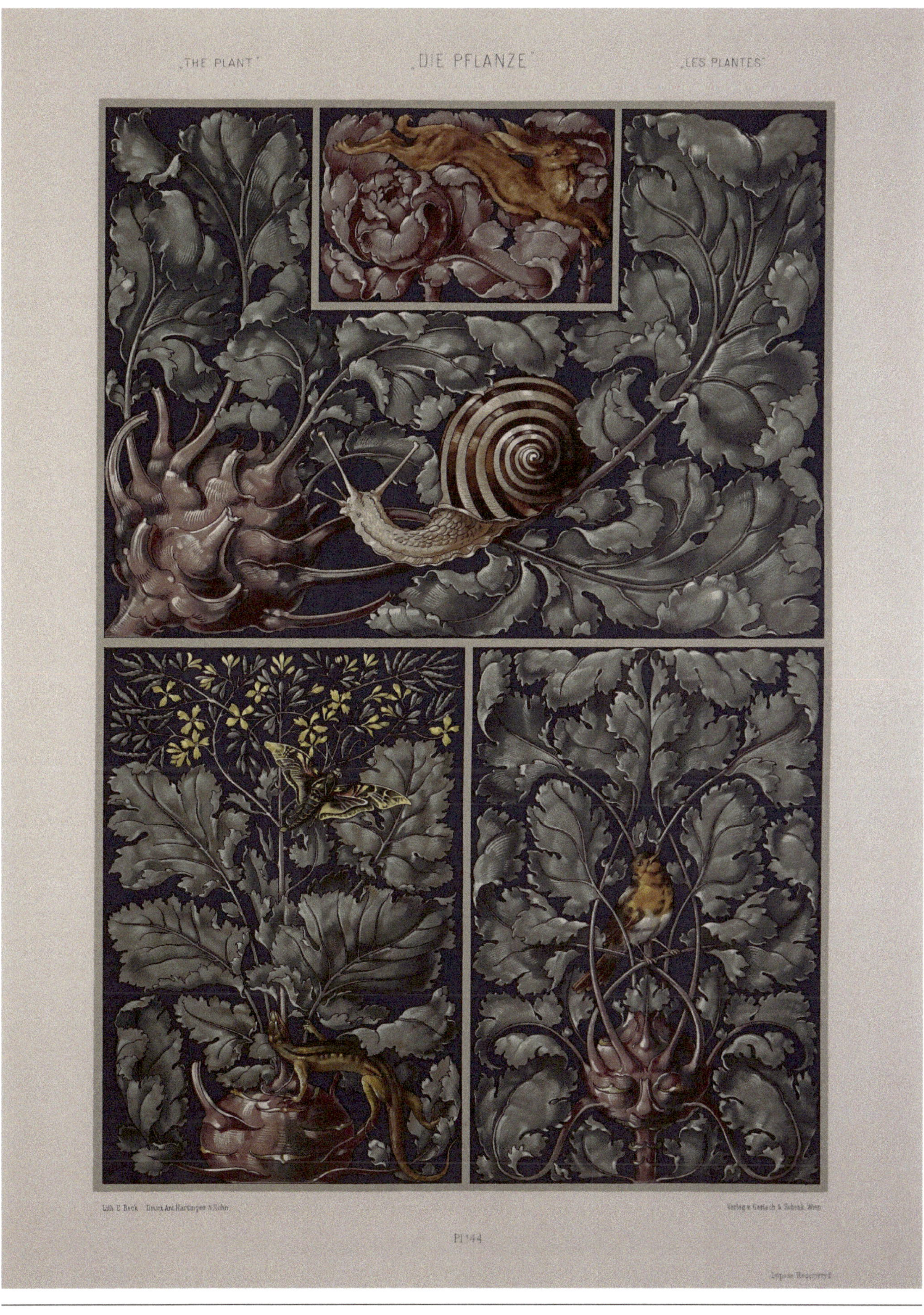

ANTON SEDER

Lith. E. Beck   Druck Ant.Hartinger & Sohn   Verlag v. Gerlach & Schenk, Wien

Pl.144

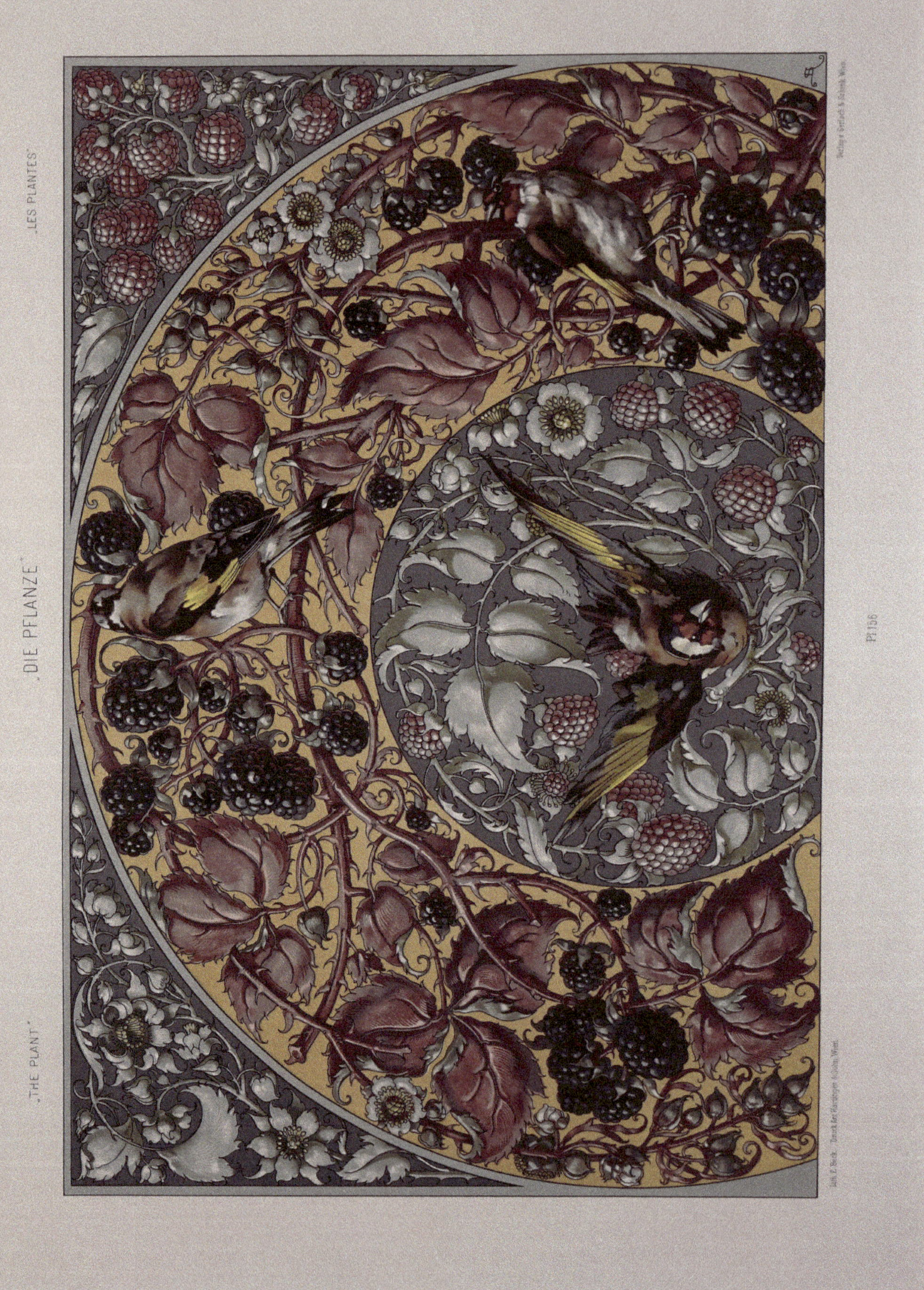

59. Plate 156, Die Pflanze in Kunst und Gewerbe
Volume 2, by A. Seder, c 1886

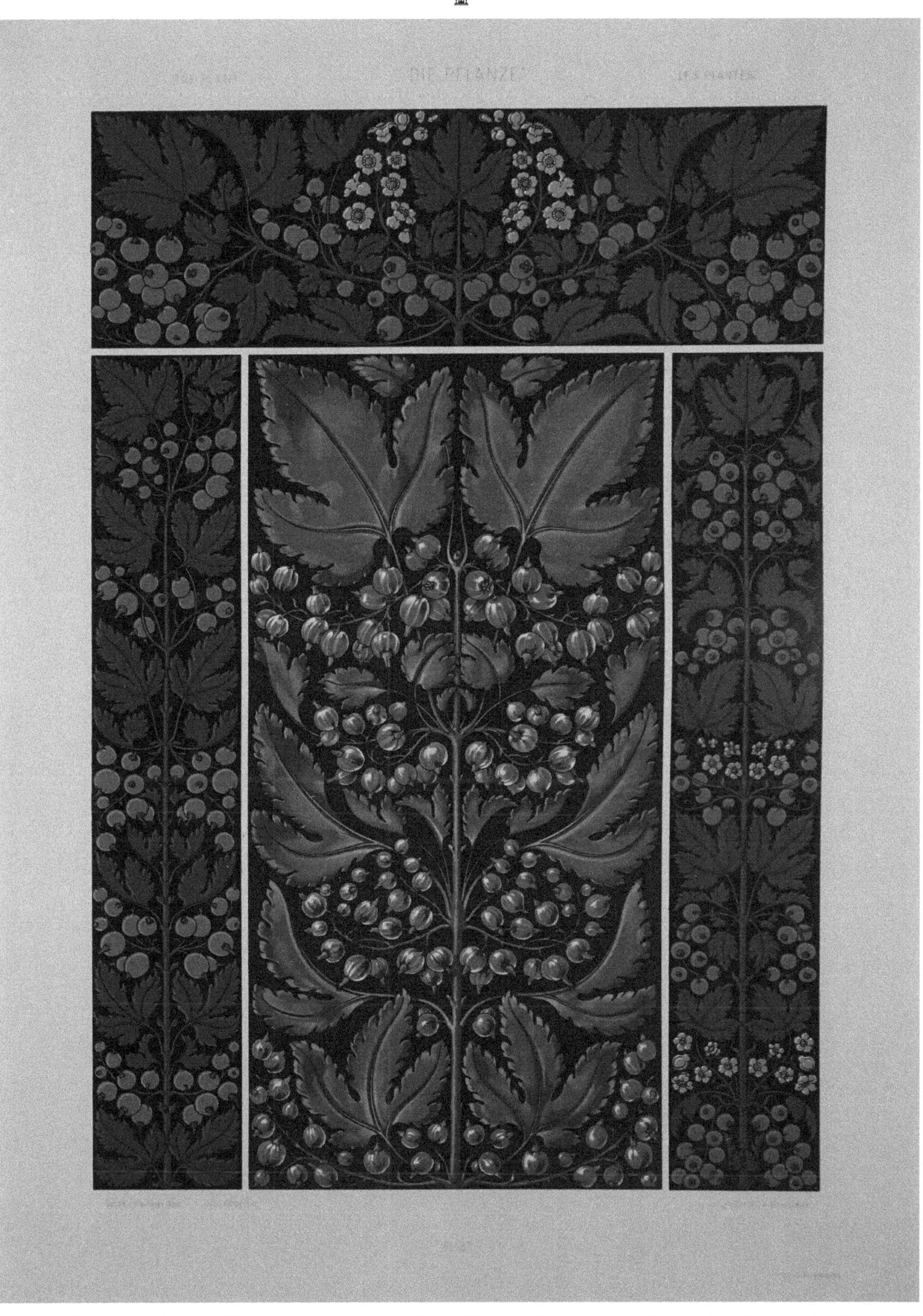

60. Plate 157, Die Pflanze in Kunst und Gewerbe
Volume 2, by A. Seder, c. 1886

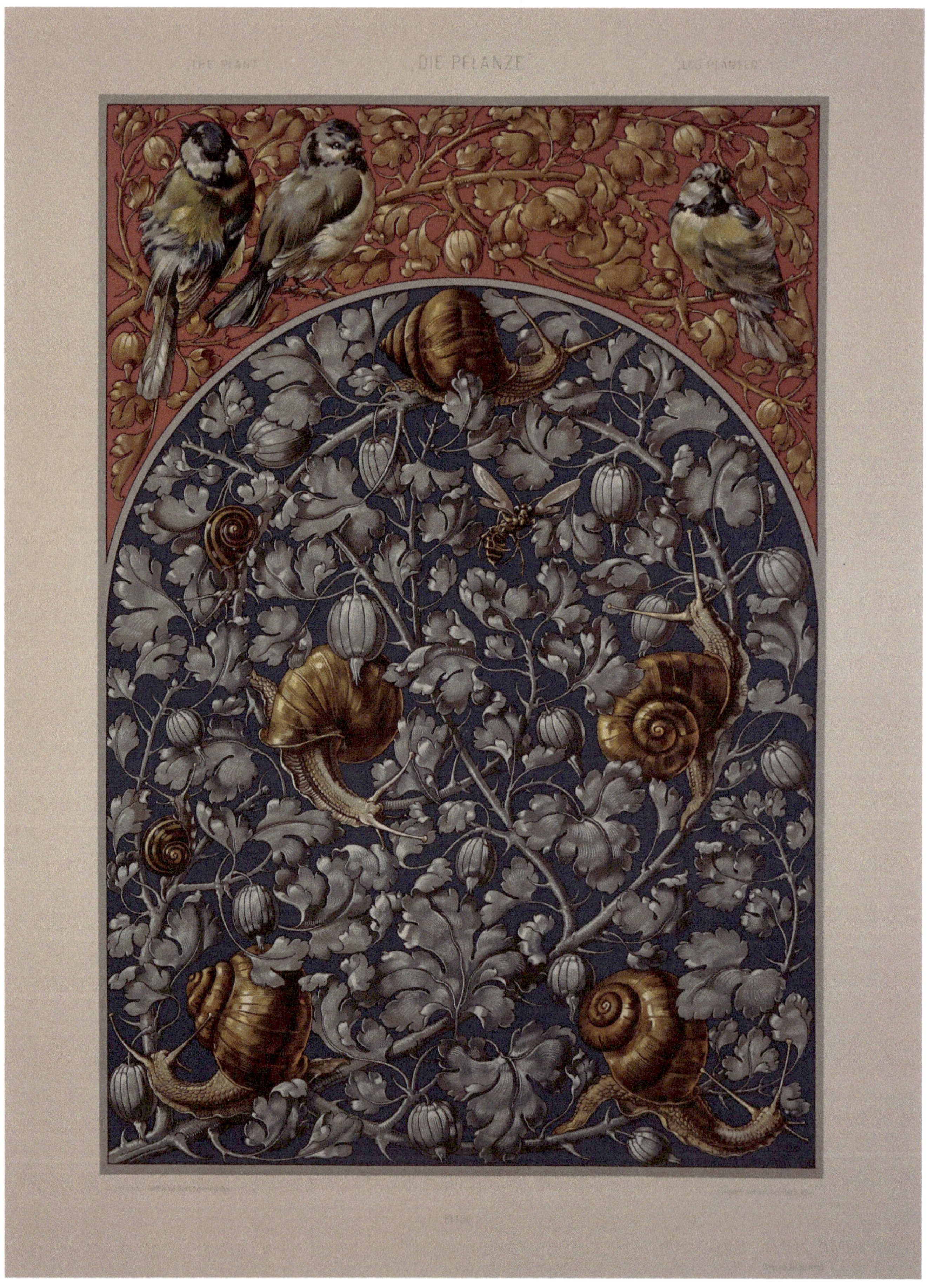

61. *Plate 158, Die Pflanze in Kunst und Gewerbe*
Volume 2, by A. Seder, c. 1886

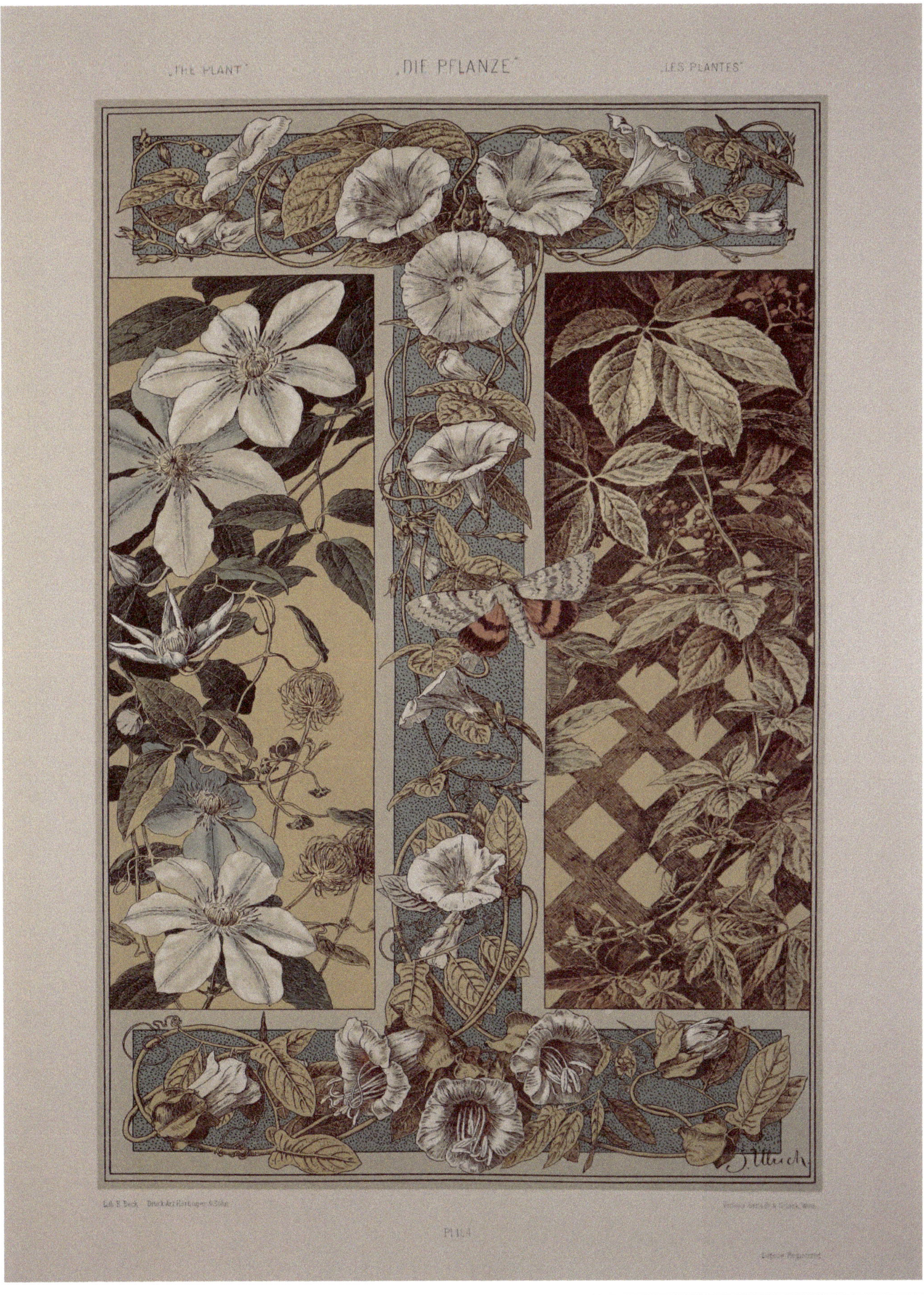

62. Plate 164. Die Pflanze in Kunst und Gewerbe
Volume 2, by A. Seder, c 1886

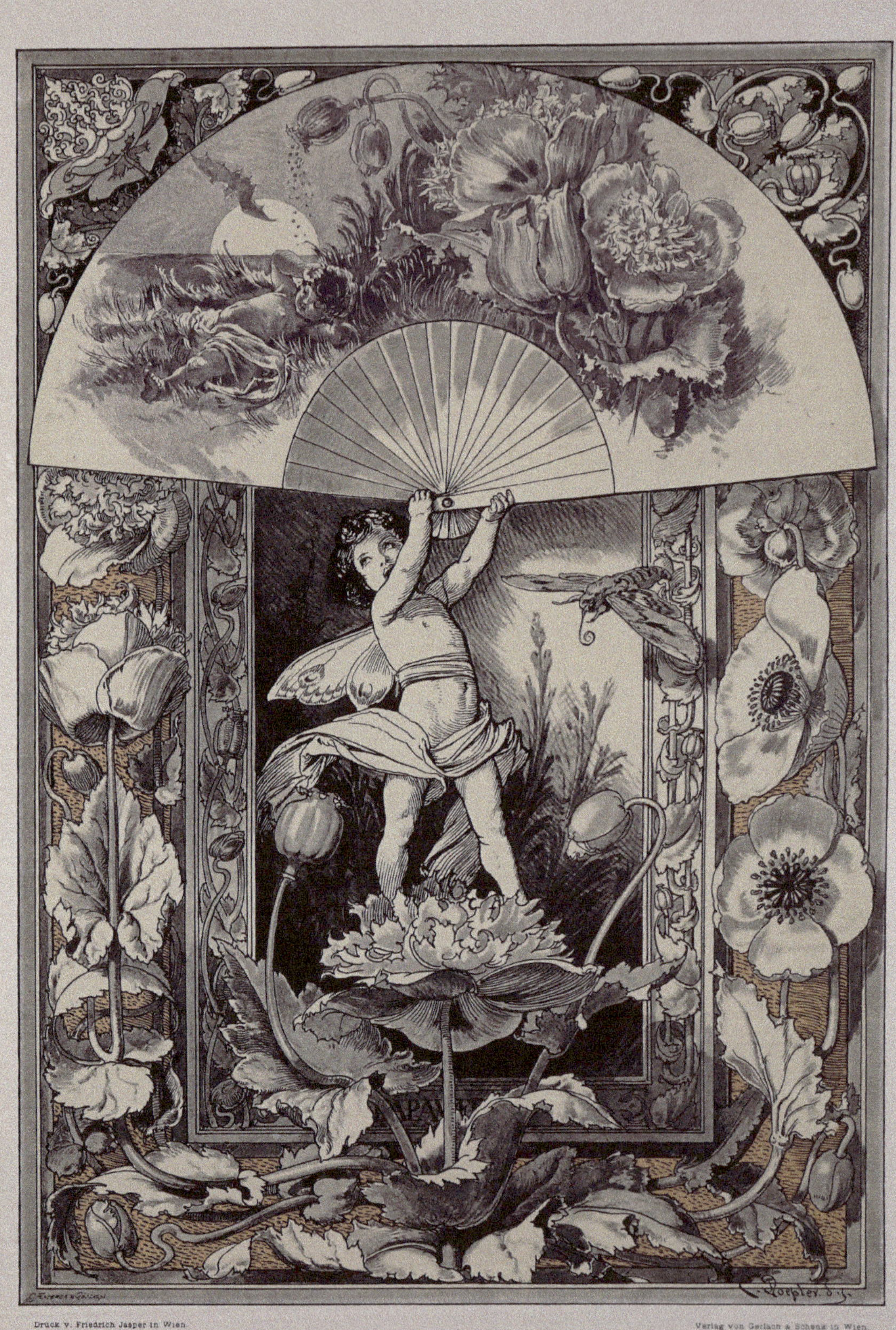

63. Plate 168. Die Pflanze in Kunst und Gewerbe
Volume 2, by A. Seder, c. 1886

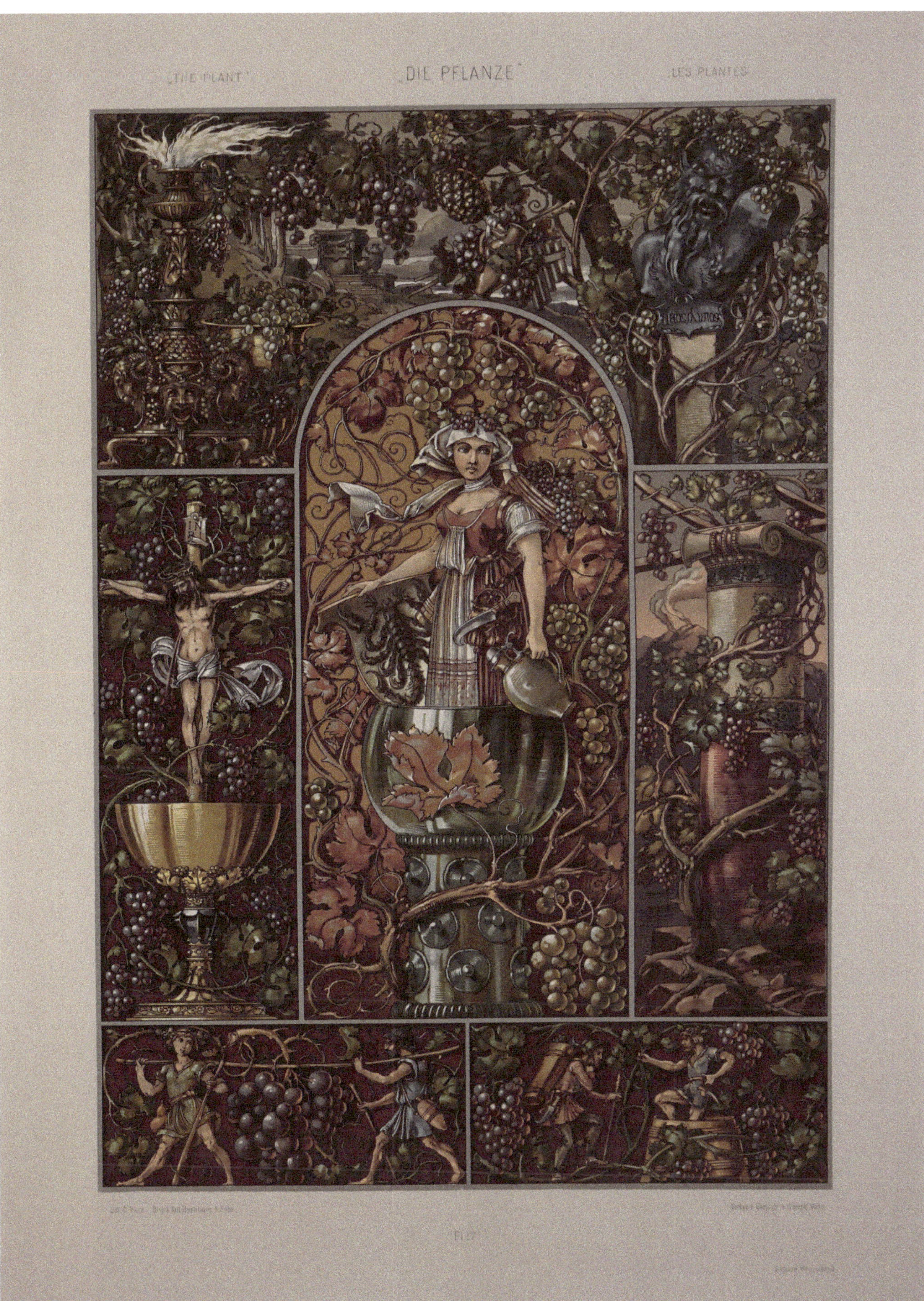

ANTON SEDER

64. Plate 171, Die Pflanze in Kunst und Gewerbe
Volume 2, by A. Seder, c. 1886

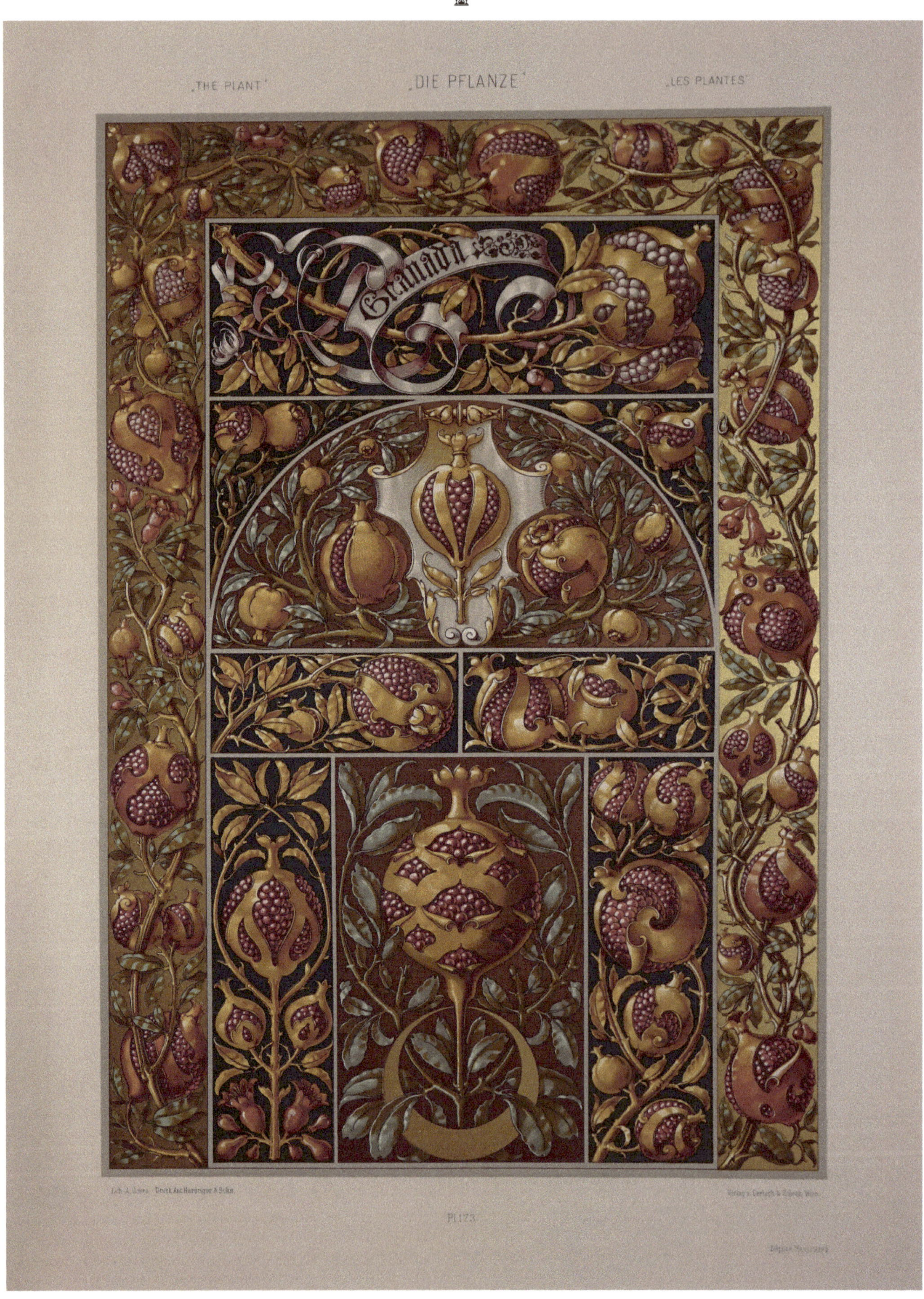

65. Plate 173. Die Pflanze in Kunst und Gewerbe
Volume 2, by A. Seder, c. 1886

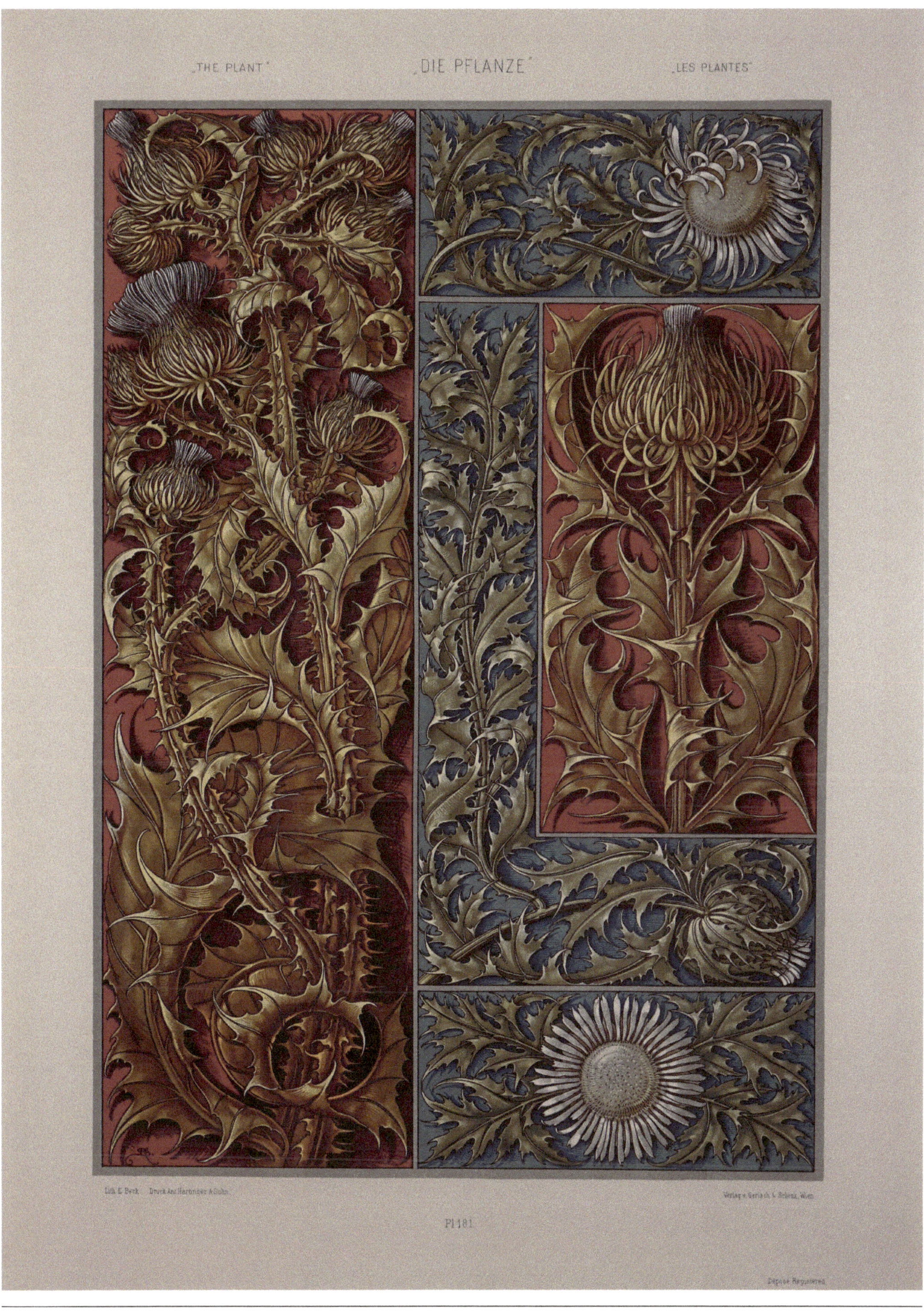

ANTON SEDER

66. Plate 181. Die Pflanze in Kunst und Gewerbe
Volume 2, by A. Seder, c 1886

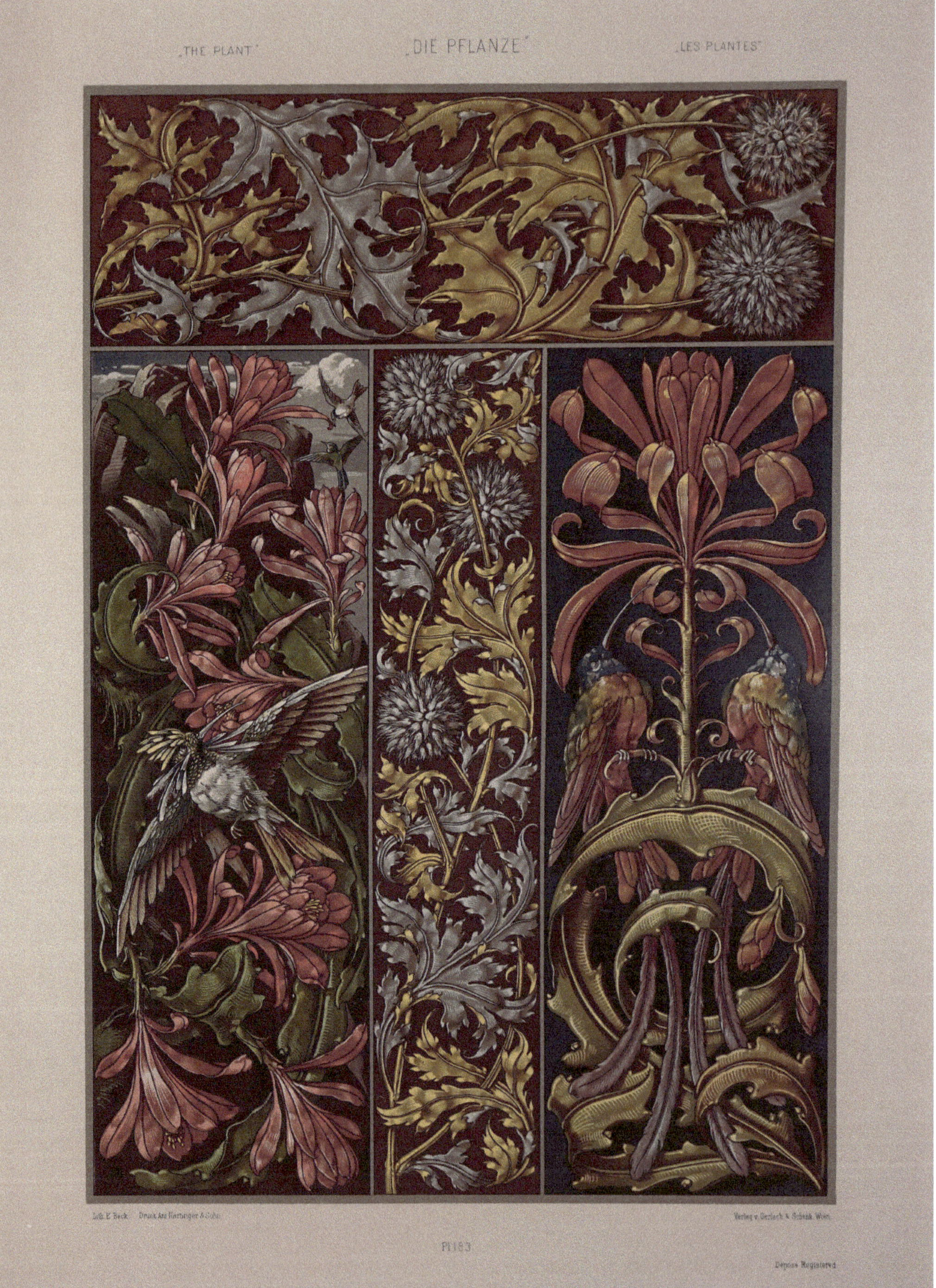

67. Plate 183. Die Pflanze in Kunst und Gewerbe
Volume 2, by A. Seder, c.1886

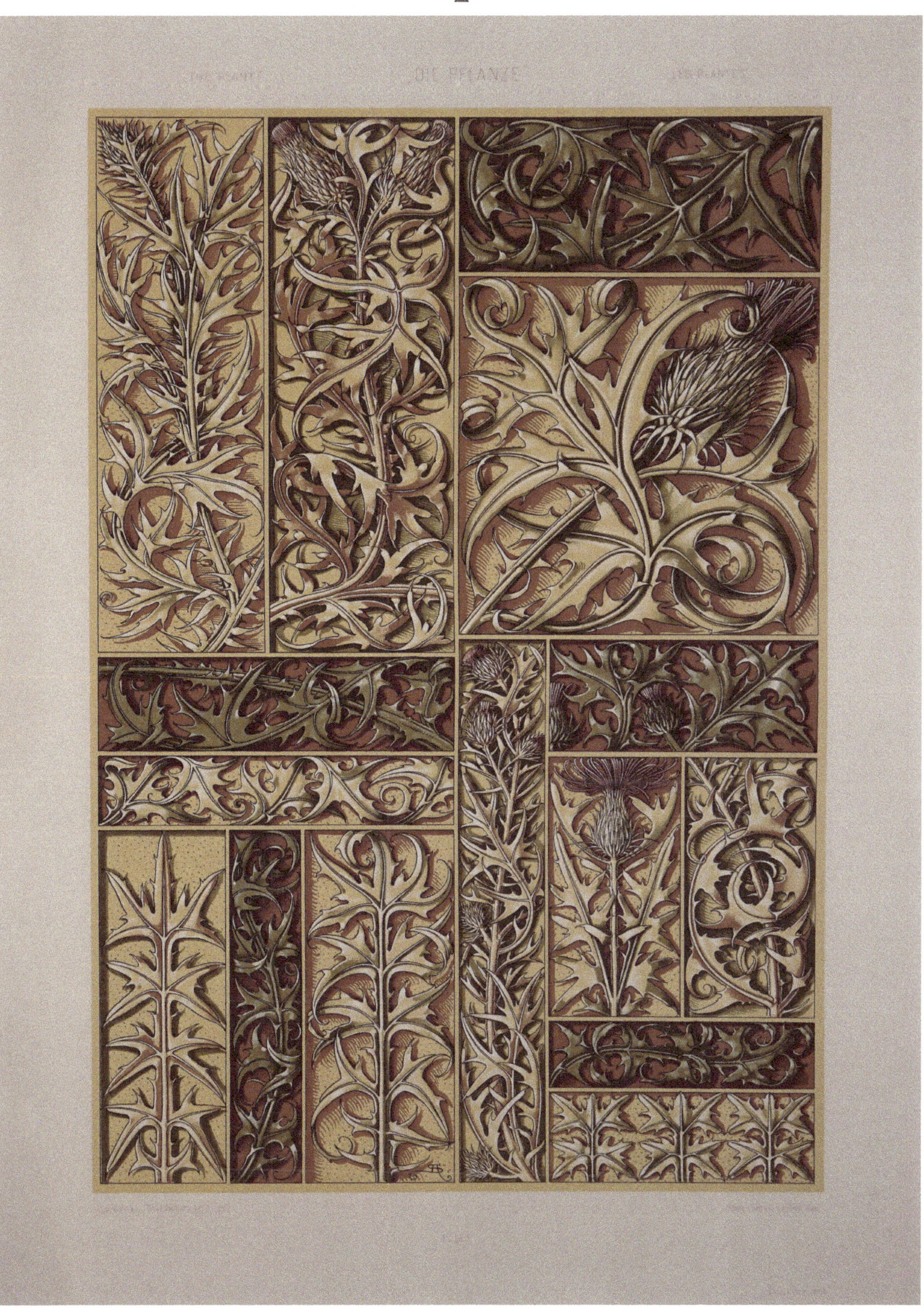

ANTON SEDER

ANTON SEDER

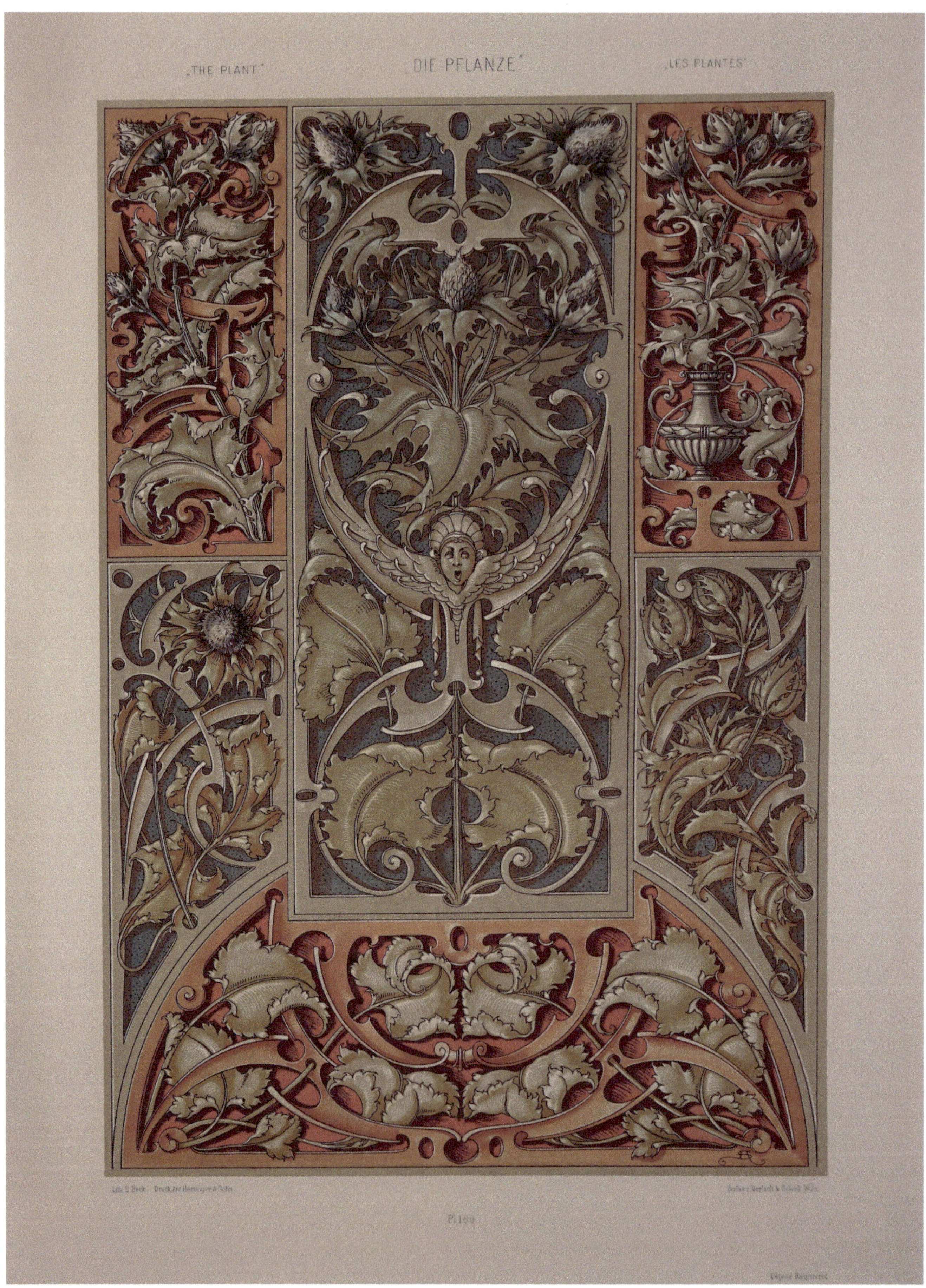

69. Plate 186, Die Pflanze in Kunst und Gewerbe
Volume 2, by A. Seder, c. 1886

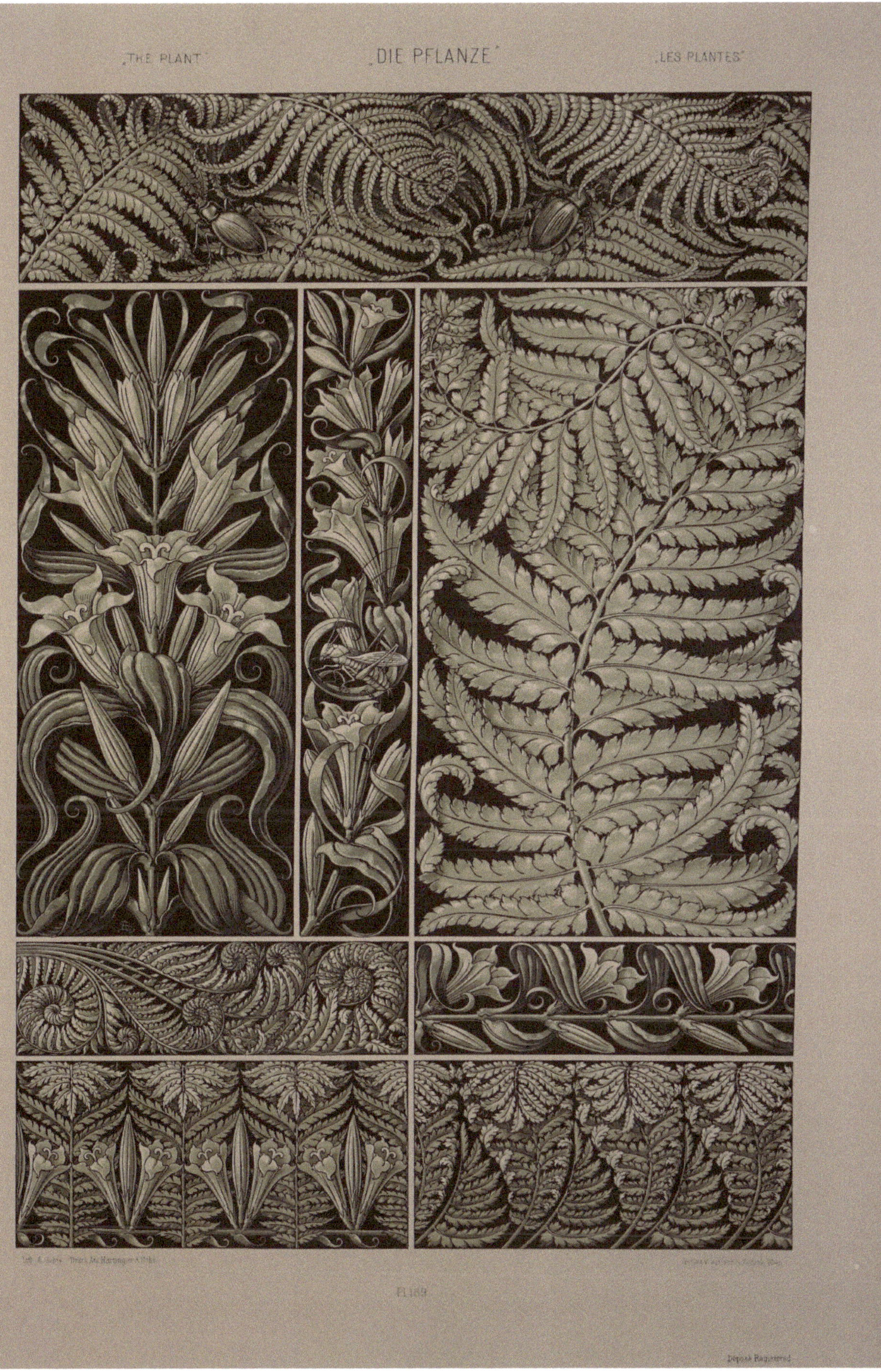

70. Plate 189. Die Pflanze in Kunst und Gewerbe
Volume 2, by A. Seder, c. 1886

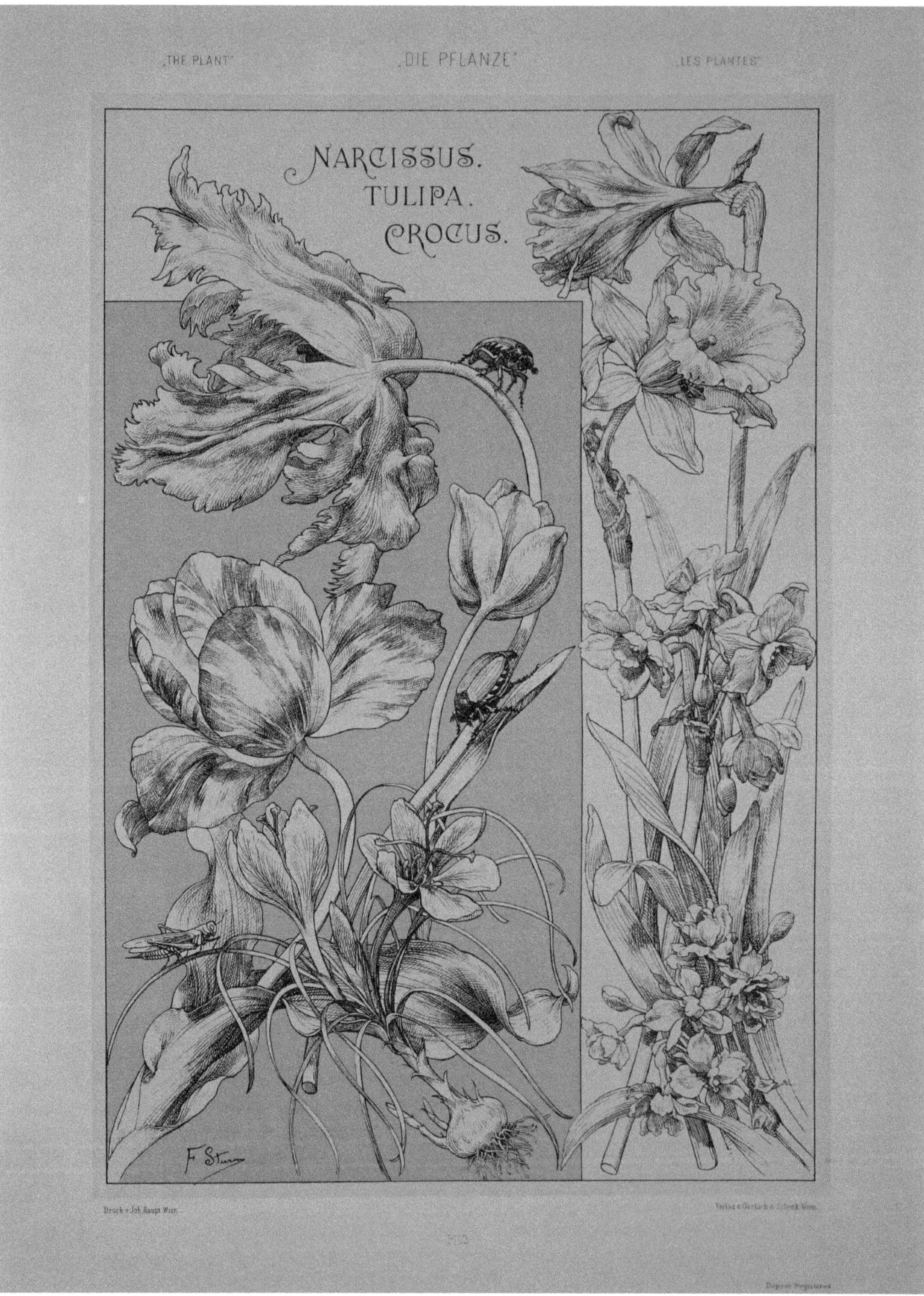

71. Plate 13. Die Pflanze in Kunst und Gewerbe
Volume 1, by A. Seder, c. 1886

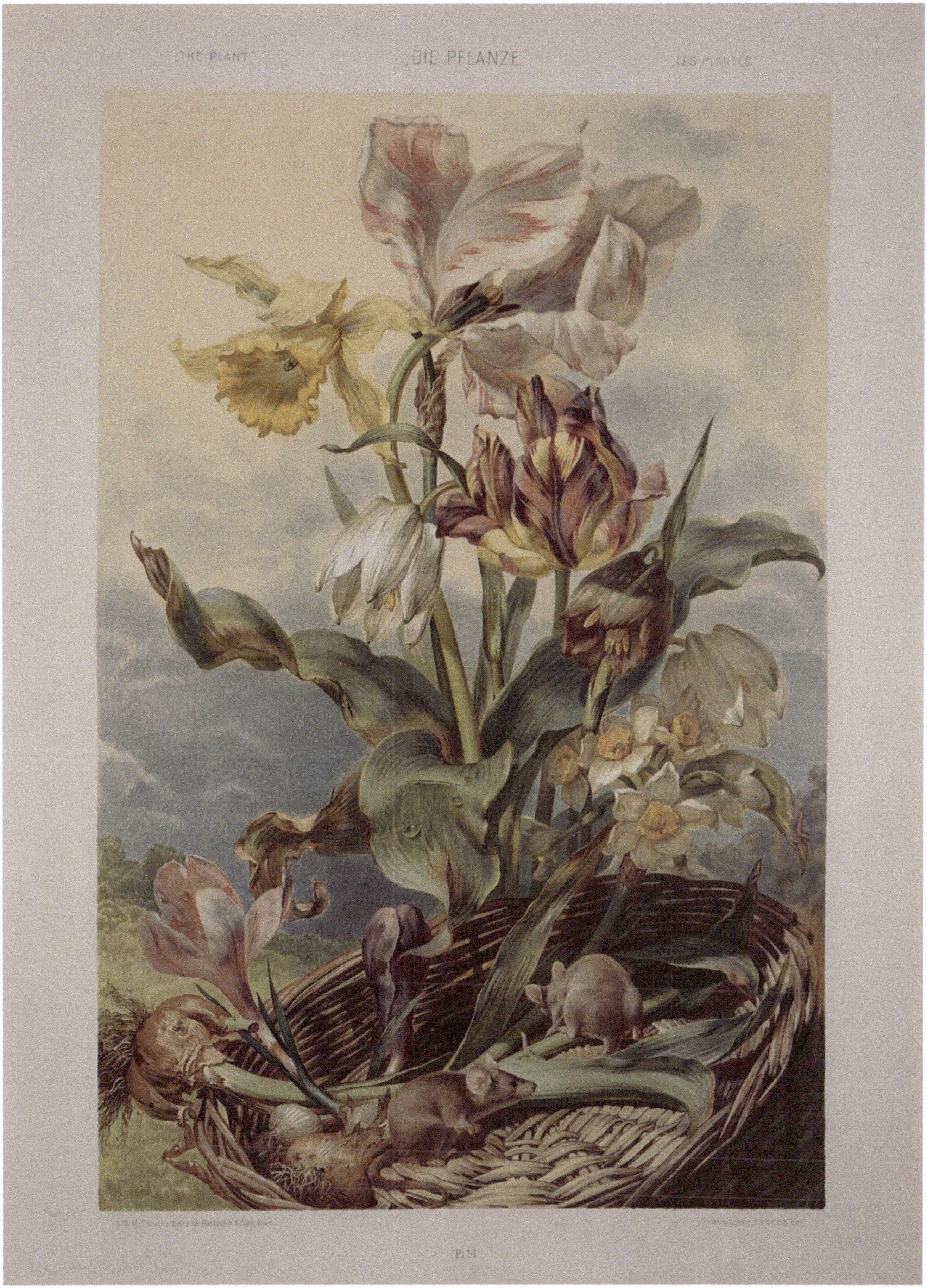

ANTON SEDER

72. Plate 14. Die Pflanze in Kunst und Gewerbe
Volume 1, by A. Seder, c. 1886

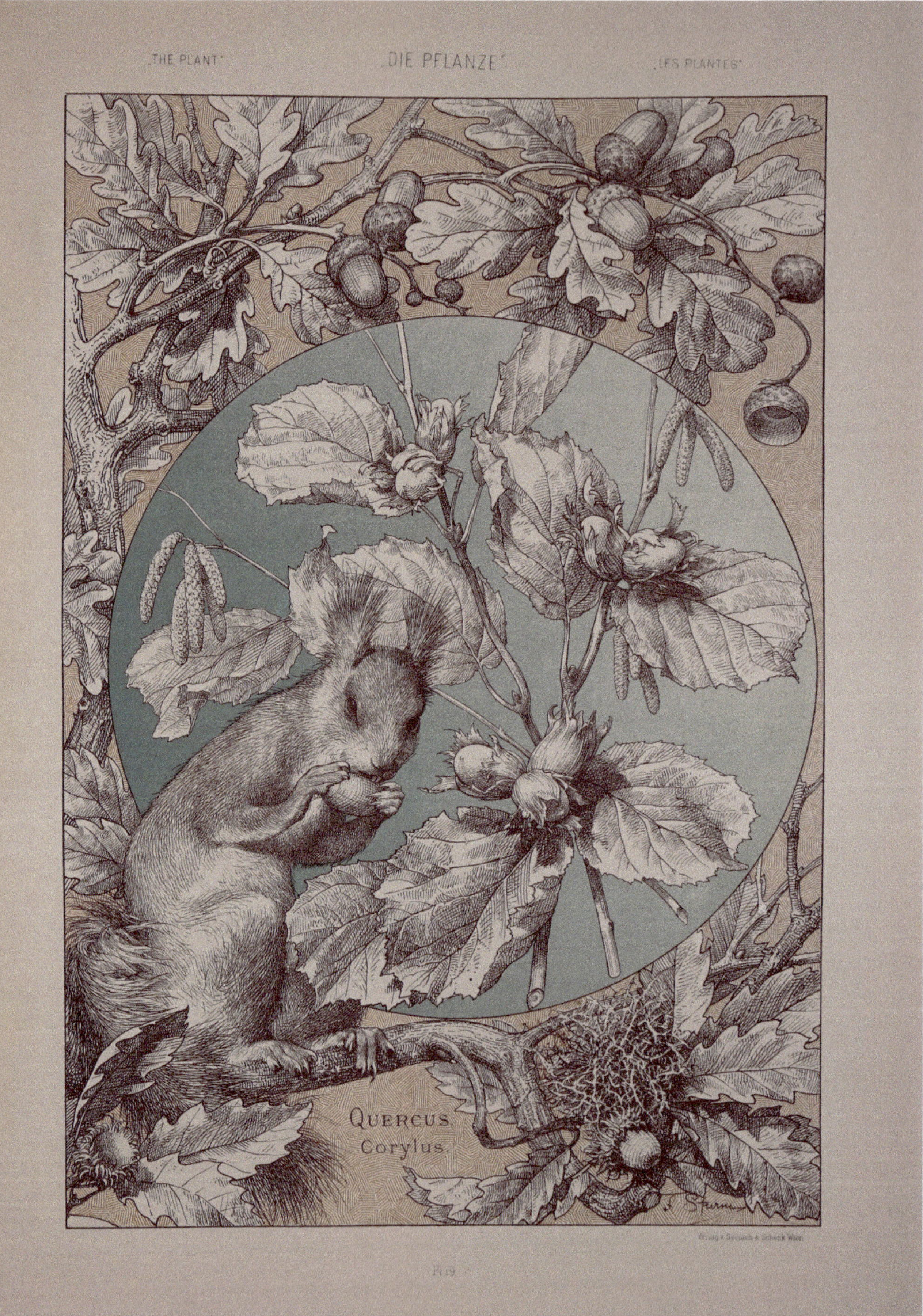

73. Plate 19. Die Pflanze in Kunst und Gewerbe
Volume 1, by A. Seder. c.1886

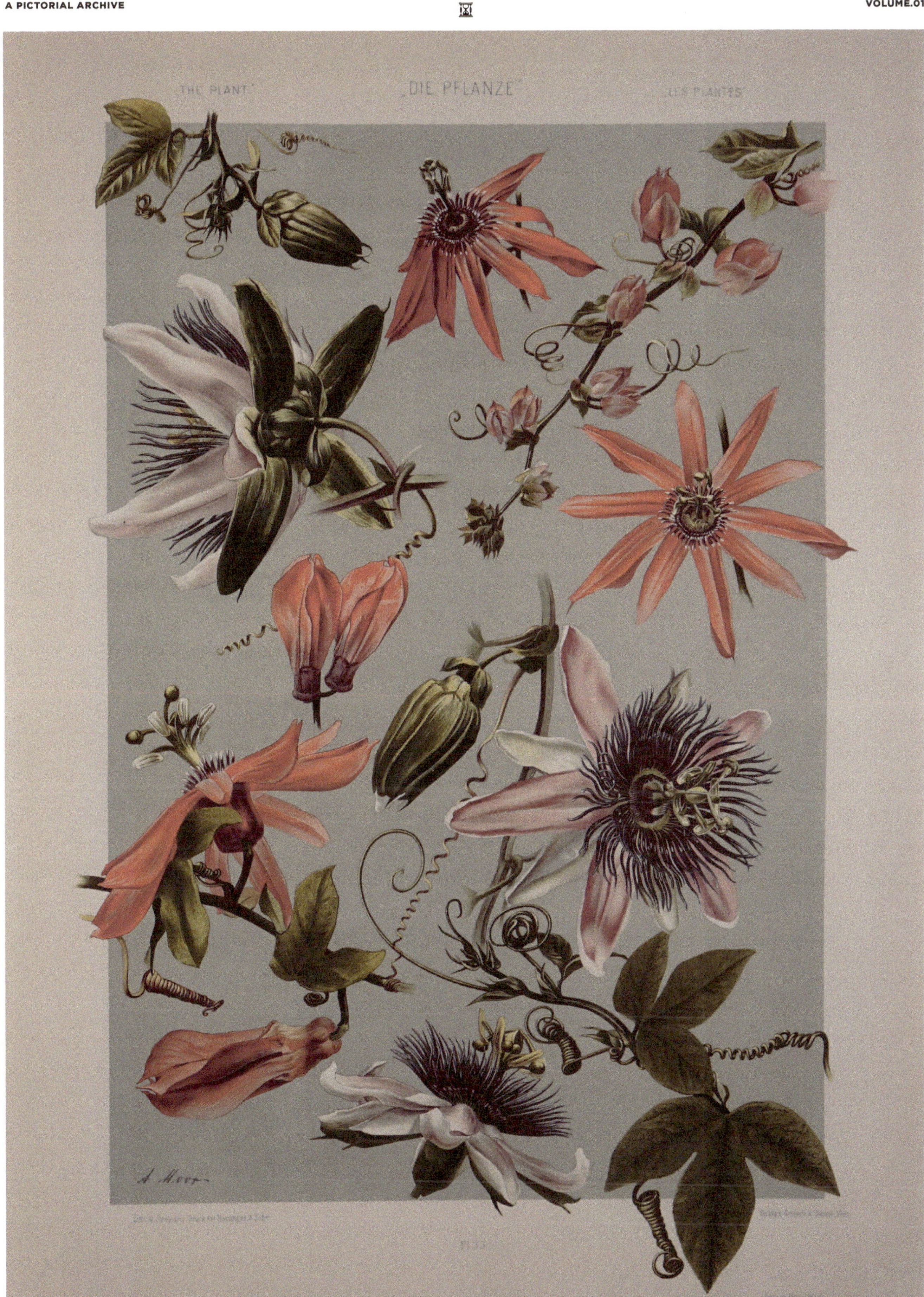

74. Plate 33. Die Pflanze in Kunst und Gewerbe
Volume 1, by A. Seder, c. 1886

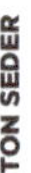

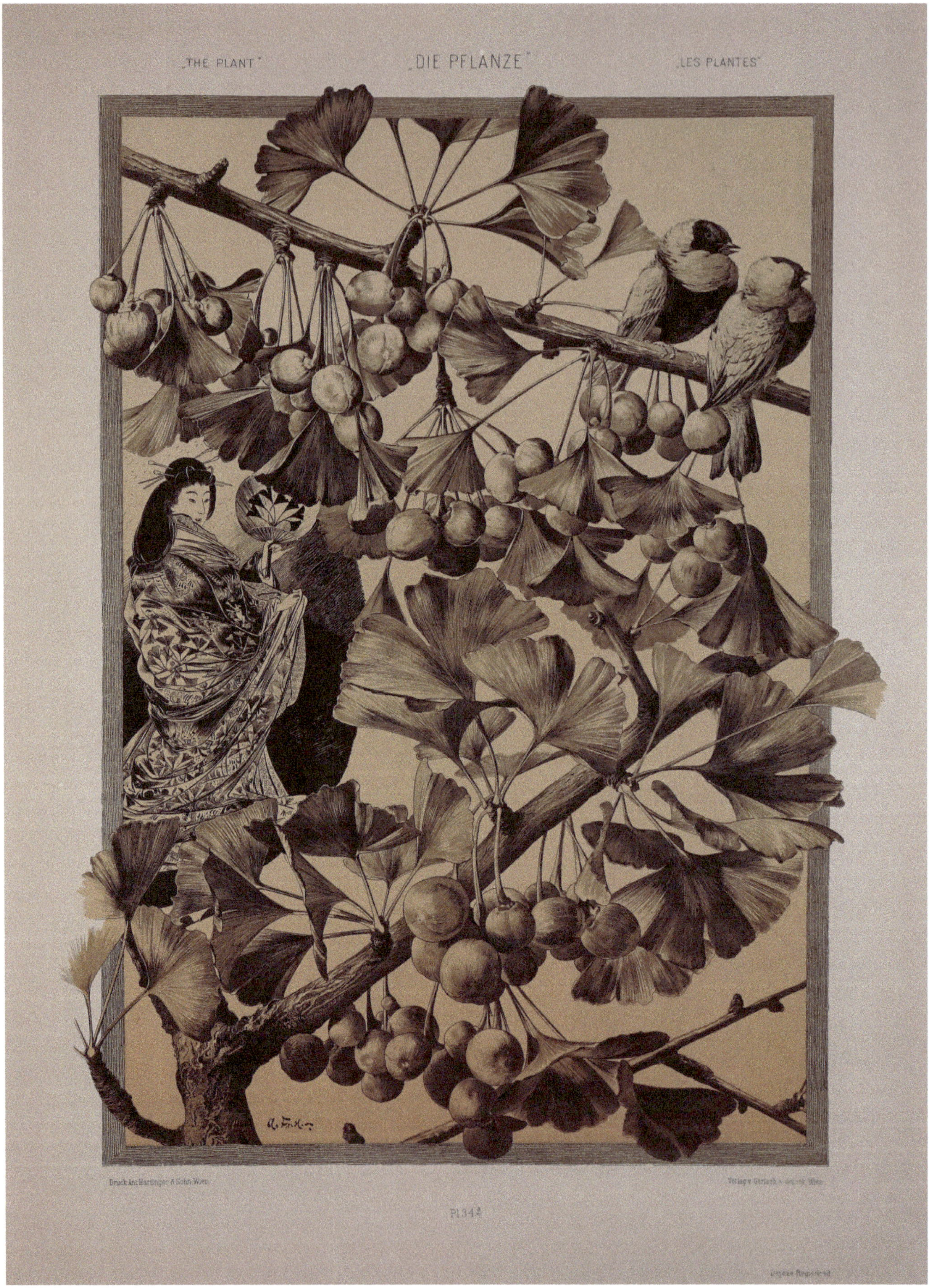

75. Plate 34a. Die Pflanze in Kunst und Gewerbe
Volume 1, by A. Seder, c 1886

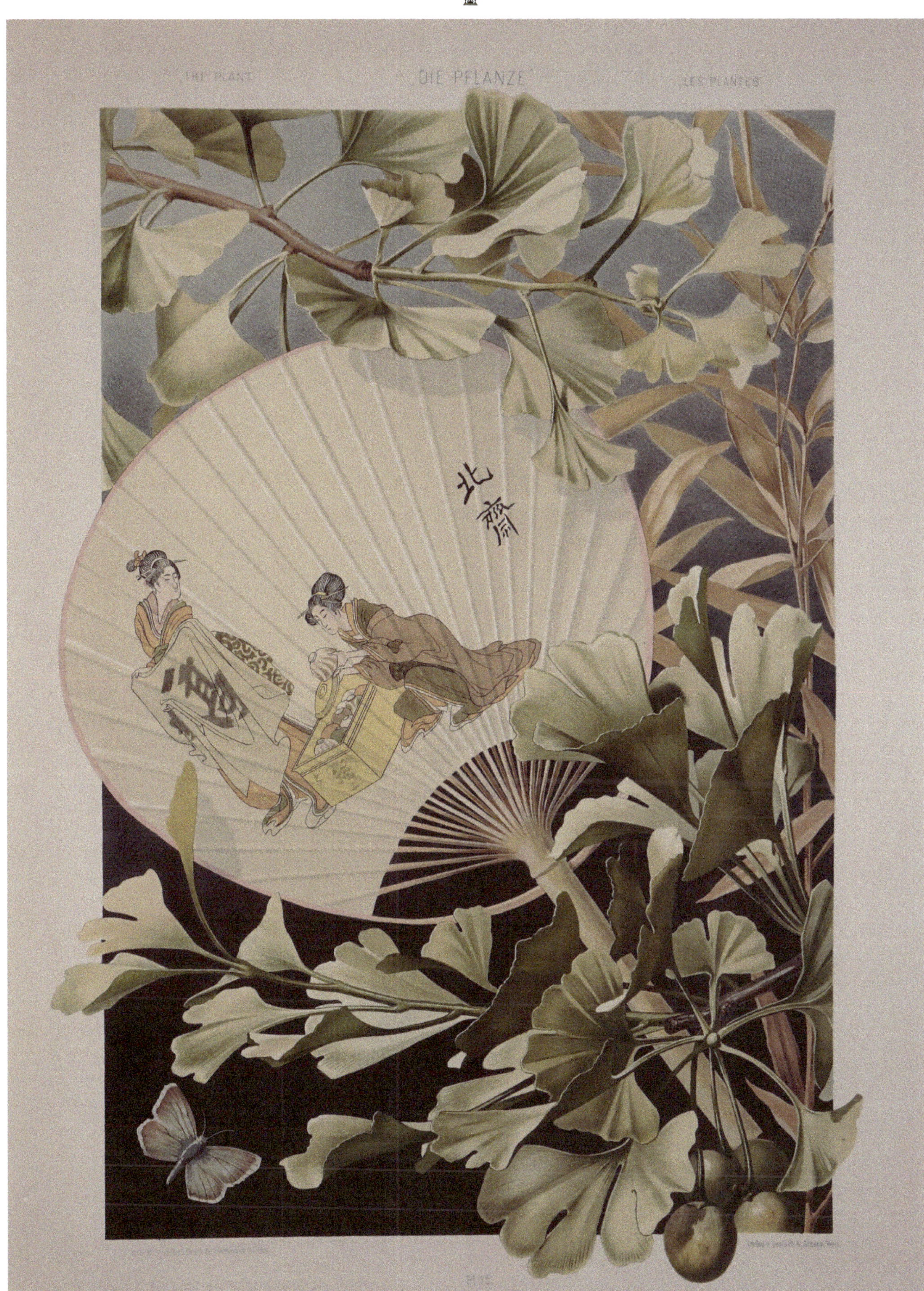

76. Plate 35. Die Pflanze in Kunst und Gewerbe
Volume 1, by A. Seder. c 1886

ANTON SEDER

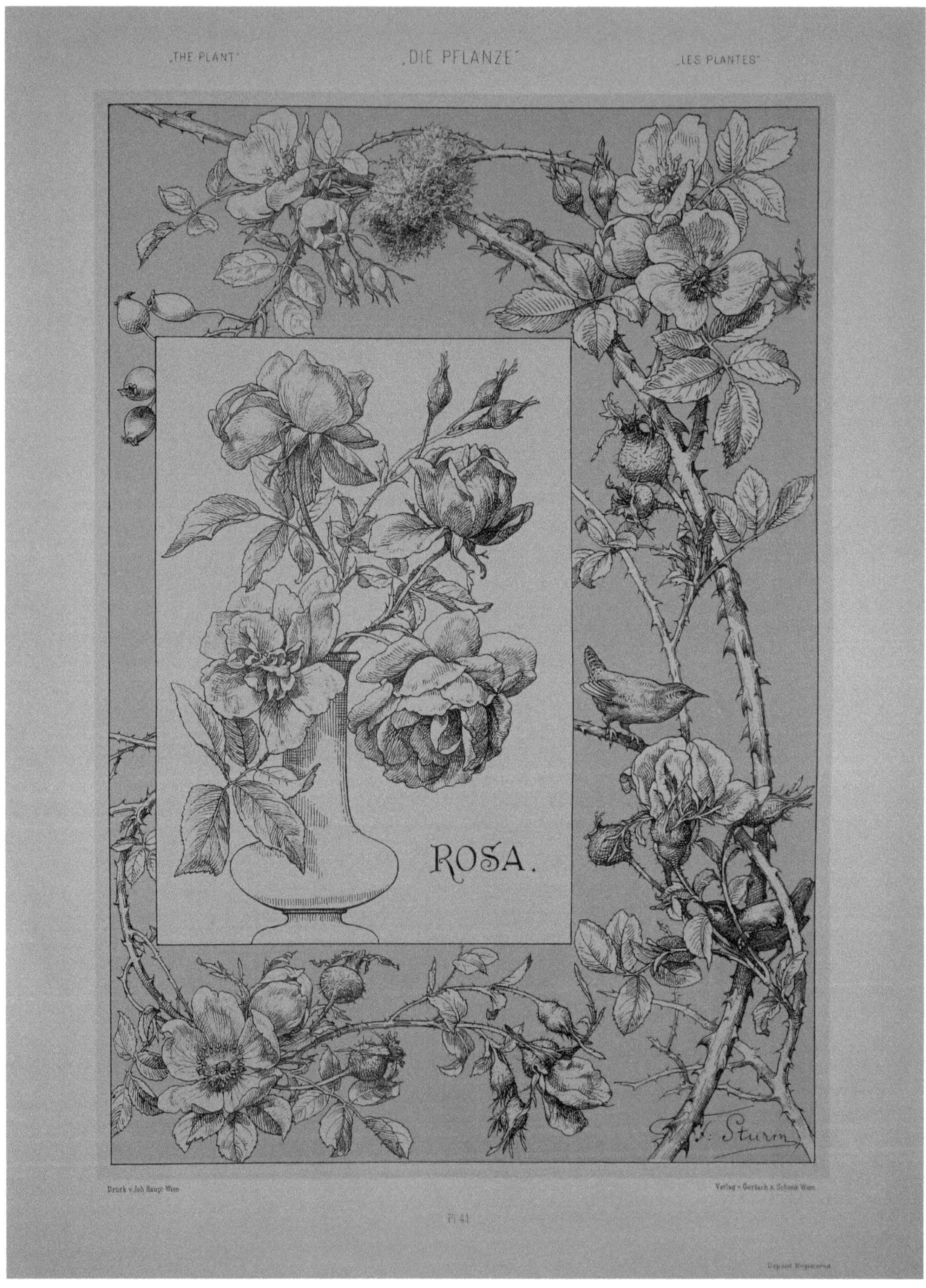

77. Plate 41, Die Pflanze in Kunst und Gewerbe
Volume 1, by A. Seder, c. 1886

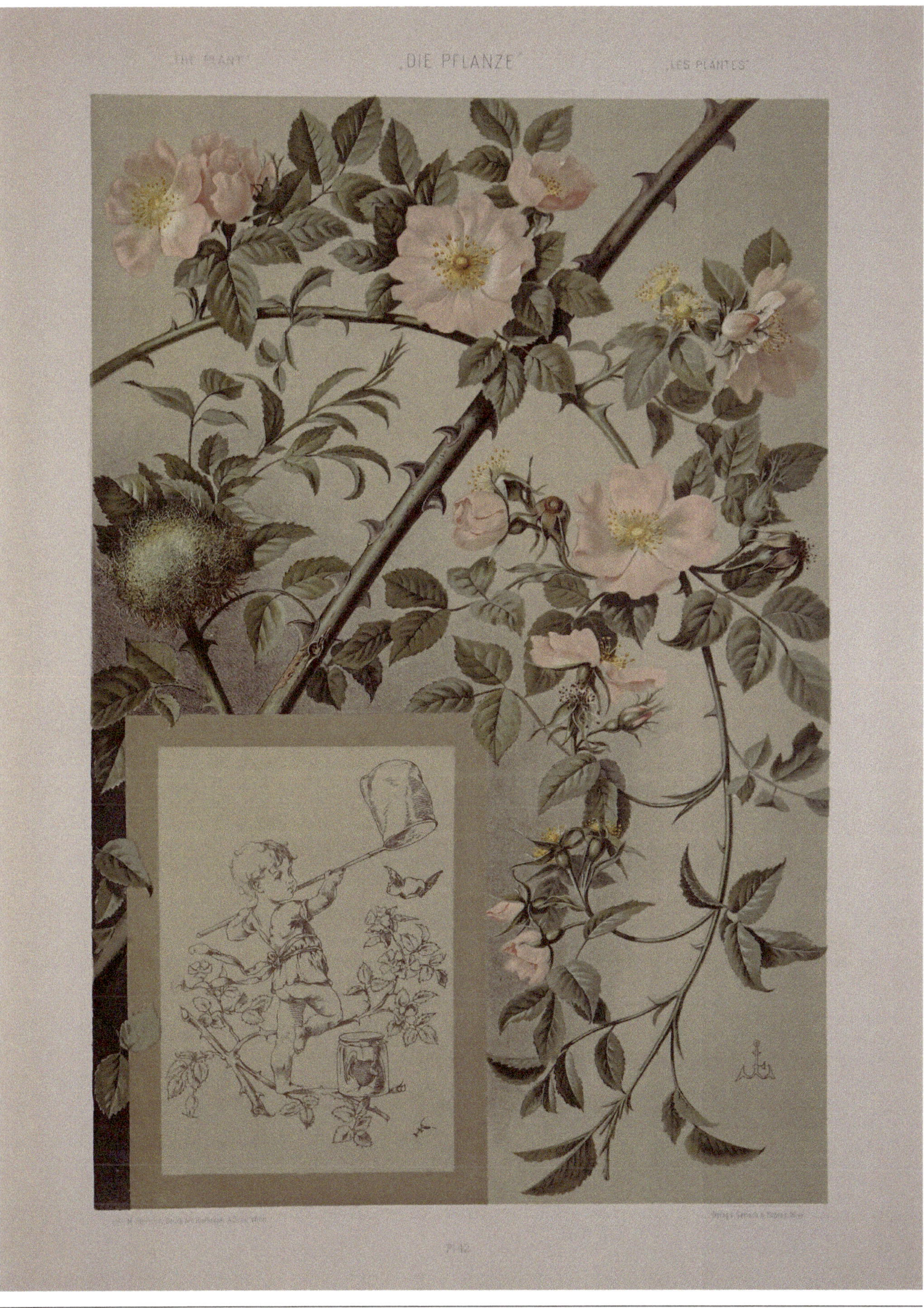

78. Plate 42. Die Pflanze in Kunst und Gewerbe
Volume 1, by A. Seder, c. 1886

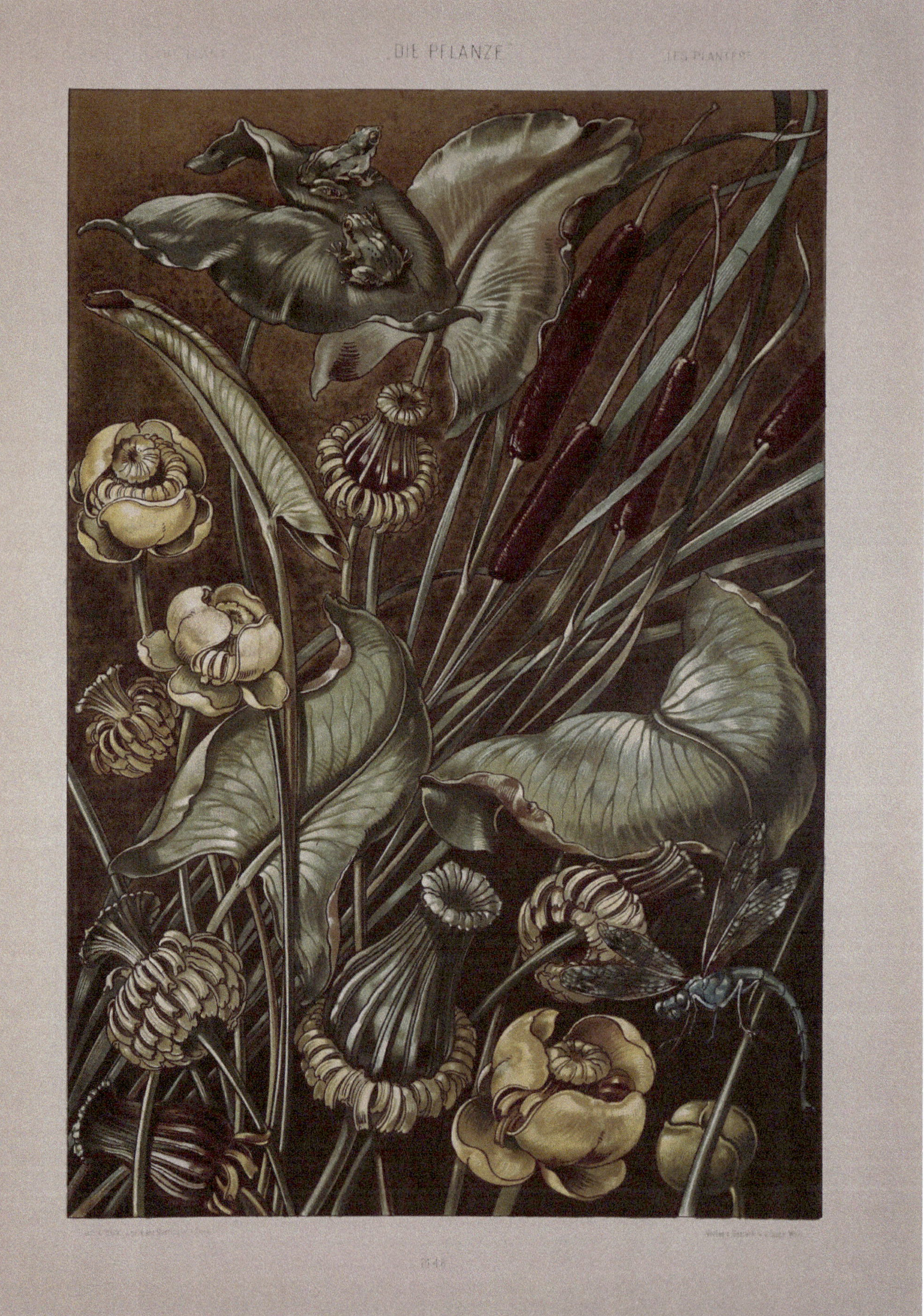

79. Plate 48, Die Pflanze in Kunst und Gewerbe
Volume 1, by A. Seder, c. 1886

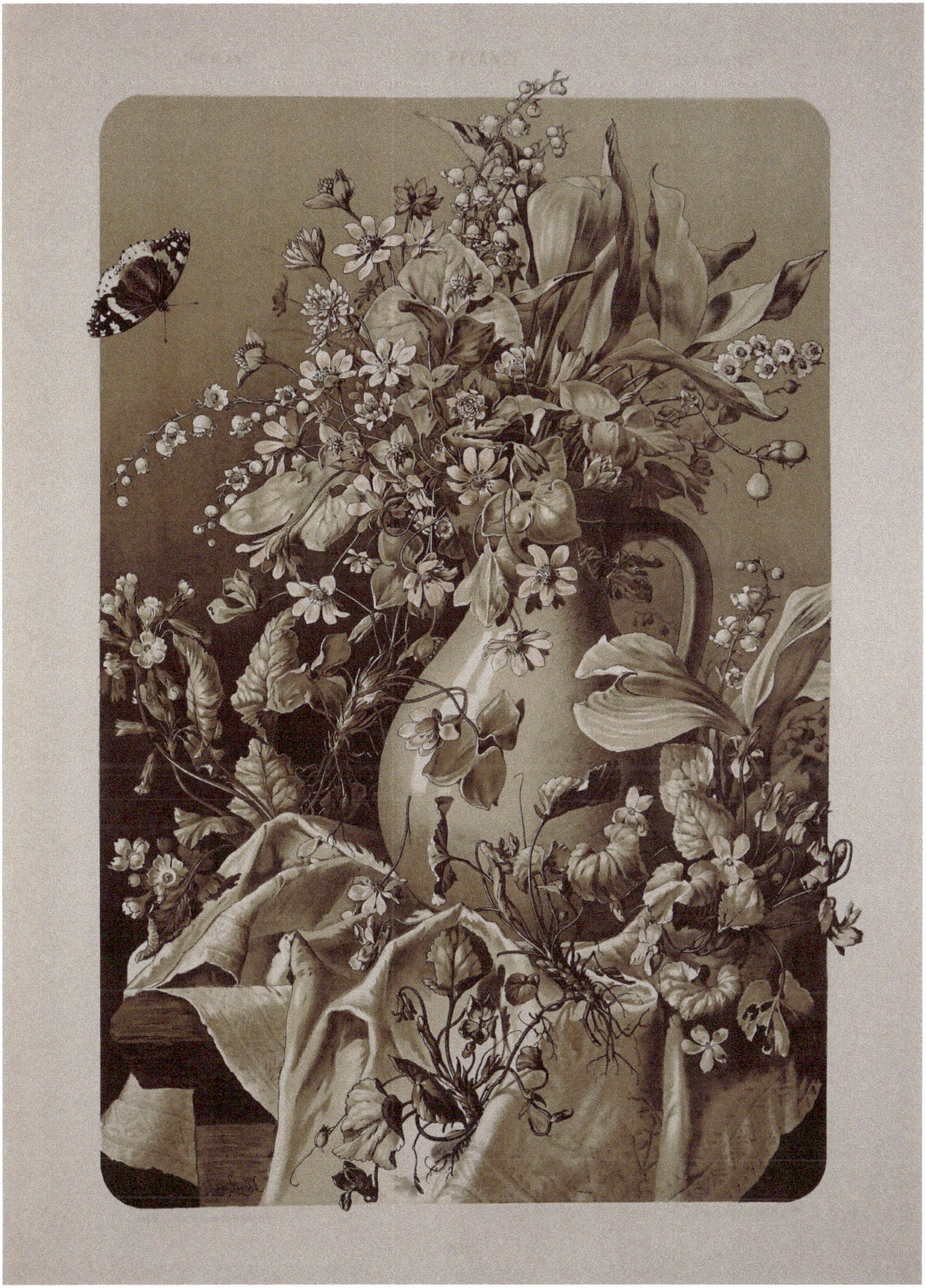

ANTON SEDER

80. Plate 56, Die Pflanze in Kunst und Gewerbe
Volume 1, by A. Seder, c. 1886

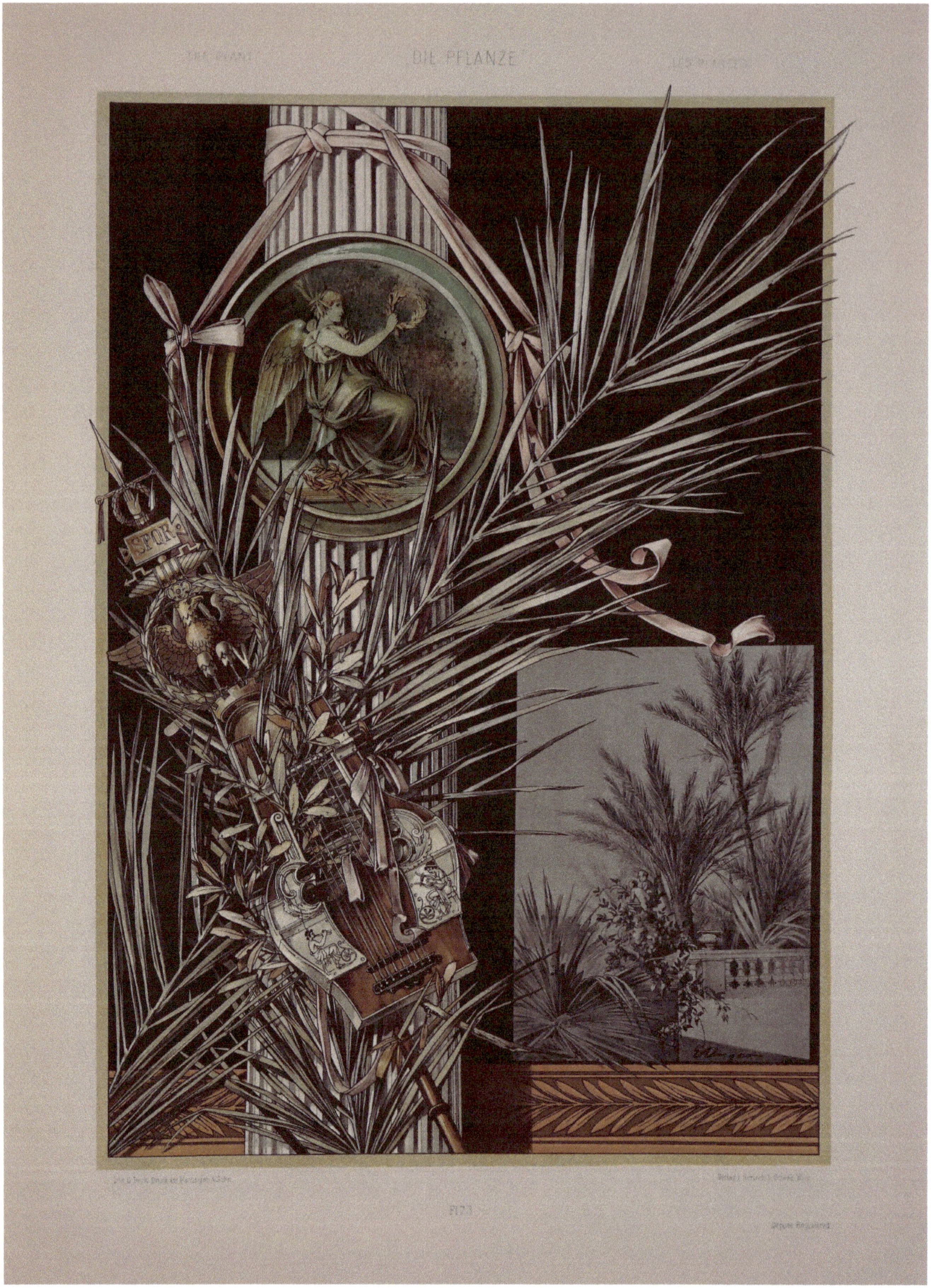

81. Plate 73, Die Pflanze in Kunst und Gewerbe
Volume 1, by A. Seder, c. 1886

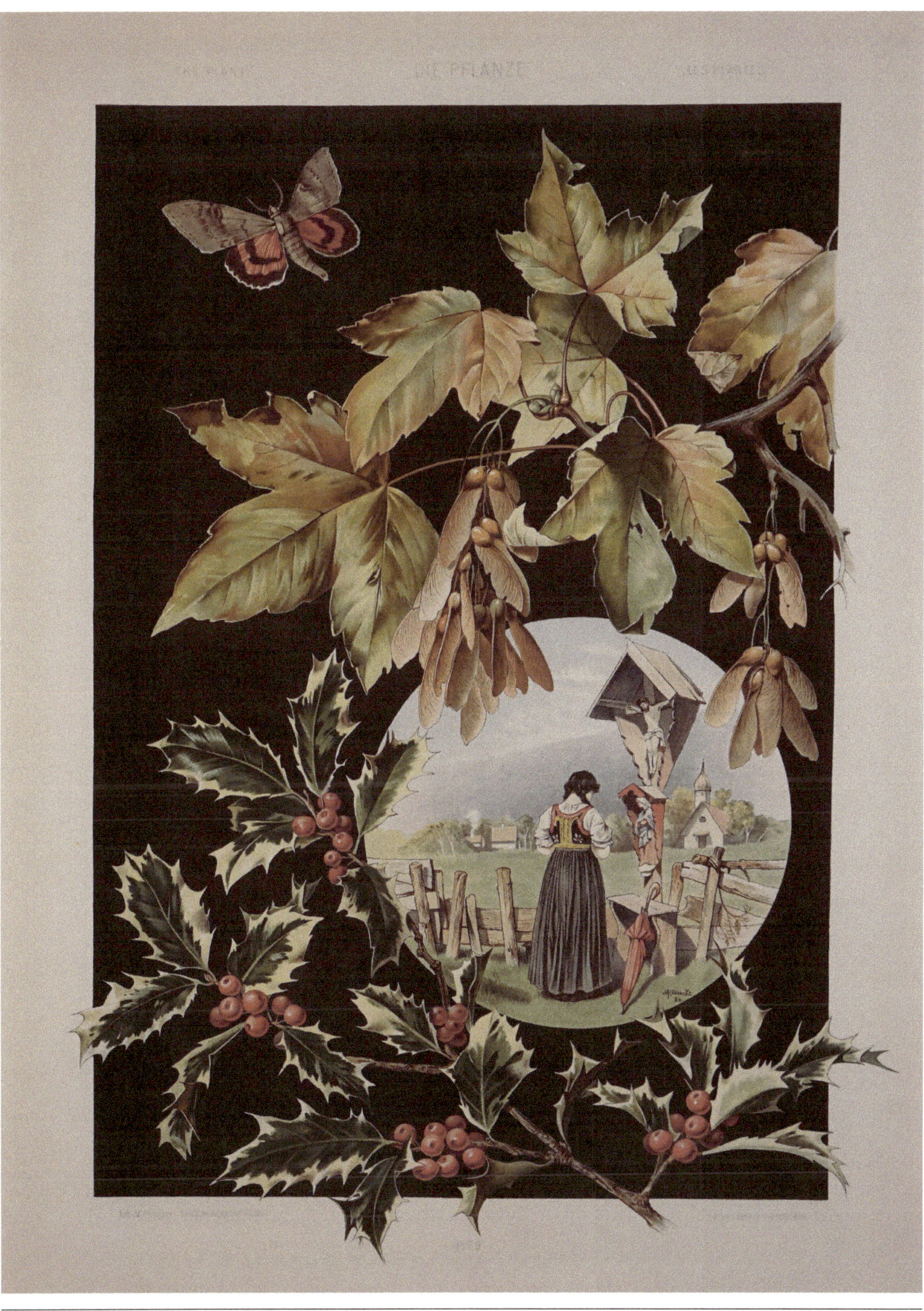

ANTON SEDER

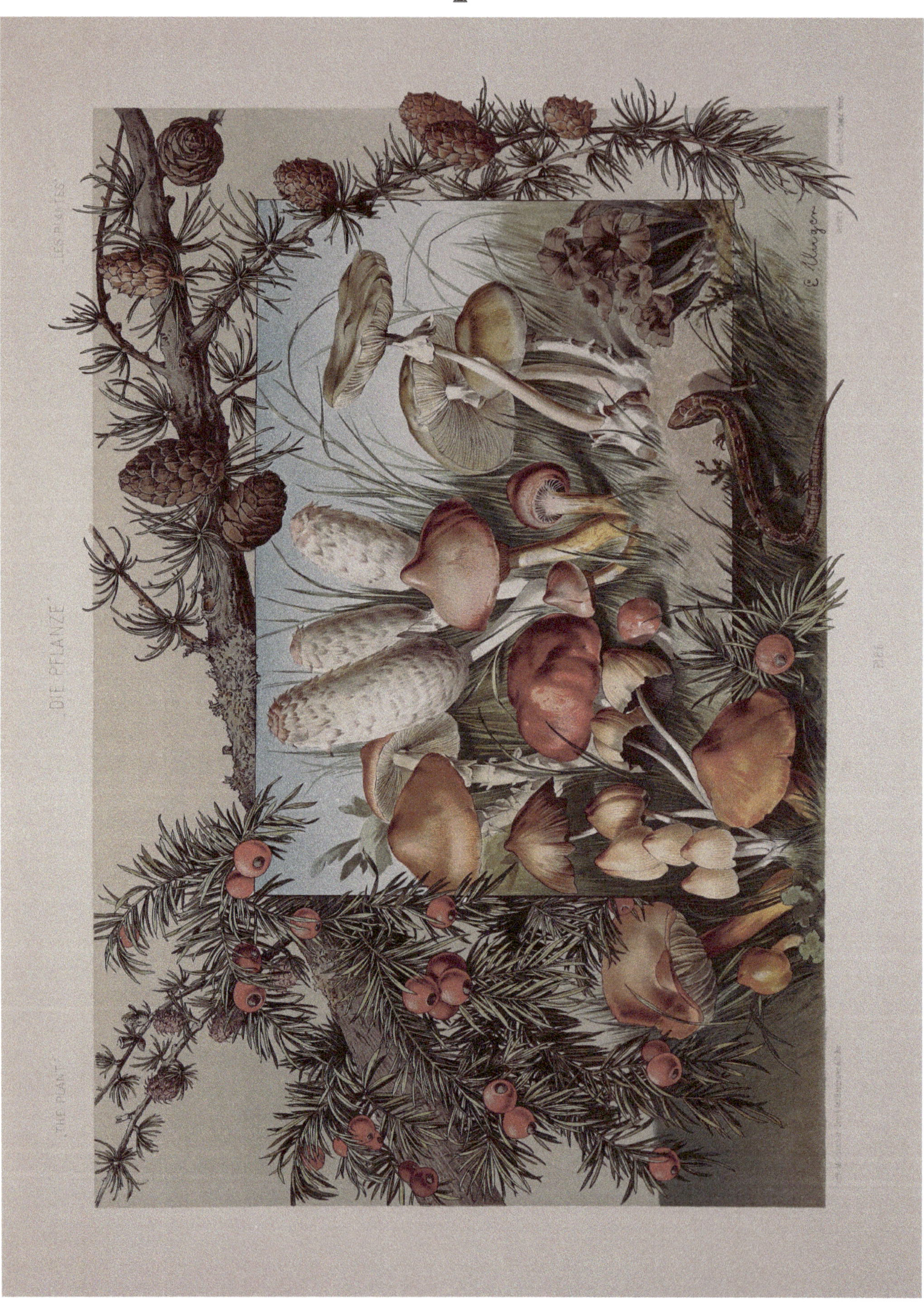

83. Plate 86. Die Pflanze in Kunst und Gewerbe
Volume 1, by A. Seder, c. 1886

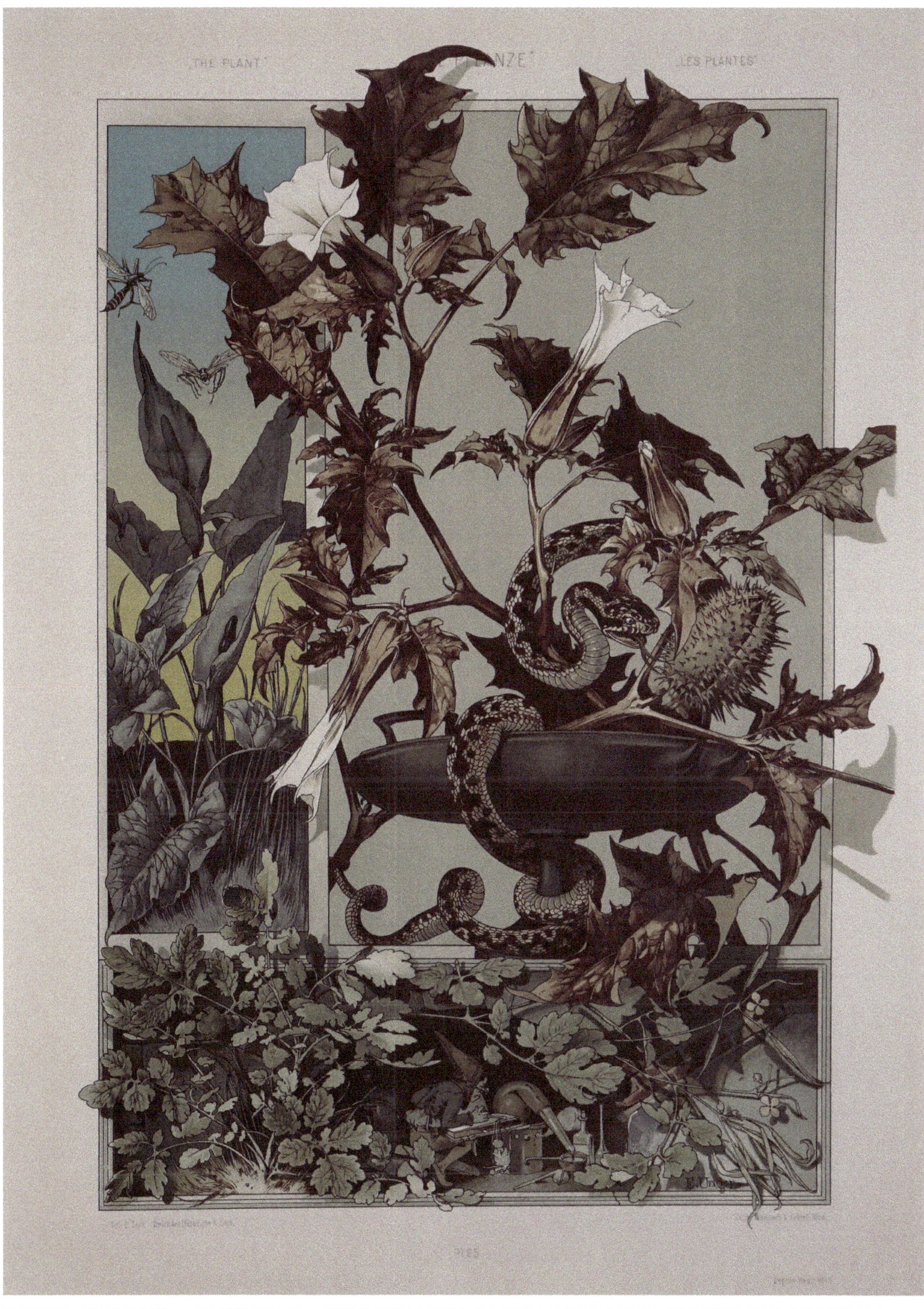

ANTON SEDER

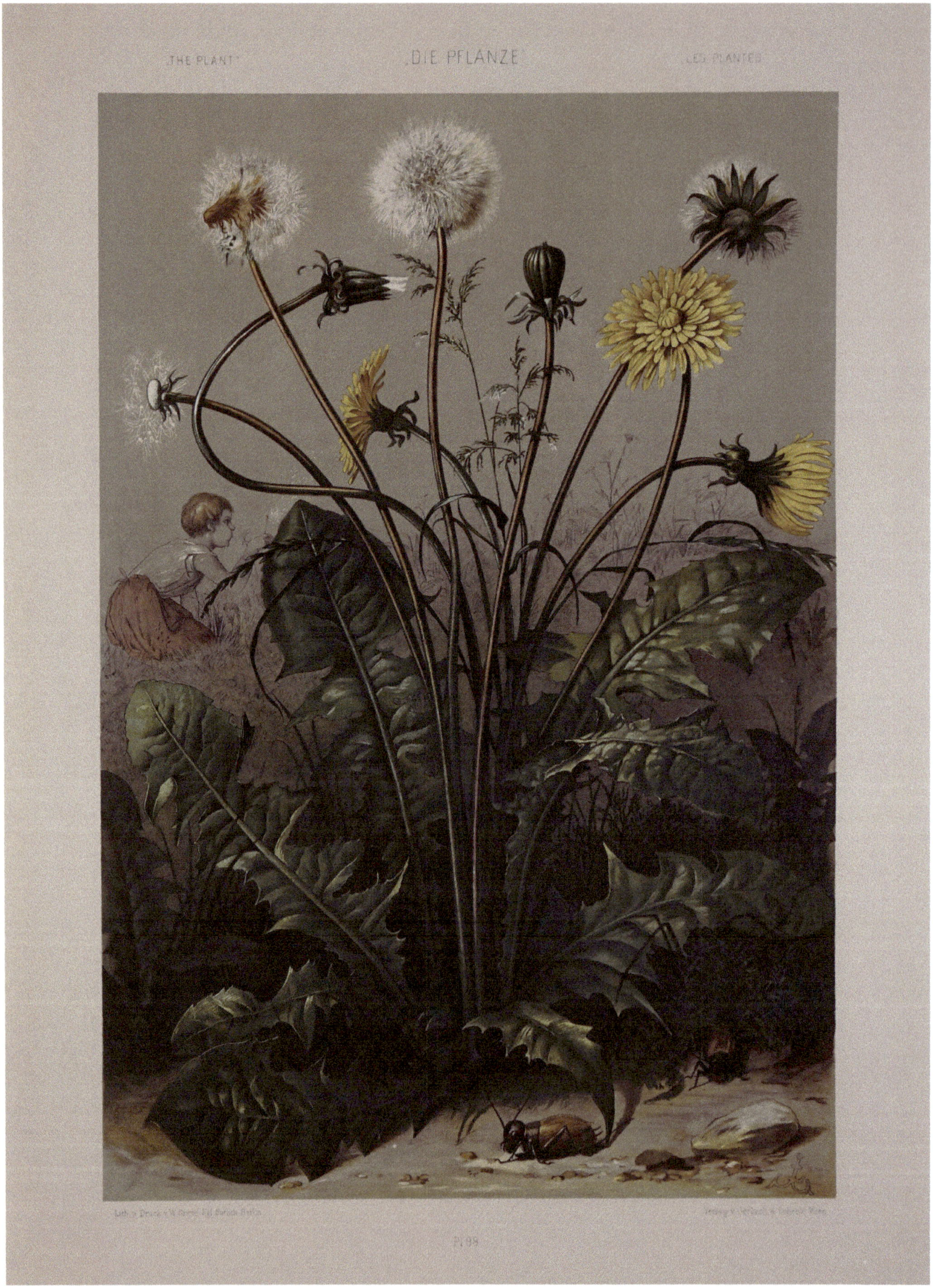

85. Plate 98. Die Pflanze in Kunst und Gewerbe
Volume 1, by A. Seder, c. 1886

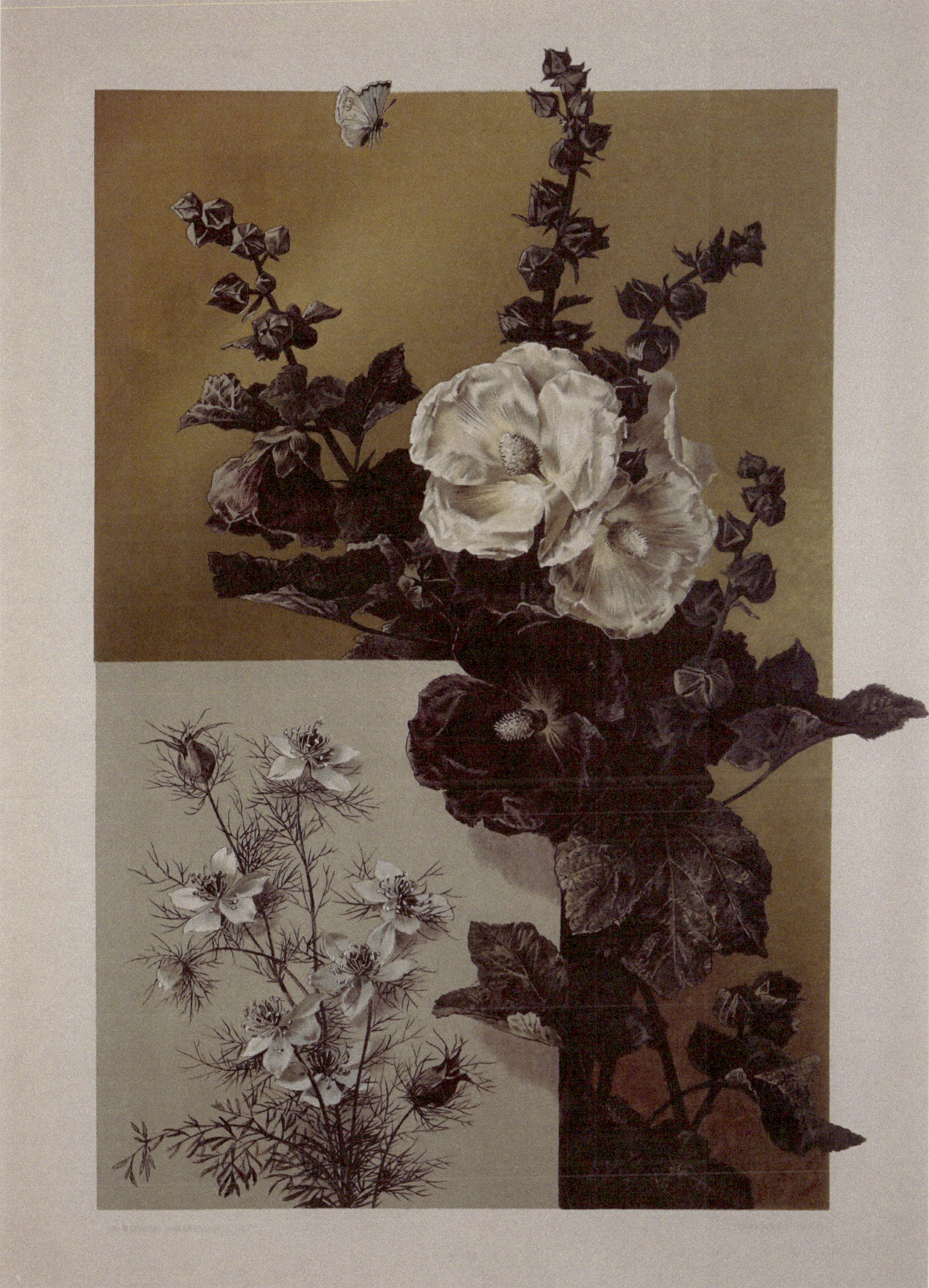

86. Plate 103, Die Pflanze in Kunst und Gewerbe
Volume 1, by A. Seder, c. 1886

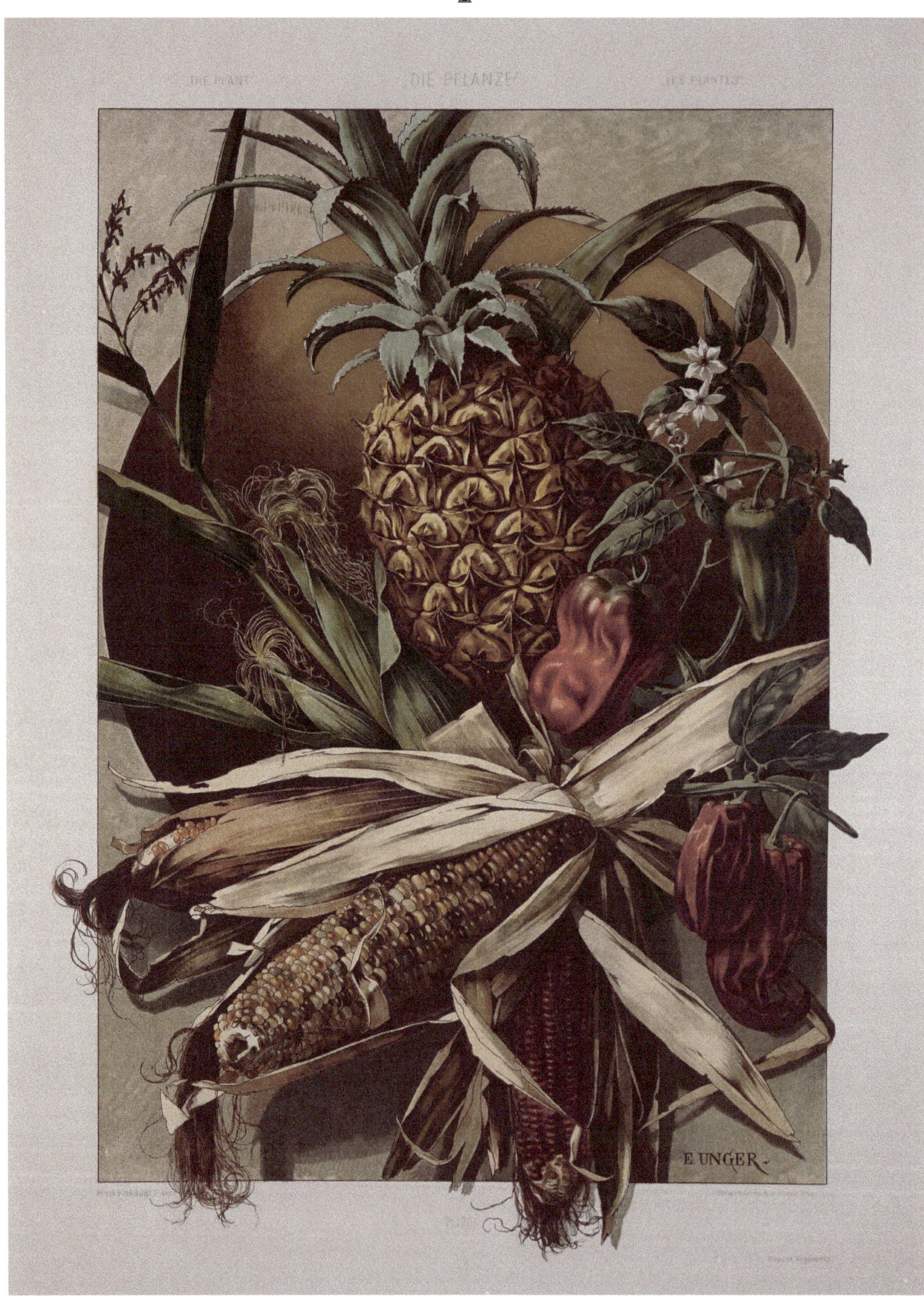

87. Plate 120. Die Pflanze in Kunst und Gewerbe
Volume 1, by A. Seder, c 1886

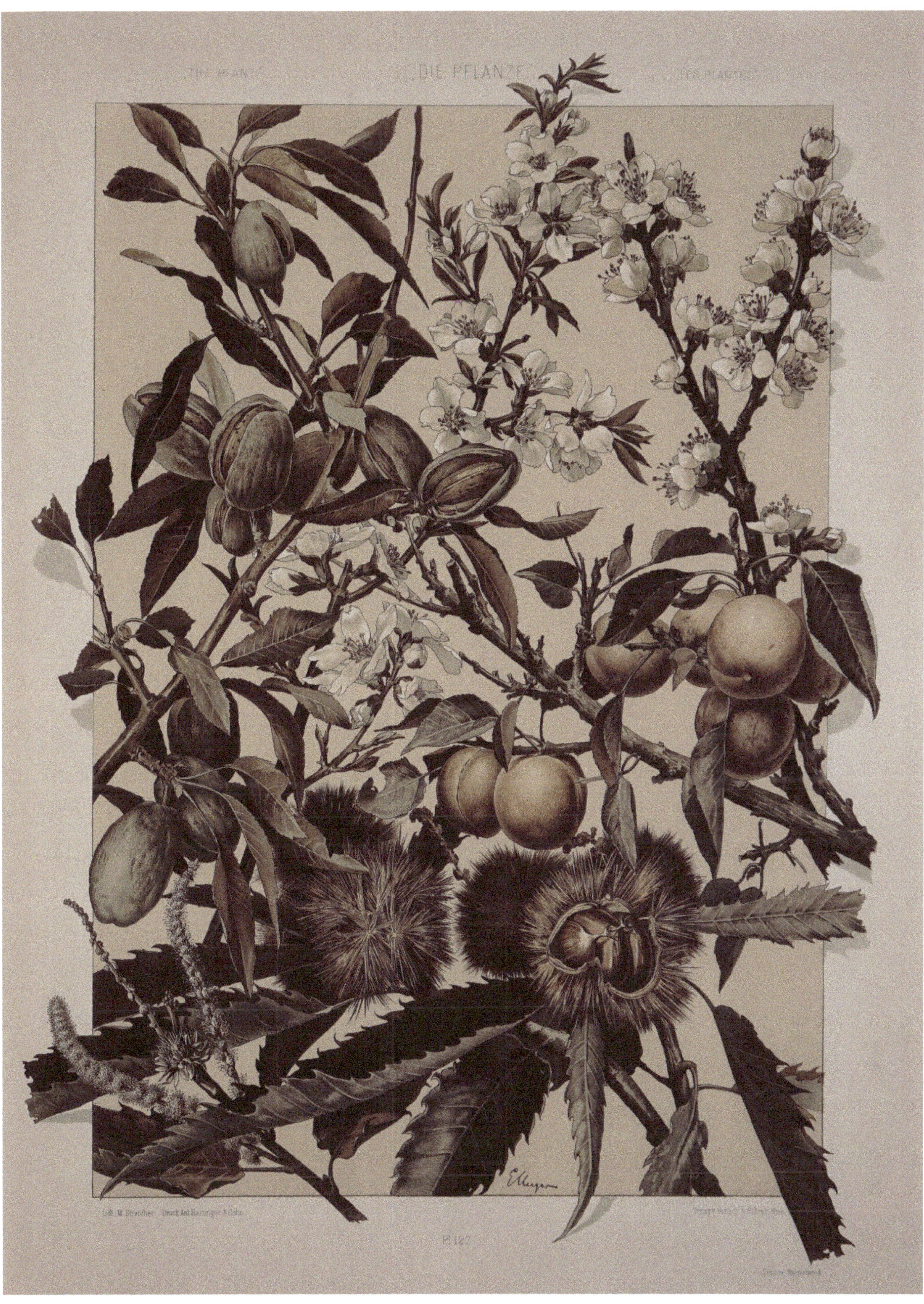

88. Plate 127, Die Pflanze in Kunst und Gewerbe
Volume 1, by A. Seder, c. 1886

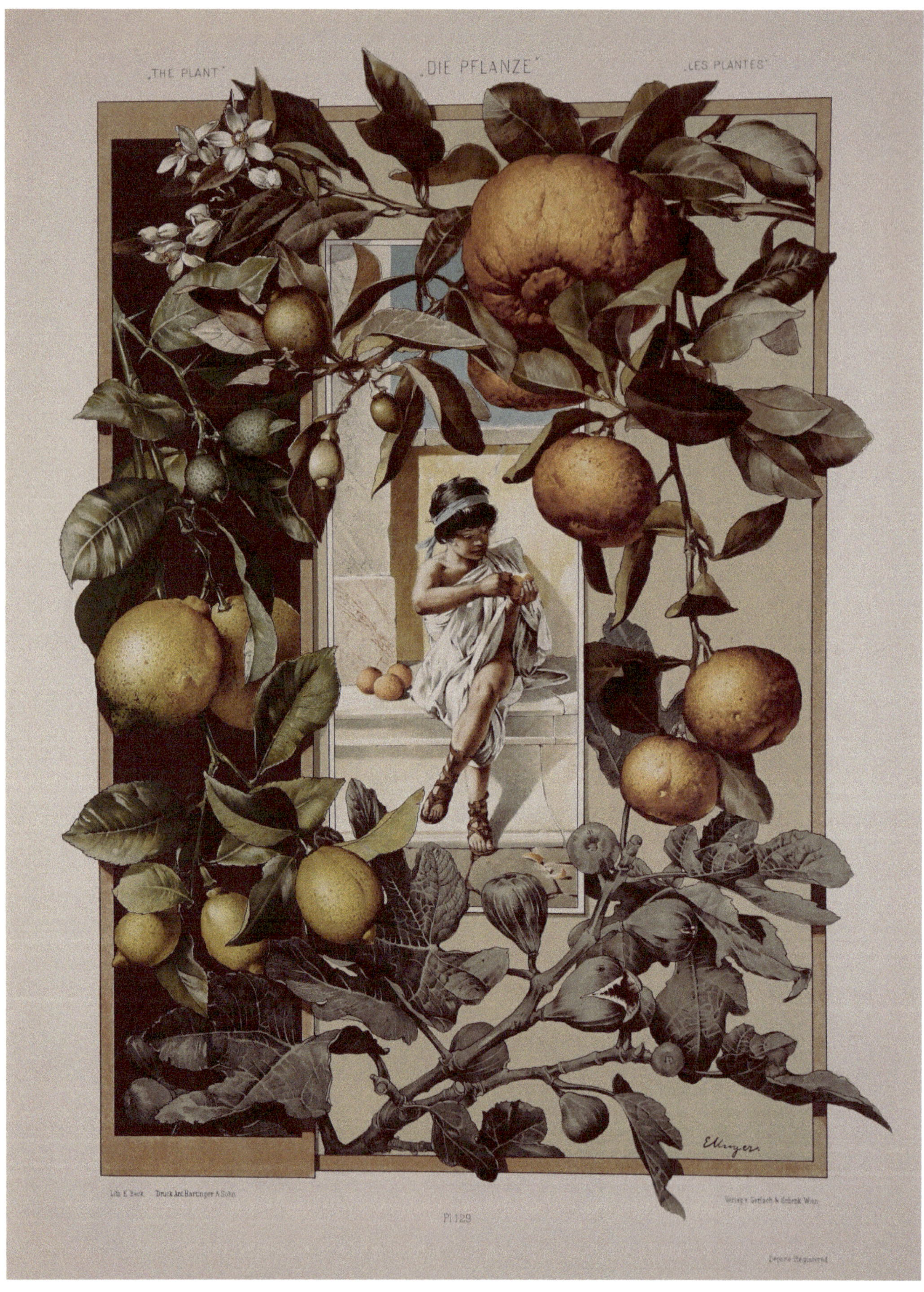

89. Plate 129, Die Pflanze in Kunst und Gewerbe
Volume 1, by A. Seder, c. 1886

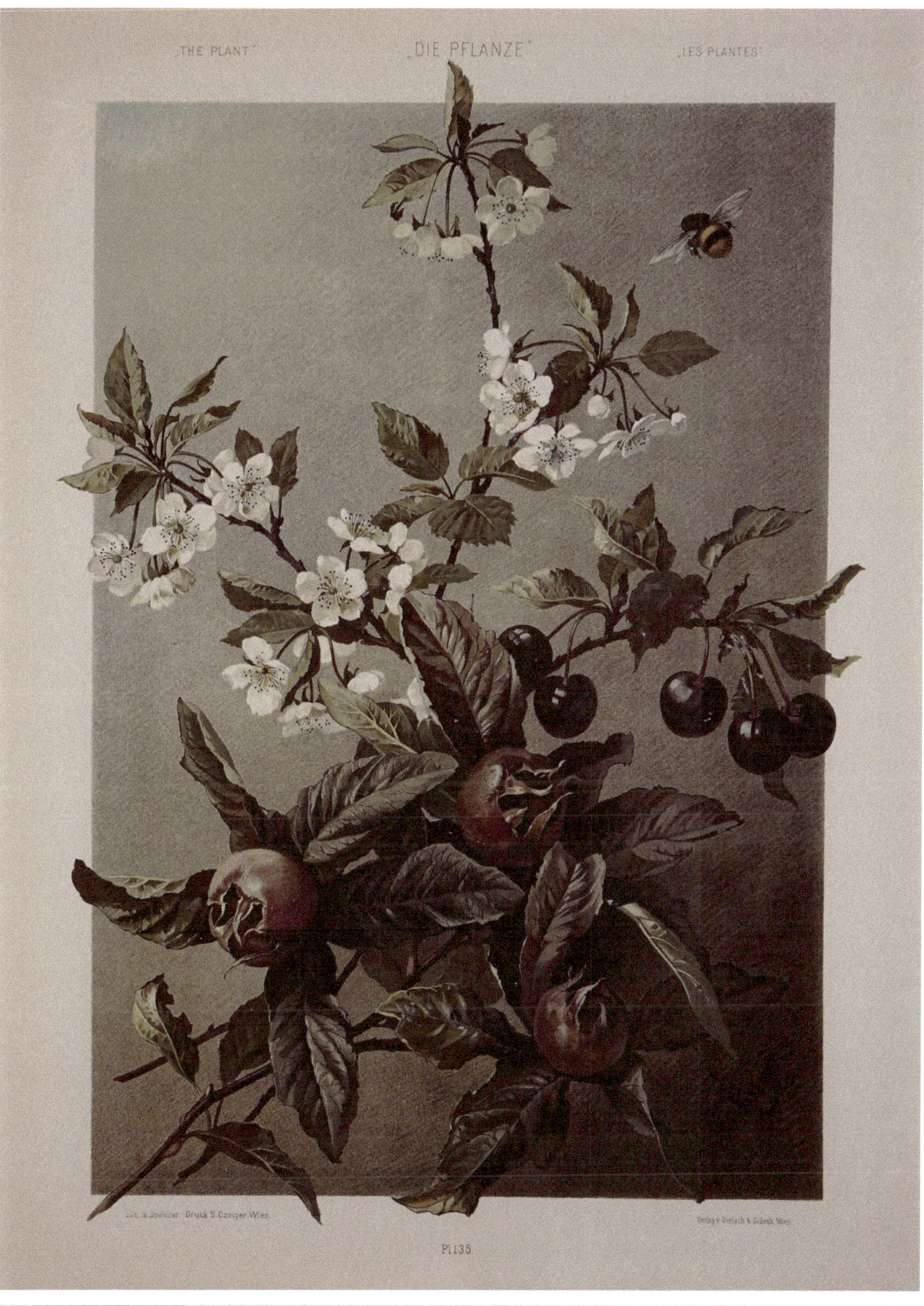

ANTON SEDER

90. Plate 135, Die Pflanze in Kunst und Gewerbe
Volume 1, by A. Seder, c 1886

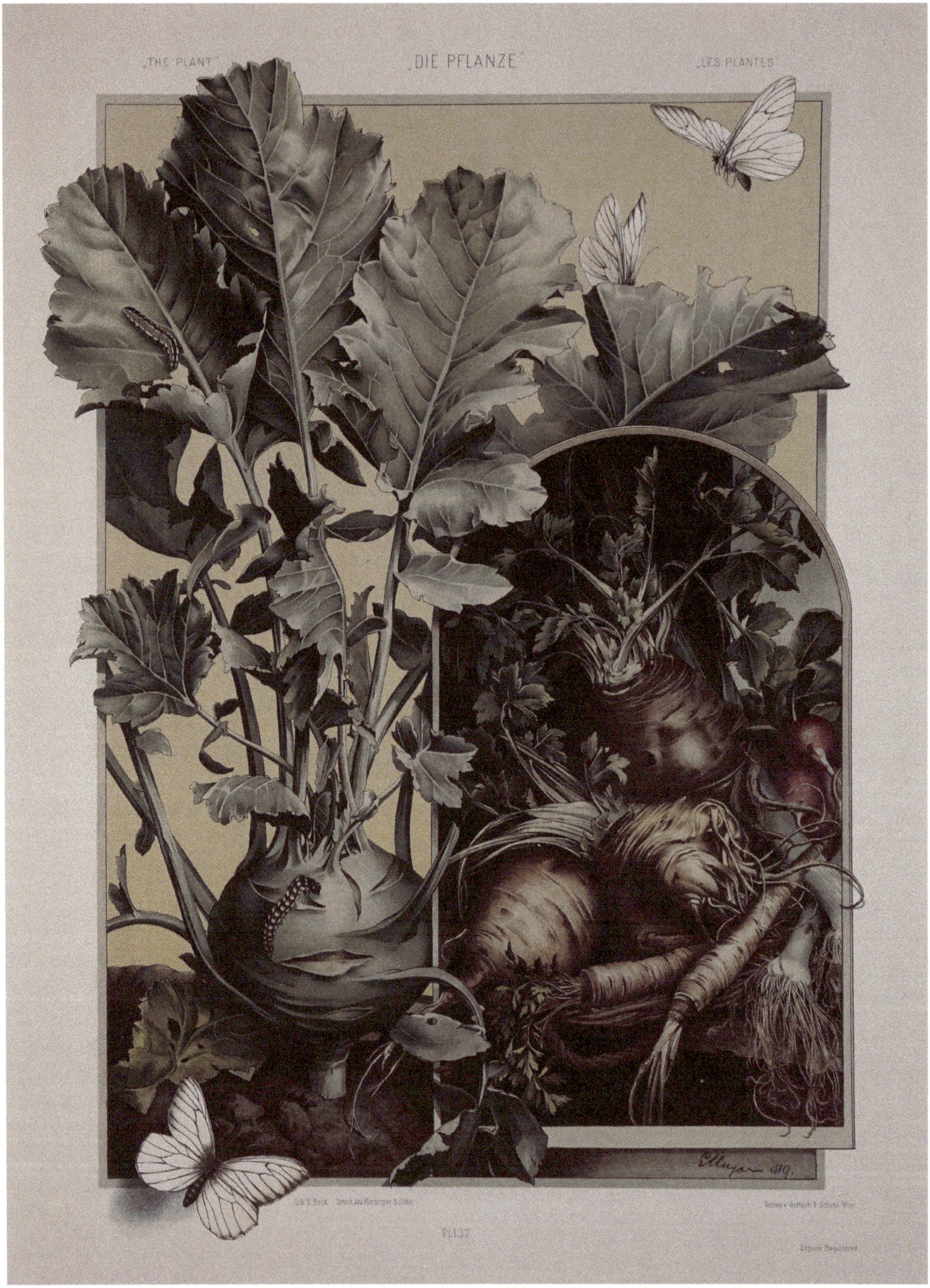

ANTON SEDER

91. Plate 137. Die Pflanze in Kunst und Gewerbe
Volume 1, by A. Seder, c. 1886

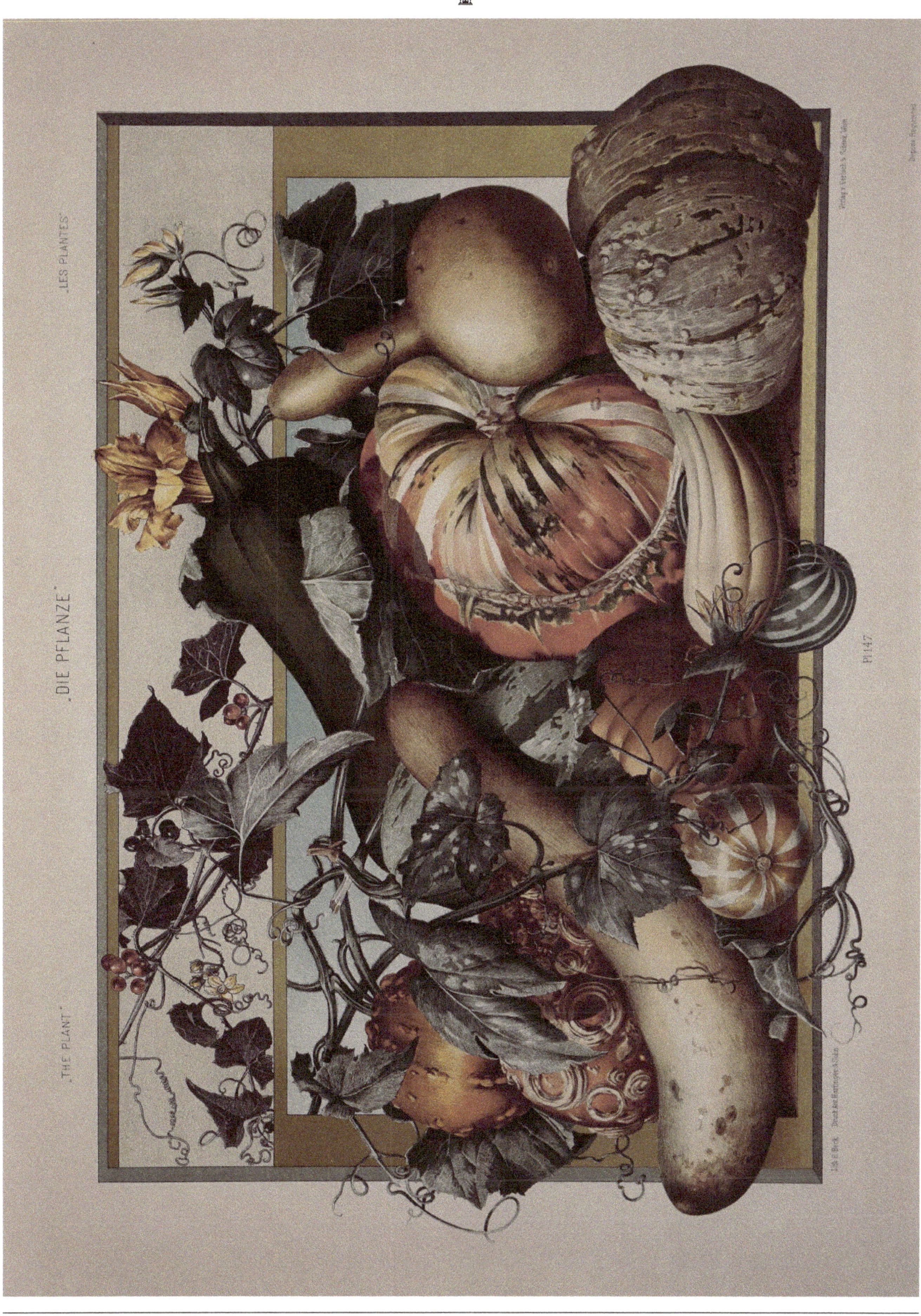
„LES PLANTES"
„DIE PFLANZE"
„THE PLANT"
Pl.147
ANTON SEDER

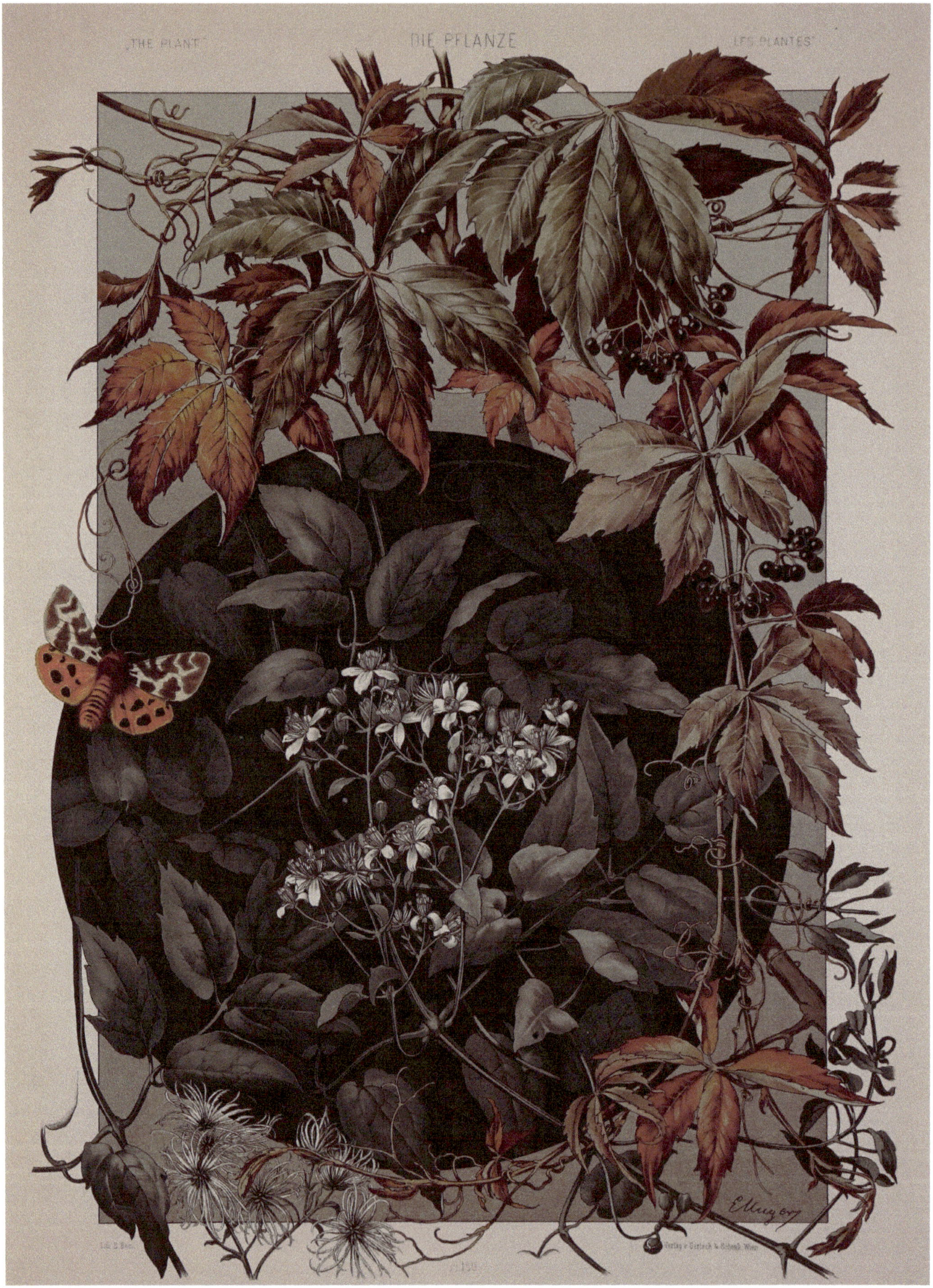

93. Plate 159. Die Pflanze in Kunst und Gewerbe
Volume 1, by A. Seder, c 1886

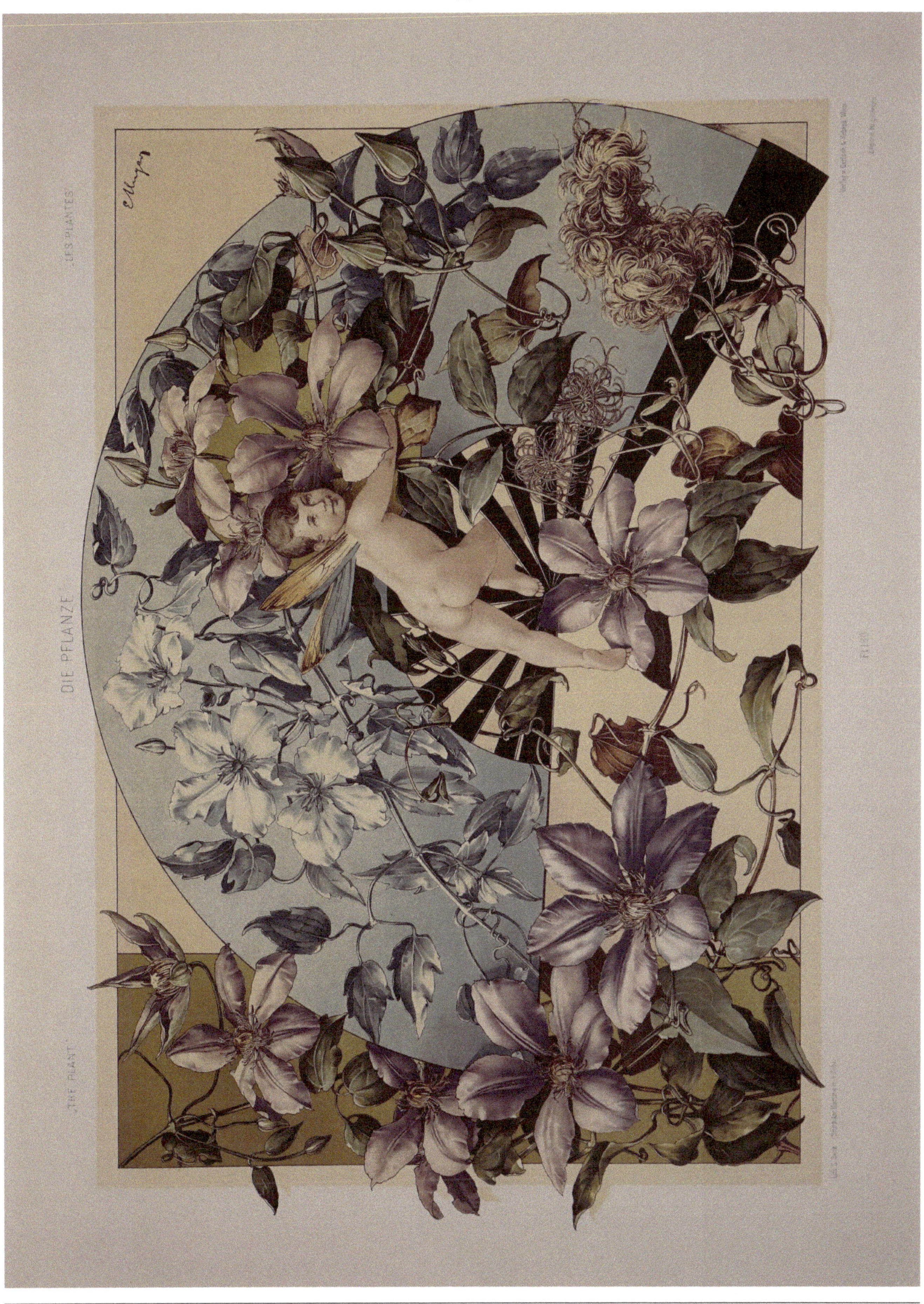

94. Plate 160, Die Pflanze in Kunst und Gewerbe
Volume 1, by A. Seder, c. 1886

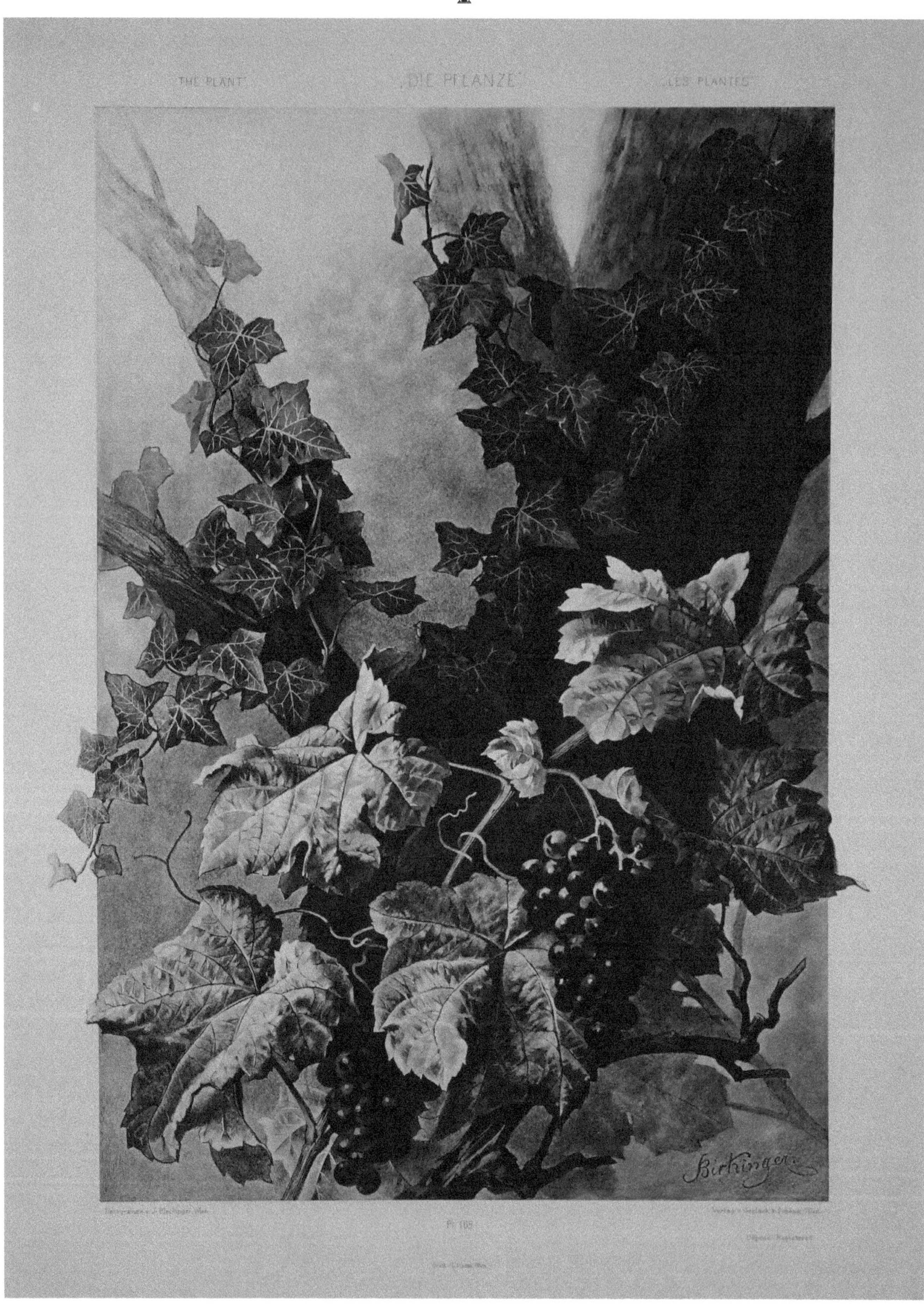

95. Plate 165. Die Pflanze in Kunst und Gewerbe
Volume 1, by A. Seder, c. 1886

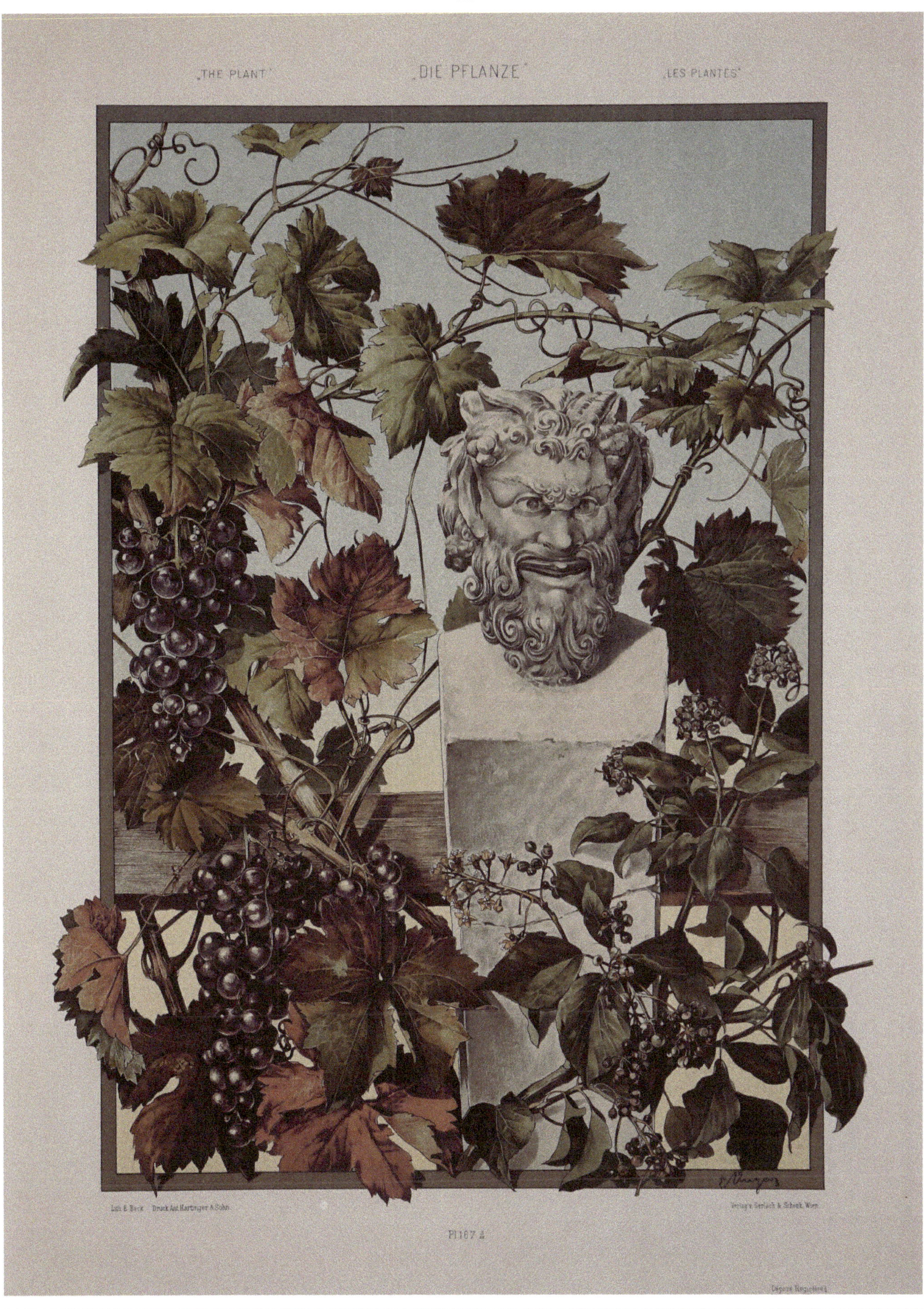

96. Plate 167a. Die Pflanze in Kunst und
Gewerbe Volume 1, by A. Seder, c. 1886

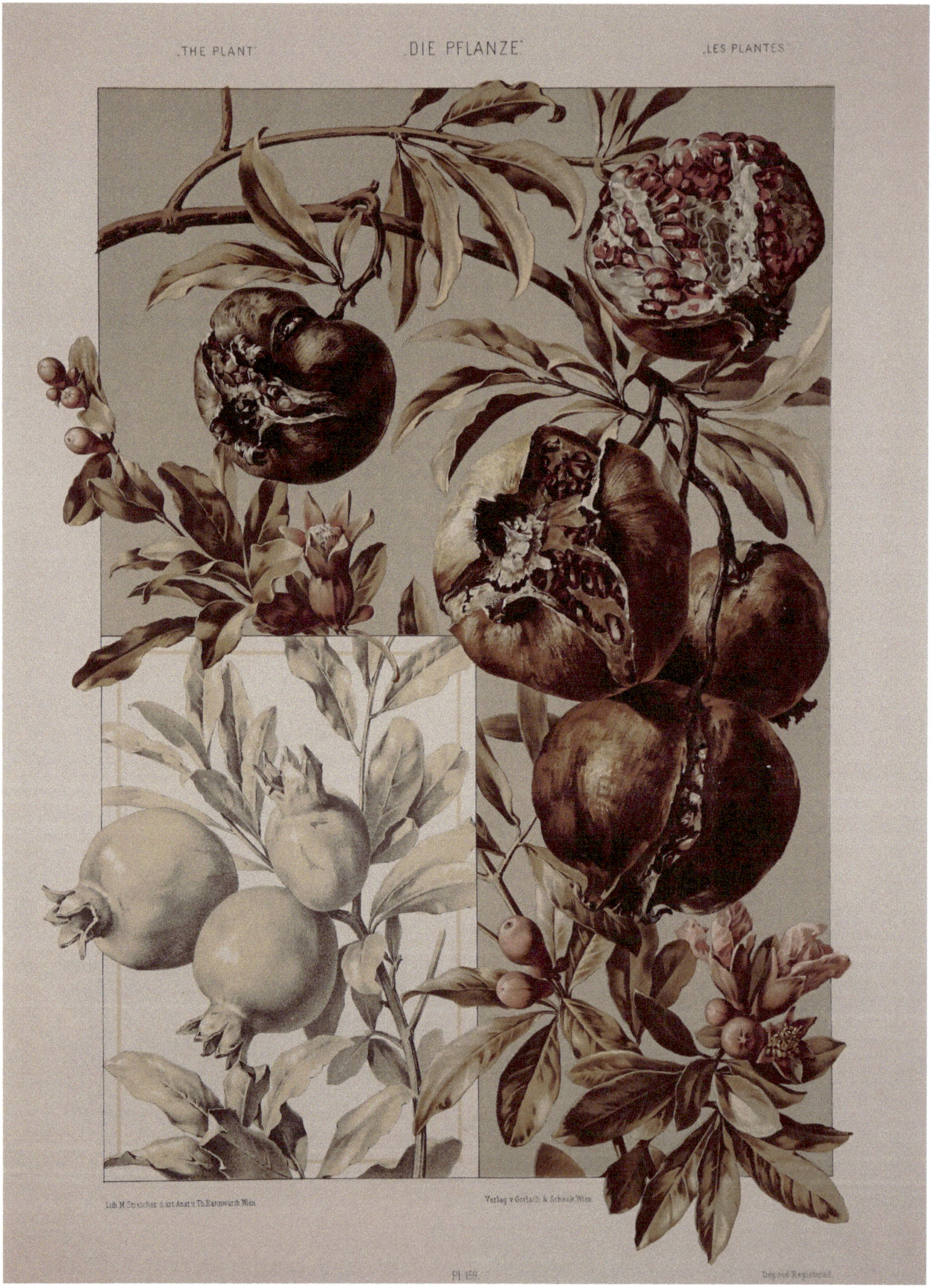

97. Plate 169. Die Pflanze in Kunst und Gewerbe
Volume 1, by A. Seder, c. 1886

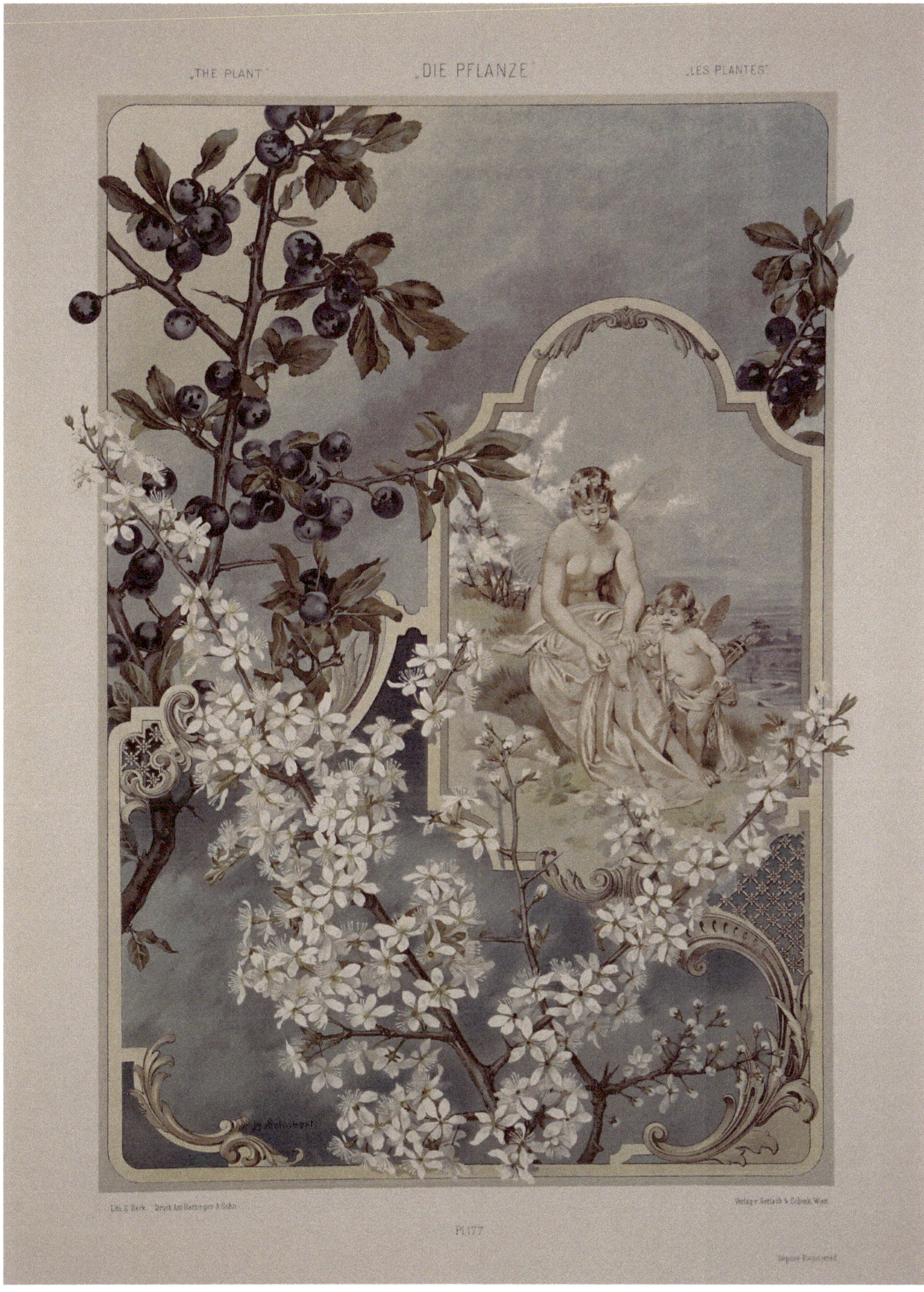

98. Plate 177, Die Pflanze in Kunst und Gewerbe
Volume 1, by A. Seder, c. 1886

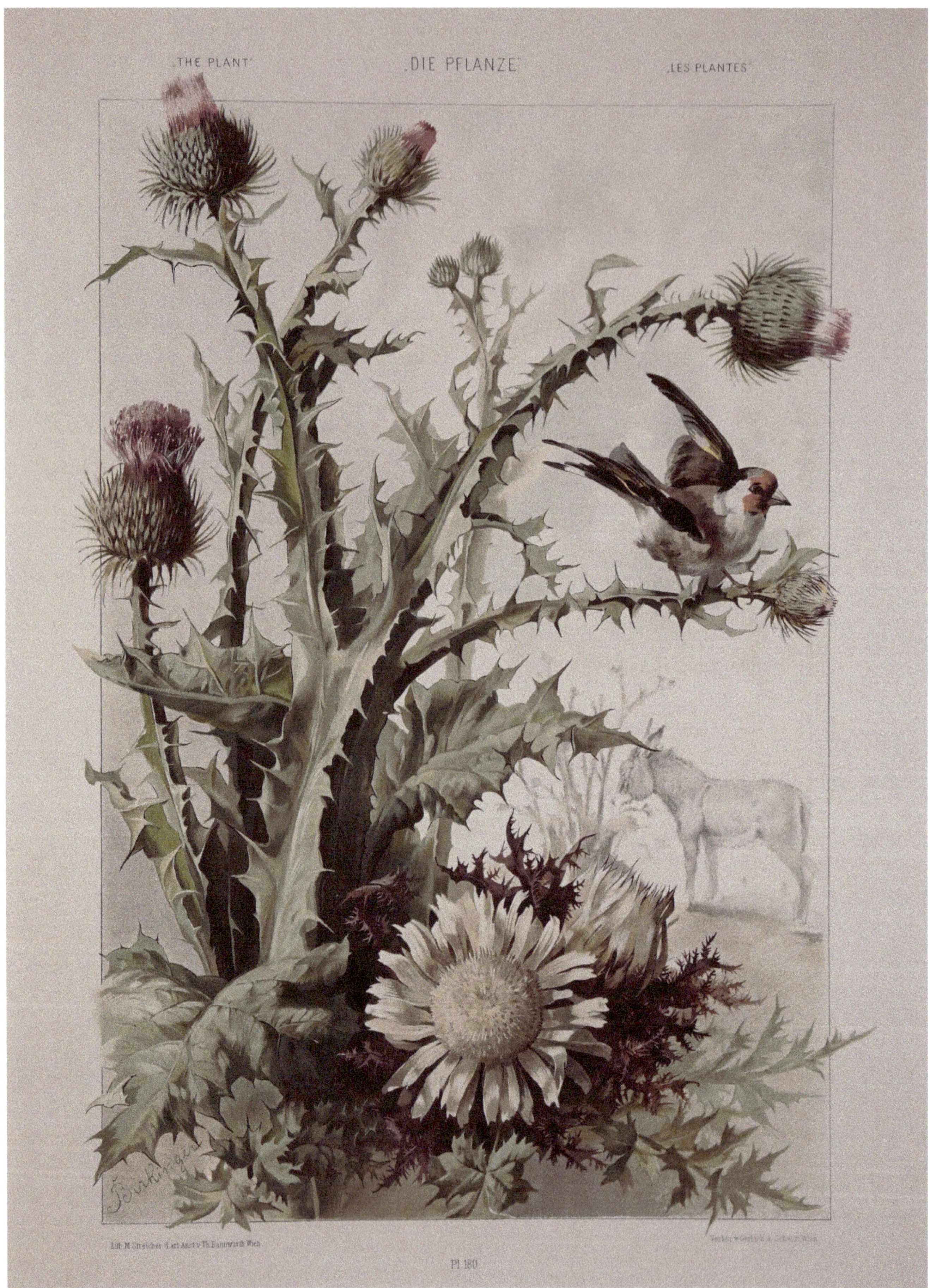

99. Plate 180, Die Pflanze in Kunst und Gewerbe
Volume 1, by A. Seder, c. 1886

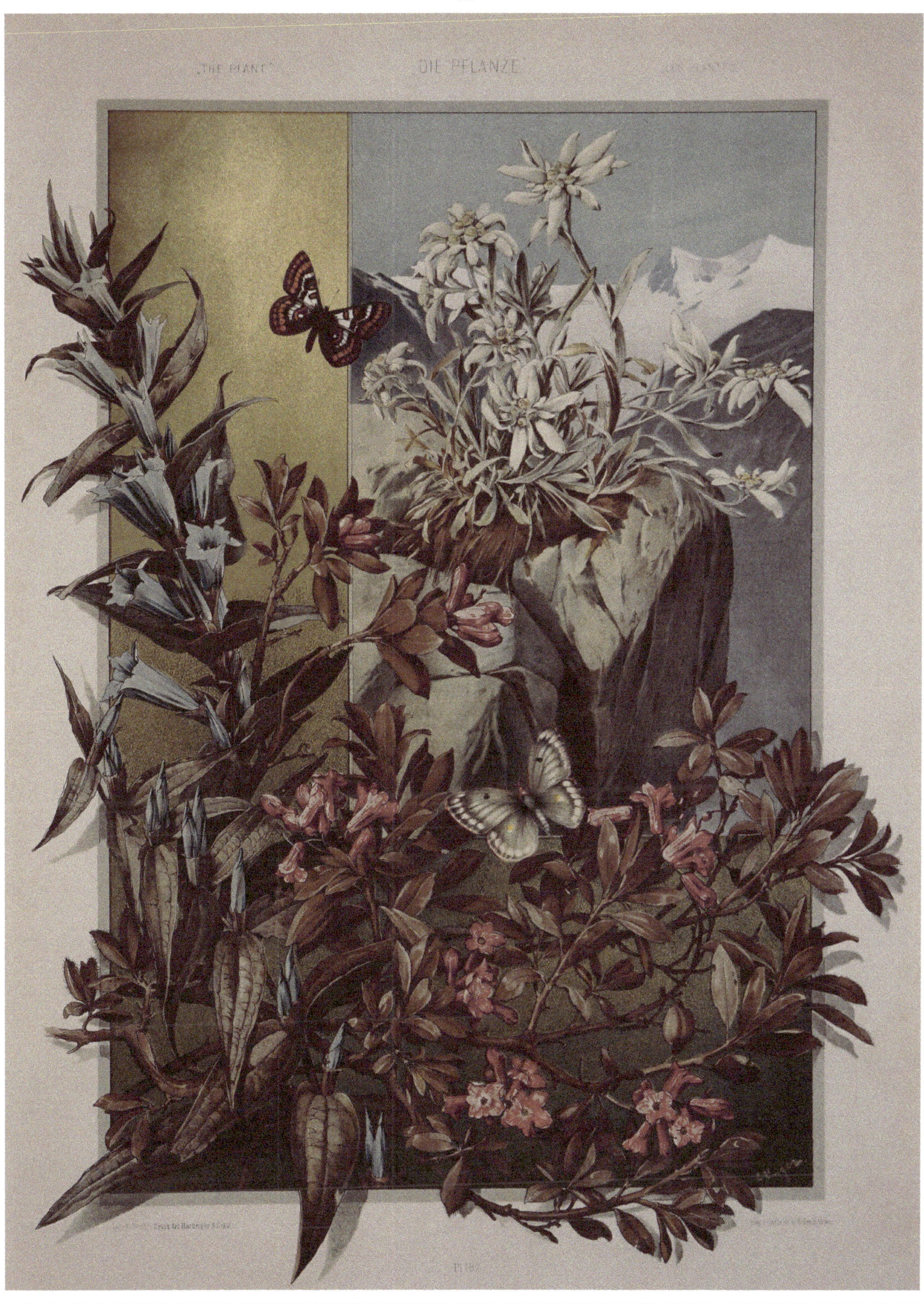

ANTON SEDER

100. Plate 187. Die Pflanze in Kunst und
Gewerbe Volume 1, by A. Seder. c 1886

04

DOWNLOAD YOUR FILES

START HERE
Enter the following URL
in your web browser:
www.vaulteditions.com/pages/asa

STEP 2
Enter the following password to
access the download page:
asa62829sxda

STEP 3
Enter your email address
where requested and submit
your details. A download link
will be sent to your inbox.

TECHNICAL SUPPORT
Please email:
info@vaulteditions.com